Danish Reactions to German Occupation

Danish Reactions to German Occupation

History and Historiography

Carsten Holbraad

UCL PRESS

First published in 2017 by
UCL Press
University College London
Gower Street
London WC1E 6BT

Available to download free: www.ucl.ac.uk/ucl-press

Text © Carsten Holbraad, 2017

A CIP catalogue record for this book is available from The British Library.

This book is published under a Creative Common 4.0 International license (CC BY 4.0). This license allows you to share, copy, distribute and transmit the work; to adapt the work and to make commercial use of the work providing attribution is made to the authors (but not in any way that suggests that they endorse you or your use of the work). Attribution should include the following information:

Carsten Holbraad, *Danish Reactions to German Occupation*. London, UCL Press, 2017. https://doi.org/10.14324/111. 9781911307495

Further details about CC BY licenses are available at http://creativecommons.org/licenses/

Front cover image: Headquarters of the Schalburg Corps, a Danish SS unit, after 1943. The occupied building is the lodge of the Danish Order of Freemasons located on Blegdamsvej, Copenhagen. Courtesy of Nationalmuseet, licensed under CC BY-SA 3.0.

ISBN: 978–1–911307–51–8 (Hbk.)
ISBN: 978–1–911307–50–1 (Pbk.)
ISBN: 978–1–911307–49–5 (PDF)
ISBN: 978–1–911307–52–5 (epub)
ISBN: 978–1–911307–53–2 (mobi)
ISBN: 978–1–911307–54–9 (html)
DOI: https://doi.org/10.14324/111.9781911307495

To the memory of Jørgen Hæstrup – who started it all.

Preface

In *Danish Neutrality: A Study in the Foreign Policy of a Small State* (Clarendon Press, Oxford 1991), I identified and analysed certain ideas and attitudes behind Danish foreign policy in modern and contemporary history. Focusing on situations of crisis or war in the region, I detected two opposing tendencies in Danish reactions, namely towards engagement in and withdrawal from international conflict.

At one stage, I considered the idea of following up with a briefer work which would explore a similar duality of attitudes to foreign affairs to be found in some modern Danish fictional literature. Instead, I decided to narrow the historical focus, and examine Danish reactions to the country's most traumatic experience in recent history: the five years of German occupation during the Second World War. There were two reasons for this choice.

In a conversation with my son and his friend Morten A. Pedersen – both members of the small and exclusive group of Danish anthropologists with a PhD from King's College, now known as the Cambridge Danes – Morten pointed out that there was a need for someone to get on top of the ongoing debate among historians and others about Danish conduct during the German occupation.

On a more personal level, a topic focusing on that relatively brief period had the attraction of taking me back to the subject matter of my initial introduction to historical research. As a high-school student at Sct. Knuds Gymnasium in Odense who had mastered the skills of stenography and typing, I spent most of my spare time in 1947–48 working as a secretary to Jørgen Hæstrup, a young and dynamic history master who recently had started collecting material about the resistance movement for the Danish Public Record Office. Destined to become the leading historian of Danish resistance and its links with Britain, he was in the process of locating secret archives and securing written verbal reports from key resistance figures.

Taking down reports and typing out archival material, I met quite a few members of the resistance and gained some knowledge of its activities. I also formed a good working relationship with Hæstrup. Though I was unable to accept repeated invitations in later decades to join his group of young occupation historians, my friendship with him lasted till his death in 1998. Thus, it is appropriate to dedicate this work to the memory of Jørgen Hæstrup. It offers a spectral analysis of Danish reactions to the German occupation and presents a critical overview of subsequent and recent historiographical debate about a crucial national experience not yet fully digested.

The first part of the book presents Danish conduct in the Second World War in a historical context by sketching out the foreign relations of the country in modern times and tracing its reactions to successive crises and wars in the region. For its earlier sections, I draw on my first book about the history of Danish foreign policy, mentioned above.

The second part lays out the historically attested and widely known reactions to German occupation from the invasion on 9 April 1940 to the liberation on 5 May 1945. However, for analytical reasons, the order of presentation is logical rather than chronological, ranging from willing cooperation at one end to armed resistance at the other. Yet, that order happens to correspond fairly well with the actual chronological development over the five years.

The third part of the book deals with the historiography about the occupation period, from the first post-war decades till well into the present century. Three waves of writings have been distinguished. The post-war works, mostly written by historians and other writers who identified with the resistance movement, tended to present a picture of growing resistance backed by increasing public support. Subsequently a revisionist wave of scholarship took a more critical view of resistance, perhaps at the same time adopting a more sympathetic attitude to cooperation. More recently, a second wave of revisionism, less interested in the history of resistance, took up the cases of various groups of individuals who had engaged in some form of collaboration with the occupiers. That part closes with a tentative overview of recent trends in scholarly debate and a brief presentation of recurrent public discourse about Danish reactions to the occupation.

Though Norway occasionally has been brought into the picture, no attempt has been made in this book to make comparisons and draw parallels with other countries under German occupation. Each such country was in a geopolitical situation of its own in relation to the European conflict, and had its own history of interacting with rivalling great powers and its own tradition of dealing with a preponderant and threatening power. Moreover, the policy and conduct of the occupying power varied from country to country. Thus, as for both its situation and its conduct during the Second World War, Denmark was a special case, which should be examined separately rather than fitted into some quasi-comparative framework.

Much of the book was researched and written while I was Honorary Research Associate in the Department of Scandinavian Studies at UCL. As such, I much enjoyed the use of the UCL Library's excellent collection of books about the history, politics and culture of Denmark and other Nordic countries.

I am grateful to Knud J.V. Jespersen, professor emeritus at the University of Southern Denmark in Odense, for generous and useful comments on an early draft. The constructive criticism and good advice of the anonymous reviewers are also much appreciated. In particular, I am indebted to the expert on Danish occupation historiography for helping me find a way through recent literature.

London
C. H.

Contents

Introduction

For Denmark, the most momentous experience of the twentieth century was the five years of German occupation during the Second World War. As a crisis in the political history of the country, it was in some respects comparable to the two major traumas of the nineteenth century, namely the unfortunate involvement in the later stages of the Napoleonic Wars and the disastrous defeat in the war with the German Confederation half a century later. As in those earlier crises, the impact of the war profoundly affected the Danish conception of the international situation of the country and influenced its foreign policy for a long time.

But the nature of the experience of invasion, occupation and liberation, and its effects on the national psyche and future foreign policy, made it very different from the two low points in the earlier century. Both the involvement with Napoleonic France and the war with Bismarck's Prussia in 1864 led to defeat and very substantial losses of territory and population. After 1814 and, even more so, after 1864 Denmark went through a crisis of anxiety about survival as a sovereign state. In both situations the most significant political outcome was a reinforcement of an already existing tendency to try to steer clear of European power politics. On the other hand, the period of German occupation, which was marked initially by reluctant cooperation with the authorities of the occupying power but later also by growing active resistance, led to a national soul-searching and a reconsideration of the country's role in international relations. One outcome was a tentative revival of a much older tradition of Danish foreign policy, which had been characterized by a more active engagement in the international politics of the region. However, the inclination inherited from the nineteenth and early twentieth centuries, towards disengagement and neutrality in international conflict, survived. Thus the years of occupation became a quasi turning-point in the history of Danish foreign policy.

For much of the second half of the twentieth century Danish politics became marked by a recurrent debate between those who sought a fuller and more committed involvement in the policies and activities of the Western alliance and a more willing participation in the drive towards a degree of European integration and, on the other hand, those who stuck to a more cautious and hesitant line in both NATO and EC relations. Thus, in periods of the East–West conflict, the alliance and security policies as well as the European policy of the country often came to appear half-hearted. The debate continued, though in a lower key, after the end of the cold war, when it at stages came to focus on Danish participation in the US-led wars against Iraq and Afghanistan.

Throughout, the issue was essentially between those who recognized that the wider issues of international politics were crucial enough for Denmark to engage actively in the conflicts and pursuits of the region and those who were content with guarding customary Danish values and interests by keeping a low profile in international politics. In terms of party politics, the division between the former and the latter was largely between right-of-centre and left-of-centre sections of the Danish political spectrum.

On a more intellectual level, the debate may even be seen as roughly reflected in the works of historians and other writers dealing with the Danish reactions to German occupation. The first post-war writings on that subject, most of them written by people who identified with the resistance movement, tended to present the period of occupation as a picture of growing resistance backed by wide popular support, and to give less attention to the presence of cooperation with the German authorities and divisions of opinion in the country. The first wave of revisionist writings queried the strength and efficacy of the resistance, cast doubt on the degree of support it enjoyed and often took a more sympathetic view of the policy and practice of governmental and administrative cooperation with the enemy. A later revisionist wave subjected the resistance movement to criticism more on moral grounds, condemning in particular the practice of shooting informers, and dealt sympathetically with various sets of individuals who, in one way or another, had engaged in personal collaboration with agents of the occupying power. The first post-war historians, to the extent that they accepted the goals and means of the resistance, were in tune with those who advocated a more active engagement in international politics. The revisionists, judging by their antipathies as well as their sympathies, on the whole seemed closer to those who kept an eye on the narrow and immediate interests of the Danish people and opted for a more passive or minimal role in foreign politics.

In more recent years the historical debate intensified, with not only historians and writers but also some politicians and other prominent persons, including a few survivors of the resistance, taking part. The behaviour of the Danes during those five years, at official as well as more private and individual levels, once again became the subject of heated exchanges in the media. Now, more than 70 years after the end of the occupation, the politics and morality of the people who lived through it still seem to be divisive issues, for scholars as well as a wider public.

That the conflict between cooperation and resistance under occupation remains unresolved may be seen as evidence of a profound ambivalence in the mentality of a people conditioned by traumatic defeats and losses and split between opposite reactions to conflict and crisis. On a deeper level of analysis, however, the issue can be understood in terms of the history and geography of a country for centuries burdened with the predicament of being a small state in an exposed strategic location.

The aims of the present study are, first, to consider the whole range of Danish reactions to German occupation, from willing collaboration at one end to armed resistance at the other; then to examine the long debate since 1945 and explore the political and moral dimensions of both the policy of cooperation and the course of resistance; and finally to view those opposite positions in the context of traditional ideas and attitudes relating to conflict and war. It follows that a brief preparatory overview of the trends of thought and tendencies of behaviour that came to characterize Danish conduct of external relations in the centuries preceding the invasion of Denmark in 1940 will be useful.

1
Traumas and trends

The foremost watershed in the history of Danish–Norwegian and Danish foreign policy is the end of the Great Northern War in 1720. In the centuries before that year Denmark–Norway, with Iceland and Greenland, colonies in the Caribbean, India and West Africa and a powerful navy, played a very active part in the politics of the region. As a major power situated by the Baltic Sea, it fought aggressive and defensive wars, mostly against Sweden, and gained and lost territories. In the centuries following 1720 Denmark–Norway, and later Denmark, adopted an increasingly passive role in European politics. Taking leave of one means after another of conducting foreign policy, the kingdom gradually resigned itself to the fate of a small state. While becoming ever more preoccupied with international trade, international law, international morality and international organization, Denmark eventually came close to turning its back on international politics.

The retreat from power politics, which went on till the middle of the twentieth century, comprised several stages. Each stage may be defined by reference to the character of the policy pursued by the kingdom in conflicts among the European powers. The first one lasted from the end of the Great Northern War to the country's involuntary involvement in the Napoleonic Wars in 1807. During this long period Denmark–Norway managed to secure neutral status in the various wars that occurred. However, while steering clear of actual hostilities between the emerging great powers, it participated in the shifting alliances of the European balance of power, which was possible under the loose and rather accommodating rules of neutrality then prevailing. The second stage began at the end of the Napoleonic Wars and finished soon after the First World War. Apart from its own wars with its southern neighbours, Denmark again stayed neutral in all wars in this period. But its position among the powers changed. While most of the time armed with fairly substantial military forces, the country was now so isolated that it played only a minimal role in the working of the balance of power. The last stage of the Danish retreat from international politics lasted from the initial years of the League of Nations to the later part of the Second World War. In this period Denmark remained diplomatically isolated, but now based its policy of neutrality on extremely weak military foundations.

Apart from 1720 itself, the most formative years in the history of Danish foreign policy were 1814, when the kingdom lost Norway to Sweden only half a dozen years after losing its navy to Britain; 1864, when German forces defeated the Danes and all of Schleswig-Holstein went to Prussia; and 1914, when Denmark declared strict neutrality in the hostilities but gave Germany certain assurances. While the events marked by the year 1814 dwarfed the kingdom and those of 1864 checked its territorial ambitions, the conjuncture of 1914 established Denmark on its course of disengagement and neutrality. Twenty-five years later, when another major war broke out in its vicinity, Denmark again declared its neutrality, in the hope that this policy would once more see the country through the hostilities unscathed. Instead, it led to German invasion and five years of occupation. That experience started a debate about the prudence and morality of Danish international conduct which is not yet over.

Though a member of one or other of the great European alliance systems most of the time since 1720, Denmark did not become involved in the actual hostilities of any of the major wars during the period. Despite several close shaves, it also managed to avoid wars with its northern and North German neighbours. Thus, much of the time during more than 80 years of peace Denmark was in the fortunate position of being able to concentrate its international efforts on the economic interests of the country. When major powers were at war, it could carry on its shipping and develop its commerce, and enjoy the advantages of increased demand for such services brought about by the war. This lenient and prolonged experience of European politics was bound to affect the style of the kingdom's diplomacy and the nature of its foreign policy, and perhaps even the Danish conception of international politics in general.

In playing the European balance of power cautiously and defensively, and exploiting the absence of established conventions of neutrality through skilful bargaining with belligerents, Denmark developed a decidedly pragmatic and opportunistic form of diplomacy. 'To plead our case and steal our way through as best we can,' as O.H. Guldberg, head of government from 1780 to 1784, once put it, became the Danish way.[1]

The circumstance that Denmark, usually enjoying the protection or support of some powerful ally, often could afford to devote its efforts to championing the rights and exploiting the advantages of neutrals tended to give its foreign policy a mercenary character. In crisis or war, when some other states might have to struggle for security and survival, Denmark could go on enriching itself. The prosperity that the kingdom enjoyed in the second half of the century helped to substantiate the notion of foreign policy as largely a pursuit of economic interests.

The long-lasting combination of peace and prosperity also helped to foster a conception of international politics as essentially a competition for economic advantage, rather than a rivalry for power and struggle for survival. Among those responsible for shaping and directing the kingdom's foreign policy it may even have given rise to a certain smugness about Danish conduct in European affairs. In a confidential letter written in 1757, J.H.E. Bernstorff, who conducted the foreign policy of the kingdom from 1751 to 1770, told a friend that 'a war started without just reason – I will go even further: without necessity, seems to me to be the most dreadful of all decisions that human beings could take'.[2] In retrospect, eighteenth-century Danish neutrality may be seen as not only the first phase of a withdrawal from European power politics, but also as the beginning of what might be described as a process of sentimentalizing the nature of international relations. Though the sovereign identity, territorial extent, political system and social structure of Denmark, as well as the international conditions of Europe, all changed, that process continued in the following centuries.

1.1 1814

In the final decades of the first long period of neutrality distinguished here, the diplomatic situation of Denmark–Norway worsened considerably. During the French Revolutionary and Napoleonic Wars it soon became more difficult to secure the basic interests of the kingdom by playing the European balance of power the way earlier statesmen had done, and sometimes also more dangerous to champion the rights and exploit the advantages of neutrals. Having tried, in rapidly changing international circumstances, to steer a safe course between great-power rivals and, at the same time, uphold its preferred principles of neutrality, Denmark ended up as an ally of Napoleonic France. The seven years of war that followed started with a major disaster for the kingdom and ended with an even greater one.

In the crises and wars of the earlier part of the period, Denmark had predominantly followed its own neutral course, which on the whole had been cautious and defensive. In the later decades, however, it moved, sometimes by force of events and sometimes deliberately, towards a collective and more offensive policy of neutrality. In 1794 Denmark and Sweden signed a neutrality convention, and in the following years demonstrated their willingness jointly to defend their neutral status in the French Revolutionary War. However, while making the most of the economic opportunities presented by a war which involved all the great powers of Europe, the Danish government refused to provide convoys for its ships and avoided challenging Britain diplomatically.

This measure of restraint disappeared after 1797, when crown prince Frederick as regent took over the direction of foreign policy. Within a year his government provided convoys and ordered commanding officers to refuse visitations by belligerent powers, and if necessary to back the refusal with armed force. Eventually the new policy led to clashes in the Mediterranean between Danish convoys and ships of the British navy. When the British government reacted, the Danes refused to back down, and maintained the principle of the inviolability of neutral convoys in the expectation that Denmark would have the support of Russia, which by then had left the coalition against France. While Denmark appealed to Russia to revive the Armed Neutrality League of 1780, Britain sent a diplomat to Copenhagen to enforce an agreement. Faced with a threat of bombardment by a squadron of the British navy, the Danish government gave way temporarily. Shortly thereafter the tsar invited Denmark, Sweden and Prussia to join Russia in re-establishing an Armed Neutrality League, a principal aim of which would be to enforce the inviolability of neutral convoys. Hopeful that such an alignment would lead to a negotiated settlement with Britain and a formal acknowledgement of the principles of neutrality that Denmark had long been championing, the Danish government decided to accept the invitation.

However, far from strengthening its bargaining position by this move, Denmark soon ended up a victim of new developments in the relationships of the great powers. While tension between Russia and Britain rapidly rose, the tsar and Napoleon moved closer to each other. Denmark, aware that Sweden had been trying to secure Russian support for an attempt to conquer Norway, recognized that it would be geopolitically dependent on Russia in an armed conflict between Britain and the two strongest powers on the Continent. So when Britain sent a fleet to Danish waters and presented an offer of a defensive alliance, the government refused, and engaged in an unequal battle with Nelson's squadron at Copenhagen. In the armistice negotiations it procrastinated, and accepted the British terms only after the death of Tsar Paul and the succession of his pro-British son Alexander I.

A few months later Denmark's diplomatic situation became even more difficult. In a Russo–British convention Alexander renounced not only the principle of the inviolability of neutral convoys but also the rather more important one of 'free ship, free cargo' which Denmark had championed for generations. Unable to secure a release of the Danish ships captured and a return of the colonies occupied by Britain during the hostilities unless it accepted unconditionally the terms of the convention, the government gave in to the pressures of the two powers and acceded to their convention. This was the end of the Danish policy of offensive neutrality. When, in 1803, the war with Napoleon broke out again, the government returned to the tradition of defensive neutrality, forbidding those practices which in the past had provoked Britain while, at the same time, taking care not to provoke France.

Thus, when four years later Denmark found itself exposed to diplomatic pressures even severer than those experienced after Frederick assumed responsibility for foreign policy it had little to do with the nature of its neutrality policy. The reason was another realignment of the great powers. Following the defeat of the Russian army by the French in 1807, the tsar signed a peace treaty by which he undertook to accede to the Continental System of blockade and to join Napoleon in forcing the remaining neutrals to close their ports to all British shipping. A month later Denmark received ultimatums from both France and Britain, each of which presented the government with the choice between becoming an ally and being treated as an enemy. For Britain, the real concern was with the Danish navy, which, if it fell under French control, would complicate British naval movements and economic warfare. Hence the British government demanded that Denmark either became an ally and put its navy under British command or handed it over as a pledge of Danish neutrality. When the crown prince turned down the ultimatum, a British fleet prepared to blockade Zealand and landed troops north of Copenhagen. The Danish government responded by declaring war. After encirclement of Copenhagen and three days of bombardment of the capital, the Danes requested a cease-fire. When the British left they took with them, as their property, the entire Danish navy and its equipment.

Without its navy, Denmark felt compelled to accept the French ultimatum and join France and its allies in the war. In the treaty alliance,

Napoleon promised his support in case of an attack on Denmark and guaranteed the territorial integrity of the kingdom, while the Danish government undertook to join the Continental System and, together with France and Russia, declare war on Sweden to force it to follow suit. Thus Denmark, after generations of neutrality, peace and prosperity, ended up actively involved in a major European war.

The later years of that war became increasingly foreboding for Denmark. In 1810, when marshal Bernadotte was made an heir to the Swedish throne under the name of Carl Johan, the old idea of taking Norway away from Denmark received new impetus in Stockholm. Over the next few years Frederick VI, as the crown prince had become in 1808, and his advisers were disturbed by news of successive Swedish plans for taking possession of Norway, and at one stage also parts of Denmark itself, with the support of one or more of the great powers. However, they were still inclined to rely on the guarantee of Napoleon, who renewed the alliance treaty in 1812. But after the subsequent defeats of the French army in Russia the insecurity of Denmark became more obvious. The king, still focusing narrowly on the possession of Norway, maintained his confidence in the military genius of Napoleon and decided to remain his ally. On the other hand, the Danish foreign minister and several other advisers, now increasingly apprehensive for the very survival of the state, feared the possibility of their country ending up as the ally of a defeated Napoleon and wanted Denmark to seek support elsewhere. The immediate anxiety about the loss of Norway and the deeper fear of a deprivation of independent statehood became the twin preoccupations in Danish circles in the final stages of the war and first years of the peace.

Early in 1814 the peace treaty with Sweden was signed in Kiel. Denmark had to hand over all of Norway, but – apparently as a result of the pressure of time and an oversight by the Swedish negotiator – kept Greenland, Iceland and the Faroe Islands. As compensation it received Swedish Pomerania, which however went to Prussia in the subsequent Vienna settlement. Instead Frederick VI was made duke of Lauenburg. In the peace settlement with Britain, various colonies were returned to Denmark, but not the navy; and the island of Heligoland went to Britain. As part of the post-Napoleonic settlement of Germany, Holstein and Lauenburg joined the new German Confederation, where their representative in the Diet became the Danish sovereign.

Thus, 1814 marked one of the lowest points in modern Danish history. Only seven years after the seizure of its navy and one year after the financial bankruptcy of the kingdom, Denmark lost about two thirds of its territory (Greenland excluded) and one third of its population. Domestically, poverty and unemployment added to the burden. As the great loser of the Napoleonic Wars, Denmark found itself isolated and exposed when peace returned. For some time, its very survival as an independent state seemed at stake. A Norwegian rebellion against the transition to Sweden, which raised doubts about the role of the Danish government and led the great powers to set up a commission to determine its responsibility for the events in Norway, gave Carl Johan another opportunity to pursue his project of securing the Danish islands, Zealand in particular, for Sweden. The Russians, too, seemed to present a threat. After their peace with Denmark they left an army in Holstein, which gradually grew bigger and eventually occupied nearly all of the duchy. Thus, on the eve of the Congress of Vienna, which the king attended uninvited, there was a real fear in Denmark that the country might be about to suffer a fate comparable to that of Poland in the eighteenth century. For a while, defeatism set in.

Only a few months later, however, the danger began to recede. The tsar, satisfied with developments in Norway, ratified the peace and started to withdraw his troops. The fear of a military attack from Sweden lingered for some time yet. However, once the central issue became payment of the Norwegian part of the debt of the Danish kingdom the tension between the two countries took on a rather different character. In the early 1820s relations with Sweden began to improve, after the great powers had put pressure on the Swedish king to settle the outstanding matter. As a co-signatory of the Final Act of the Congress of Vienna, Denmark now enjoyed the protection of what later became known as the Concert of Europe. For the following decades Denmark had no potential enemy.

From the mid-1820s Denmark became increasingly inclined to turn its back on international politics and to involve itself in domestic affairs alone. As in some other parts of Europe in the restoration period, those were the Biedermeier years in Danish political and social life. To say that Denmark had no foreign policy, a historian of the period considered, would be only partly true of the years from 1824 to 1831, but entirely true of the following years.[3] Denmark simply took care to keep its balance among the great powers. That required a little more skill in the 1830s, when tension between the two liberal powers in the west and the three autocratic powers in the east of Europe compelled Denmark to keep the lowest possible profile in diplomacy, than it had done in the 1820s. Maintaining such a balance allowed the government to concentrate its international efforts on trade and transport.

Official preoccupation with economic matters reflected not only the relative calm of European politics in those years but also a change in the character and attitudes of the foreign ministers of the country. Niels Rosenkrantz, who had advised the king in matters of foreign policy during most of the years of the alliance with Napoleonic France and had stayed in office until 1824, had been in the aristocratic, cosmopolitan tradition of the eighteenth century. His successors, the first of whom was Ernst Schimmelmann, identified more with the commercial interests of the wealthy circles at a slightly lower level of Danish society.

The age of restoration was the first part of the second long period of Danish foreign policy distinguished here, which lasted more than a hundred years. If in the eighteenth century the kingdom had been a power of the third rank, in the course of this period it became simply a small state. The most obvious reason was the succession of losses suffered. However, it was also the result of certain changes in the structure and organization of the European states system which made the difference between great powers and other sovereign states more marked than before. The four principal allies of the coalition that had defeated Napoleon, together with France itself, were clearly superior in terms of power to all other states in Europe. The dominant role assumed at the Congress of Vienna also gave them a new status in the society of states. Moreover, their subsequent efforts at joint management of European politics, initially through the congress system of the post-war decade and later through the looser Concert of Europe, lent them some of the qualities of a class in international society. Various changes of relative power among the great powers themselves, first the decline of Russia in the earlier part of the period and, more important, the rise of Germany in the later age, further weakened the diplomatic position of Denmark.

As in most of the eighteenth century, Denmark stayed out of the wars of the great powers throughout this period. But it now moved one step further away from the kind of active participation in European politics that so often had characterized its foreign policy in the centuries before 1720. It no longer entered into military alliances. One reason was that the country now had so little to offer others that it was barely worthy of an alliance. However, in the course of the century, particularly after 1870, Danish governments made a virtue of necessity by adopting a policy of isolation. Prudently staying neutral in the conflicts of others, they became increasingly inclined to present this policy in a legal and moral framework. Thus Danish neutrality, which in the eighteenth century had been more a practice of diplomacy, eventually became also an ideology of foreign policy.

1.2 1864

When Denmark did go to war again in the nineteenth century it was not as an ally of a great power in a European war but as principal in a local conflict, bent on defending or pursuing vital interests by its southern border. In the course of the quiet years in European politics tension had begun to rise again in many parts of the Continent, both within and between states. Motivated by the new forces of liberalism and nationalism, growing pressures had been directed against the dynastic and territorial order imposed by the victorious powers at the Congress of Vienna. Both the national politics and the international relations of Denmark became affected too. Early in 1848 the new king, Frederick VII, responded to political pressure by voluntarily putting an end to absolutism and starting a process that eventually led to constitutional government. One result was that National Liberal leaders soon secured a dominating influence on the foreign policy of the country. Almost immediately they became involved in a crisis in the relations between Denmark and the duchies of Schleswig and Holstein.

Nationalist stirrings in the two duchies had given rise to a movement which sought to separate Schleswig from Denmark, unite it with Holstein under a joint constitution and take it into the German Confederation. The policy of the new Danish government, on the other hand, was to unite Schleswig with Denmark. After a rebellion in the duchies, the government went to war on the programme of 'Denmark to the Ejder', the river separating Schleswig from Holstein. Shortly it found itself engaged in hostilities not only with the recalcitrant duchies but also with Prussia and the loose German Confederation. The Danish forces fought with patriotic enthusiasm and wide popular support. But, as the war progressed, disagreement about its aims developed among the Danish government, the armed forces, the diplomatic service and even the king, who found it difficult to accept his new constitutional role. The disagreement became even more pronounced in the peace negotiations. Eventually, after the Conservatives had gained more influence in the government at the expense of the National Liberals, the Ejder programme was abandoned. Instead the government accepted an arrangement which gave the kingdom three separate units: Denmark, Schleswig and Holstein. This outcome, agreed in 1852, presented a constitutional problem for the government, the solution of which became the principal concern of Danish foreign policy for the next dozen years.

The general idea behind successive Danish attempts to solve the problem was to order relations between the three units of the kingdom in a way which could provide a lasting framework for national development and the best possible protection against German interference. Reflecting a revival in the influence of the National Liberals, the efforts became increasingly aimed at tying Schleswig closer to Denmark and giving Holstein a separate status. This revival of the Ejder policy was in conflict with the agreement of 1852, and acceptable to neither Holstein nor the German Confederation, which threatened to occupy Holstein. Prussia favoured a solution which involved a division of Schleswig. The Danish government, expecting that long-standing rivalry between Austria and Prussia would prevent the Confederation from intervening militarily, persisted with its policy, in the hope that a crisis would lead to a great-power conference and a satisfactory settlement. Here it had the support of the press, the people and most politicians. Following a German invasion of Schleswig, war broke out again in 1864. Denmark fought defensively with a view to bringing about an international conference. But when a conference eventually did meet, the Danes again found it difficult to agree on a policy. In the course of the conference, the differences between the king, the government and the foreign ministry became increasingly marked. In the end Prussia and Austria imposed a peace of their own, with the result that two years later Schleswig-Holstein became a province of Prussia.

When the king, following the defeat of the Danish forces and the poor performance of the diplomats, had to give up the two duchies and cede Lauenburg, the kingdom lost about two fifths of its territory and approximately one million of its inhabitants. The loss of Schleswig was particularly painful to the nation. A despair of the sort that had set in 50 years earlier returned. Among politicians it was widely feared that Denmark might not be able to survive as an independent state. Since so much of Danish territory had been lost already, perhaps all of Jutland would be taken on some future occasion.[4] Such fears reasserted themselves half a dozen years later, when some thought that Bismarck, following his defeat of France and the unification of Germany, might go on to conquer all of Denmark. Gradually, the darkest forebodings receded. Yet, some events in the next few decades, in particular the repeal of paragraph 5 of the Peace of Prague of 1866, which had allowed for the possibility of Denmark some time in the future regaining part of Schleswig through a plebiscite, and the treatment of the Danish minority south of the new border, did little to remove Danish anxiety. In the longer run, of course, the sources of lasting Danish insecurity in the half century after 1864 were not merely the growing strength and self-assertive policies of Bismarckian Prussia and imperial Germany but also the rising tension among the great powers of Europe.

Whereas Danish concerns about survival after 1814 could be put to rest within a few years thanks to the territorial stability introduced by the Vienna treaties and maintained through the relative solidarity of the great powers, after 1864 it became much more difficult to rely on the great powers for ultimate security. While the development of Bismarck's alliance system tended to divide Europe, his successors' excursions into world politics helped to intensify rivalry among the great powers in global as well as European politics. A further source of insecurity for Denmark was the relative decline of Russia as a great power. In the earlier part of the century after 1814 the kingdom had sometimes relied on the tsar for diplomatic support in critical situations, even as late as the difficult years from 1848 to 1852. After the Russian setback in the Crimean War this was no longer quite so possible. The Russian defeat in the war with Japan in 1904–05 left Denmark even more isolated diplomatically. By then Danish governments could not escape the conclusion that their country was firmly within the German sphere of influence, in a Europe which seemed to be growing increasingly dangerous for a small state.

In the long run, Danish reactions to the trauma of 1864 were of several kinds. First, there was a marked introversion of national efforts. 'What is lost outwards must be gained inwards' became the watchword of the nation. Through education – of adults as well as children – religion, literature and art, the spiritual level of the people was raised. Through land reclamation, more efficient agriculture, improved transport, modernized commerce and industrial initiatives the material resources of the country were developed. In the later decades of the century the foundations were laid for the prosperous and egalitarian Denmark that was to take shape in the twentieth century.

Second, there was a thorough adjustment to the external situation of the country after the Prussian victories and the establishment of the German *Reich*. Bismarck's defeat of France in the war of 1870–71 soon put an end to Danish dreams of taking revenge for 1864 and recovering Schleswig – or a substantial part of it. Instead rules were developed for living next to a forceful and assertive great power. As early as 1878 J.B.S. Estrup, Conservative president of the council, asserted that Denmark in its diplomacy ought to move close enough to Germany to leave no doubt that it would be on the side of this power in a major war – 'in any case *never* against it'.[5] In the following decades Denmark, out of respect for the preponderance of its neighbour, desisted from pursuing the cause of the Danes living south of the border. After 1901 Liberal governments, in particular that formed by J.C. Christensen in 1905, found it necessary to steer so close to Germany in their foreign policies that they in effect compromised the neutral position of the state. This policy of accepting German hegemony came to a head with the outbreak of major war in 1914.

Third, in the last decade of the nineteenth and first decade of the twentieth centuries some politicians tried to secure permanently peaceful relations with all other states through the introduction of two measures available under international law, namely neutralization and arbitration. In Danish political thought, the idea that a country might save itself from the worst calamities that could befall a member of an anarchical society of states by declaring itself perpetually neutral in the conflicts of others, and having such status recognized or even guaranteed by the great powers, can be traced back to 1864. Amid the despair following the defeat, the government instructed its representatives at the peace negotiations to seek a permanent neutralization of the country. The victors rejected the proposal; and the idea played no real part in politics again till the 1890s. By then the idea, together with that of arbitration, had become part of the programme of the Danish peace movement. The Liberal party adopted it, and had it included as a goal in the foreign policy and defence programme drawn up for a landmark parliamentary agreement reached in 1894. But it was not until after 1901, when the parliamentary system finally gained acceptance and the Liberals formed a government for the first time, that the party was able to pursue the status of neutralization actively. The Hague Peace Conference in 1899 and certain other developments a few years later gave some encouragement to those working for the idea. But by 1905, when the government resigned, it was clear that it was not possible to obtain adequate great-power support for its realization. Though the goal had to be dropped, pursuing it in a critical situation of European politics had underlined Denmark's determination to remain neutral in any future military conflict of the great powers.

While the quest for neutralization may be seen as inspired by a disposition to contract out of international politics, the pursuit of arbitration was motivated more by a desire for the reform of international society. The idea of reducing the occurrence of violent conflict in international society by signing treaties for the settlement of disputes through the process of arbitration had been developed and canvassed by the international peace movement in the later part of the century and had been given some impetus from a diplomatic initiative by the United States in 1890. While the initial aims were to set up a network of arbitration conventions and establish a European or international court of arbitration, the ultimate goal was an international society regulated by law, rather than by force. For Denmark, a small state in a precarious geopolitical situation, this was a particularly attractive goal. Having previously been brought up for public discussion in the 1880s, after 1890 the principle of arbitration became a subject of more serious debate between parliament and government. The principal champions were members of the Liberal party, who demanded that the government enter into treaties of arbitration with other countries. But the Social Democrats and later also the Radical Liberals, who formed a party in 1905, gave their support too. After the Hague Peace Conference of 1899 Denmark signed a considerable number of permanent treaties of arbitration. By then many Liberals, Social Democrats and Radical Liberals, representing, respectively, the farmers, the workers and the smallholders of the nation, were inclined to see the twin principles of arbitration and neutralization as offering an alternative to traditional defence and security policy.

In most of the post-Napoleonic period of European restoration, which had been an age of international order, peace and security, the concerns of Danish foreign policy had been largely of an economic nature, relating to commerce and prosperity more than anything else. In the middle part of the century, a period of growing nationalism in Europe and moderate rivalry and limited wars among the great powers, the goals had been essentially political, concerned with vital interests and national security. In the later decades of the nineteenth and first part of the twentieth centuries, when tension among the great powers was rising and Danish dependence on Germany increasing, the ends often pursued most vigorously were of a more ideological kind. They were addressed to the quality of external relations and the norms of international society. While both of the earlier sets of goals had been confined within the current state of the international system – the first aimed at drawing advantage from it and the second at providing security against it – the later set transcended the international conjuncture. It not only proposed legal measures for improving the existing situation of the country but also projected ideals for international society in general, pre-eminently peace and justice.

Thus, while the governmental response to the external pressure presented by German preponderance in the late nineteenth and early twentieth centuries stayed within the narrow limitations of geopolitical considerations, some projections of the goals of Danish foreign policy in the same years transcended the usual confines of international politics and soared into the spheres of international law and international morality. A remarkable optimism in the framing of ideological goals coexisted with a marked pessimism in the formation of security policy. In retrospect, both attitudes may be seen as indicating a reluctance, or inability, to accept the basic terms of international politics. While the more idealistic pursuits of reform in international relations seem to have taken too little account of the limitations imposed by the nature of politics among sovereign states, the ultra-realistic acceptance of the confined external situation of the country apparently left little room for exploring the diplomatic opportunities presented by an international system of rivalling great powers. Danish attitudes to, and thoughts about, foreign affairs in the period leading up to the First World War suggest that an over-optimistic idealism, apt to encourage futile pursuits, and an over-pessimistic realism, conducive to fatalistic passivity, can be alternative, and complementary, ways of contracting out of the international politics of a given historical situation.

1.3 1914

The real test of Danish neutrality came in 1914. Towards the end of July, when a great-power conflict seemed imminent, the Radical Liberal government consulted the leaders of the other parties, and found they all agreed that the only possible policy for Denmark would be a strict and impartial neutrality. When war broke out, early in August, the government issued a series of declarations of neutrality, relating to the several great-power conflicts. However, a number of contacts with German authorities had already indicated the nature of Danish neutrality. As early as 30 July a message from Berlin requested 'a favourable neutrality', to which the foreign minister Erik Scavenius replied 'yes of course – to the extent that this can be reconciled with the concept of neutrality itself'.[6] On 2 August, before Britain had entered the war, the German minister in Copenhagen asked the foreign minister how Denmark would react to a possible violation of its territorial waters. After intense discussions with the king and representatives of the armed forces, Scavenius presented his answer the following day. The government hoped, he said, that such a violation would not take place. If, through no fault of Germany's, it nevertheless did, that would make no difference to the position of neutrality assumed by Denmark. 'In no case,' he asserted, 'would Denmark ally itself with the enemy of Germany.'[7] Thus the government made its position quite clear. Whoever might violate its neutrality, Denmark would not go to war. It followed not only that the country in no circumstances would be the enemy of Germany but also that it could never become its ally.

On 5 August, after Britain had entered the war, the German minister enquired whether Denmark intended immediately and effectively to close the Great Belt, one of the straits providing access to the Baltic Sea. As the German navy had already started mining the area south of that passage, decision-makers in Copenhagen were inclined to regard the enquiry more as a demand. A refusal, they thought, would be likely to lead the Germans to complete the mining by themselves, in the process perhaps occupying a couple of strategic points in Denmark. All of them anxious to avoid any kind of involvement in the war, most were inclined to accept the demand. But when the parliamentary opposition showed reluctance to support such a decision, the government changed its mind. At this stage the king, encouraged by the chief of the navy who believed in accommodating the Germans, intervened to make the government reverse its decision again. The German minister was given an affirmative answer, and the mines were laid. To assuage the British government, the king, apparently under the impression that the mines would not be charged, sent a message of explanation to his British counterpart. George V was very understanding, as was the British minister in Copenhagen. At this stage of the war Britain had no real intention of entering the Baltic. But now Danish neutrality, in contrast with earlier wars between great powers, rested on closed straits.

The war itself provided further examples of Danish willingness to adjust to German needs. In the autumn of 1914 the government, concerned about the possibility of the war moving into the Baltic, which might lead Germany to occupy some Danish territory, made an attempt to mediate between the various belligerents. When it became clear that there was no way of bringing about a general peace, the Germans encouraged the Danes to explore the possibility of a separate peace between Germany and Russia. Although such a peace could not be in the interest of the Western powers, Denmark maintained its mediating efforts till the summer of 1915, all the time, however, discreetly keeping Britain informed. In 1917, when the intensified naval warfare enhanced the strategic importance of southern Norway and Germany feared a British action in that area, the prospect of a German occupation of Danish territory arose again. To forestall it, the foreign minister offered to put certain Danish islands at the disposal of Germany if the need arose, and once again assured the Germans of his government's intention to resist any British violation of Danish neutrality. However, while the political leaders broadly accepted the need to pursue a policy of pro-German neutrality, the sympathy of the king (personally quite critical of Germany), the army, the press and the people was overwhelmingly on the side of Germany's enemies. With Britain in particular there were many unofficial contacts throughout the war, the flow of military and political intelligence to London from highly placed Danish sources being especially important.

The bias towards Germany did not stop Denmark from championing the rights of neutrals and exploiting the advantages of non-belligerents. In its former efforts, Denmark collaborated with the other Scandinavian countries, mainly through consultation and coordination of attempts. In the first few years of the war the Scandinavian countries, and other small European neutrals, repeatedly approached the United States with a view to gaining American protection for the rights of neutrals. The minimal response of the Americans did not make it any easier for weak European neutrals to resist the diplomatic pressure of belligerent great powers and maintain a strict and impartial neutrality.

In drawing on the economic advantages of non-belligerent states, Denmark was rather more successful. Though highly dependent for its foreign trade on both Britain and Germany, it had considerable bargaining power over each, which it used with remarkable skill. Its negotiators could argue that unless Denmark kept up its exports to Britain, it would not be able to receive the raw materials needed to maintain the supply of agricultural products to Germany. Thus they convinced the Germans that it was not in their interests to continue the embargo on Danish exports to Britain that had been imposed at the outset of the war. Britain, on the other hand, wanted Danish exports enough to accept that an increasing share went to Germany. Within Denmark, the pattern of foreign trade that emerged was of particular benefit to the agricultural interests. But the shipping section, too, benefited from the war, even though a very large part of the merchant navy was requisitioned by the allied powers and many ships were lost.

Notwithstanding the various concessions to Germany, Denmark remained a neutral state. Whereas the Conservative Estrup in 1878 and the Liberal I.C. Christensen in 1907 had envisaged an alliance with Germany as a possibility in an extreme situation, the Radical Liberal leaders of 1914–18 did not go beyond a fairly passive and guarded compliance with German requirements in specific matters and never really considered engaging in the war. Though the government carried out a partial mobilization at the beginning of the war and repeatedly expressed its intention to resist a British violation of Danish neutrality, the Radical Liberal lack of faith in military resources qualified its determination to defend its position with physical means. The anti-militarism of the governing party, which was shared by many Social Democrats, pointed to the security and defence policy that would take its final form in the following decades.

So did another characteristic of Danish neutrality in the First World War, namely a suggestion of intellectual and moral superiority. As upheld by the Radical Liberal leaders, the policy reflected an inner confidence that the principle of non-involvement in the violent struggles of great powers was in harmony with the intellectual and moral forces that they, in common with a growing number of Social Democrats, believed would be shaping international relations in the twentieth century.

After the end of the war most Danes regarded the policy of neutrality as having been successful. It had kept the country out of war and given it substantial economic advantages, and had done the same for Sweden and Norway. The Radical Liberal government, which remained in office till 1920, now wanted to obtain some lasting protection for the international status of neutral states. Following an abortive revival of the old ideas of neutralization and arbitration, its representatives, together with those of the other Scandinavian nations, concentrated their efforts on influencing the drafting of what became known as the Covenant of a League of Nations projected by the victorious allies. Danish attention focused on the plans for a system of collective security, in particular on article 16 of the draft Covenant, which set out the obligations of members of the proposed League in dealing with a state in breach of the Covenant. The main concern of the government was that a member might find itself automatically obliged to participate in military sanctions. However, it received assurances that, while participation in economic sanctions would be obligatory, in the application of military sanctions the duties of members would not go beyond granting right of passage to those engaged in imposing them.

Early in 1920 the parliament unanimously approved Danish membership of the League of Nations. Yet the new Liberal government continued the endeavours to ease the role of small states in the new organization, and did achieve a few concessions regarding the obligations to participate in economic sanctions and to grant right of passage. Three of the four parts of the programme for maintaining peace among nations laid down in the Covenant, namely peaceful settlement of disputes, disarmament and peaceful change, were in harmony with most Danish thinking about international relations. But the principle of solidarity against aggression and war, on which the fourth part, collective security, rested, remained difficult to accept for large sections of a nation which for more than a hundred years had stayed out of alliances and escaped involvement in major wars.

1.4 1940

As early as the Crimean War, a French critic of Danish policy had described the country as '*craintif et optimiste*' at one and the same time.[8] That description would apply equally well to Denmark in the late nineteenth and early twentieth centuries. Indeed, it was in the decades before the First World War, when the concern to reform international society was more urgent and the need to adjust to geopolitical conditions most pressing, that the psychological and philosophical dichotomy in the Danish approach to foreign affairs became most pronounced. The coexistence, in a duality of hope and fear, of a tenacious faith in the advance of international law and order and gloomy apprehensions of war and invasion marked the pre-1914 Danish mind.

The attitudes and policies of Denmark in the third historical period distinguished here, which started a few years after the First and led up to and included most of the Second World War, again contained opposite strands. On the one hand, there was a marked tendency to draw inspiration from the goals and principles of internationalism, of both the liberal and the socialist kind. On the other hand, there was a compulsion to respond to the necessity of geopolitics. In the 1920s, when the state of the world in the eyes of most people in many countries seemed to present substantial grounds for optimism about the consolidation of international society, the former set of ideas was clearly the prevailing influence. But in the 1930s, when Denmark again was exposed to pressure from a powerful and aggressive neighbour, the internationalist creed was soon cast into the shade by a geopolitical determinism more pessimistic than ever before.

In the early 1920s the international situation of Denmark seemed safer than it had been for centuries. The collapse of the Russian government in 1917 and the establishment of five states round the eastern part of the Baltic had reduced Russian pressure on the region. The defeat of Germany in 1918 had removed the pressure from the south. And the subsequent signing of the Versailles peace treaty and setting up of the League of Nations had restored a formal concert of great powers and provided a machinery for maintaining peace among nations. Even later in the post-war decade the situation seemed fairly safe. The Soviet Union did not yet appear to present a serious danger. The eastern boundaries of the two central European powers were protected by the alliance system formed by France and the new states in eastern Europe, while the western borders of Germany were guaranteed by the Locarno system set up in 1925. The following year the pacification and rehabilitation of

Germany was sealed when the Weimar Republic joined the League of Nations. As late as the beginning of the 1930s the international political situation still seemed calm.

A further source of satisfaction for Denmark was the redrawing of its southern boundary in 1920, when, following a plebiscite, North Schleswig was reunited with the rest of the country. At last Denmark could count itself a satiated state. However, the circumstance that the reunification had been effected as part of the Versailles settlement, and not been explicitly endorsed by Germany, was a matter of some concern to the Danish government. When it subsequently attempted to confirm the new border by securing a formal recognition, no German signature was forthcoming. In the 1930s, when Germany increasingly showed signs of its intention to overthrow the Versailles settlement, the status of South Jutland, as the province was known to the Danes, became a source of considerable nervousness in Denmark.

With no threat looming on the political horizon and no further revisionist goal preoccupying the country, it seemed safe for Denmark to reduce its post-war military establishment. In 1922 parliament passed a new defence act, which reduced the number of battalions from 52 to 35, gave up the concentration on the defence of Zealand and confirmed the demolition of the fortification of Copenhagen, which had been carried out already. The act, which was based on the work of a committee set up in 1919, represented a rather one-sided compromise between the Liberal party, in government since 1920, and the Conservatives, who had found it expedient, in terms of parliamentary politics, to accept most of the Liberal proposals. It entailed a sharp reduction in the budgets of both the army and the navy. While the spokesmen of the navy had exerted some influence on the negotiations, the army chiefs had suffered from internal divisions and had played only a minor role in the decision-making. The Radical Liberals and the Social Democrats voted against the bill. While the former wanted an even severer reduction of defence expenditure, the latter advocated disarmament. However, in neither theory nor practice was there much difference between the positions of the two parties. Basically, the leaders of both believed not only that Denmark would be quite unable to defend itself against Germany, the only potential enemy, but also that maintaining armed forces of any significant size would be more likely to provoke than to deter an attack on Denmark. During the 10 years that followed the 1922 act, the two parties repeatedly put forward proposals for unilateral disarmament.

With security and defence not matters of pressing concern, the governments of the 1920s were able to concentrate their efforts in other fields. In diplomacy, they aimed at staying on fairly good terms with the great powers, particularly with Germany, and keeping out of any wars that might occur. In economic relations, they cultivated the two foremost trading partners, namely Britain, which bought nearly two thirds of Danish exports, and Germany, which supplied more than a third of the imports. In the ideological sphere, they were guided by the values and norms which the nation had inherited from the past. On one level, they upheld the democratic ideals and practices in a world in which rival political ideologies were beginning to establish themselves. On another level, they continued the pursuit of the broad internationalist goals formulated in the later part of the previous period of Danish foreign policy. Here the aim was to develop an international society which would be regulated by law rather than by power and characterized by peace instead of by recurrent wars. The League of Nations provided new machinery for the pursuit of international order. In this forum Denmark concerned itself with the rights of small states in particular. Seeking to protect and develop the rights of the lesser and more numerous members of international society could be seen as an attempt to extend democratic principles to international life.

In the early 1930s, however, signs of a rapid deterioration in the general situation of Europe began to accumulate. The economic difficulties that had plunged the world into a major crisis in the late 1920s persisted. Fascism, already triumphant in Italy, was fast undermining the political structure of the Weimar Republic, Germany's first experiment with democracy. Adolf Hitler's accession to power in 1933 signalled a new aggressiveness in German foreign policy. Within only a few years Germany withdrew from the League of Nations, introduced conscription and reorganized the army, and invaded the Rhineland. In 1935–36 Mussolini's Italy was conquering Abyssinia, and subsequently intervening in the Spanish civil war together with Germany. By the middle of the 1930s Denmark once again found itself in an exposed position.

In October 1936, when Hitler and Mussolini formed the Berlin–Rome Axis, the multiple system of five European great powers took on a triangular shape. In one corner were the two Axis powers, in another the two Western League powers and in the third the Soviet Union. The ideological struggle between fascism, liberal democracy and communism reinforced the diplomatic–strategic triangularity. The shape of the triangle changed several times. In the original configuration the three rival parties were all quite far from each other. But the Anglo–French efforts to appease the dictators, culminating in the Munich agreements of 1938, brought the two League powers and the Axis powers closer to each other. Later the Nazi–Soviet pact, signed in August 1939, and the outbreak of the war in the West established a bond between the Soviet Union and the Axis powers. Finally, after Germany invaded Russia in June 1941, the Soviet Union joined the Western powers in the military alliance against Germany and its allies.

For Denmark, one of the most significant events in the changing diplomatic alignments of the period was the signing of an Anglo–German naval agreement in June 1935. That agreement, which could be seen as an early move in the British attempt to appease Hitler, in effect left the control of the Kattegat and the Baltic Sea to Germany. Thus Denmark and Danish waters once again became part of the German sphere of influence. Subsequent changes in the alignment of the great powers did little to alter that situation.

Throughout this critical period in Danish history the country was governed by a coalition of Social Democrats and Radical Liberals. With Thorvald Stauning, leader of the Social Democrats, as prime minister and Peter Munch, Radical Liberal leader, as foreign minister, the government stayed in office from 1929 till immediately after the German invasion of Denmark in April 1940. The traditional anti-militarism of the Social Democrats and the pacifist tendencies of many Radical Liberals left their mark on the defence, the security and the foreign policy of the government.

The reduction of the military forces initiated in 1922 was continued. In 1932, at a time when the international political situation still seemed relatively safe but the economic conditions had become very serious for Denmark, a bill for a new defence act was prepared and, with a minimum of debate, passed by both houses of parliament in less than a week. The number of army battalions was reduced from 35 to 24 and the size of the navy cut severely. The army now had only two divisions, one on Zealand and the other in Jutland. Later the same year the minister of defence described the new act as amounting in reality to disarmament of the country.[9] The bill had been presented on the initiative of the Liberal party, which represented the agricultural interest, the section of the economy hardest hit by the international crisis. The two governing parties had accepted the proposal as a big step in the right direction. They were still advocating unilateral disarmament, but had failed to have their successive proposals passed by the upper house of parliament. Only the Conservatives voted against the bill.

The third set of inter-war defence laws was enacted in 1937. By then the rearmament of Germany and the ambitions of Hitler were presenting a growing threat, to the sovereignty of particular neighbouring states as well as to the peace of Europe. The League of Nations had shown itself unable to provide protection against aggression by a great power. All the political leaders in Denmark were aware of the risk of major war and the potential threat to their country. Yet the changes to the existing defence structure now proposed by the government were a mixture of fairly minimal improvements and some further cuts. While both the army and the navy received some additional funds for new *matériel*, the army incurred a reduction in size. The air force was reduced from five squadrons to four, and only three batteries were allocated for the aerial defence of Copenhagen.

The bill, which was passed with the votes of only the two governing parties, reflected more the convictions of the Radical Liberals than of the Social Democratic leaders. Since 1933 Stauning, encouraged by some influential younger members of his party, had developed certain doubts about the long-standing anti-militarism of the labour movement and had made a few tentative moves towards a strengthening of the defence of the country. But Munch, a dogmatic anti-militarist and the dominating intellectual influence on the government, had rejected or ignored such attempts to change the policy. He and some of his colleagues, and no doubt many supporters not only of his own but also of other parties, were still of the opinion that a build-up of defence would not reduce the vulnerability of the country, and might even add to it. The Conservatives, on the other hand, attacked the bill strongly and voted against it. In their view, a reasonable defence, though of course it could never be strong enough to meet a German attack in a war with Denmark alone, might well help deter an attack in the more likely situation where Germany was at war with one or more great powers and had most of its forces engaged elsewhere. The Liberals abstained from the vote. The service chiefs had had only a minor role in the preparation of the bill, mainly because of disagreement between the navy and the army, but largely shared the views of the Conservatives.

After the German annexation of a compliant Austria in 1938 the government did allocate some funds for the strengthening, as distinct from the expansion, of the armed forces. However, the effect on the military capability of the nation was of no great significance. In April 1940, when Germany was ready to invade Denmark and Norway, the Danish army consisted of two divisions, the navy was small and most of its ships old, and Copenhagen was practically without any aerial defence. It was a force capable only of dealing with incidental violations of Danish territory, not of defending the country against a proper attack. While the reduction in the defensive forces introduced in the early 1920s had been facilitated by confidence in the stability of post-war international relations, the restraint exercised in the later 1930s was conditioned more by despair about the external situation of Denmark, in a Europe of rapidly rising tension and instability.

One reason for despondency was the diplomatic isolation of Denmark. As in the nineteenth century, the government made various attempts in the 1930s to find allies or protectors. In 1933 it entertained some hope that Britain would offer military help if needed. But the British did not commit themselves. Four years later, when Stauning spoke to the foreign secretary Anthony Eden in London and voiced his concern about the Danish–German border, he received only assurances of diplomatic support against a threat from Germany. In February 1940 Winston Churchill, then First Lord of the Admiralty, confirmed verbally that, because of Denmark's proximity to Germany, Britain would be unable to provide help in case of a conflict between the two neighbours.

The other conceivable source of support was the other Nordic countries. The events in Germany in 1933 gave impulse to Danish efforts to strengthen the bonds with the neighbours in the north. But when Stauning began to explore the idea of cooperating in matters of defence it became clear that there was no prospect of establishing a Scandinavian front against German aggression. The Norwegian and the Swedish governments were against it; and the pacifist sections of Stauning's own party as well as the Radical Liberal leaders and supporters did not like the idea either. While the Danish objections were largely ideologically conditioned, the Norwegian and Swedish reactions rested mainly on strategic considerations. The two governments shared the risk assessment of the Danes, and found the strategic position of Denmark essentially hopeless. Nor did the decline of the League of Nations and the abandonment of the system of collective security later in the 1930s, or even the outbreak of war in 1939, lead to Scandinavian cooperation, whether in matters of defence or in the fields of politics and economics.

The military weakness and diplomatic isolation of Denmark were clearly reflected in the foreign policy of its government. From the mid-1930s to the retreat of the coalition government in the crisis of August 1943 Denmark's foreign policy was dominated by its fear of Germany. In the first few years of Hitler's regime it still seemed just possible that the system of collective security introduced in 1920 might offer some protection against latent German aggression. But the great powers' handling of the Italo–Abyssinian conflict in 1935–36 indicated that it could be of little help. Instead of enforcing economic sanctions against Mussolini's Italy after its attack on Abyssinia, Britain and France chose to appease Italy at the expense of Abyssinia. For Denmark, as for many other small states, that crisis became a turning-point in the attitude to the League of Nations. To its foreign minister, whose long-standing doubts about the ability of the League of Nations to check expansionistic actions by a great power temporarily had given way to a certain amount of optimism, the handling of the crisis confirmed that a small state could not rely on the League for help against a great power. Only the more traditional ways of responding to the German threat, it now seemed, were open to Denmark.

In the later 1930s Danish foreign policy increasingly followed the principle of accommodating Germany. Initially, when Denmark was a member of the Council of the League of Nations, that policy was pursued largely through the League. Danish representatives devoted much effort to attempting to improve relations between the Western great powers and Germany, and to securing a more equal position for the latter within the Versailles system. Thus, when Hitler's government in 1935 challenged the system by announcing its intention to build up the armed forces and reintroduce conscription, the Danish foreign minister tried to make the great powers tone down their condemnation of the proposed measures and, when he failed, abstained from the vote. When, the following year, Germany sent troops into the demilitarized zone of the Rhineland, the Danish line in the debate of the Council was again conciliatory. After the usual round of consultations with the other Scandinavian governments, the Danish decision-makers found that they could vote for a resolution which simply acknowledged that a breach of treaty obligations had taken place, but not for one which amounted to a censure of Germany. Guided by a wish to see all the great powers concerned take up negotiations with each other, the foreign minister recommended, in a secret meeting of the Council, that Germany should not only be allowed to participate on an equal footing in the deliberations of the Council but also be free to make proposals of its own. In the diplomacy of the next few years, after the Italo–Abyssinian crisis, Denmark continued on its course of conciliation mainly by steering close to Britain, which itself was gradually moving nearer to Germany.

In the last year of peace, after Hitler had invaded and incorporated Austria and German foreign policy had entered a more aggressive phase, Denmark had to handle relations with Germany on its own. Afraid of being drawn into a major war and anxious to have its neutrality respected, it scrupulously avoided offending Hitler's government and did what it could to accommodate German requirements. Earlier in 1938, it had already conceded Germany the right to fly over the Danish straits in times of war. In April the following year, when Hitler offered Denmark a pact of non-aggression, the government was again responsive. Such a pact, the decision-makers thought, might serve as a substitute for a more explicit recognition of the Danish–German border of 1920. At any rate, a rejection of the proposal, they feared, might offend the German leadership. While the other Scandinavian countries declined similar offers from Hitler, Denmark took up negotiations on its own. When the Germans agreed to include in the protocol of the treaty a statement which in effect allowed Denmark, in any future war between Germany and Britain, to continue trading with the latter according to the normal rules of neutrality, the pact was soon ready for signature. However, out of concern for the reactions of the Danish public, Munch declined an invitation to attend the signing ceremony in Berlin.

On 1 September, when Germany and Poland were at war with each other, Denmark issued its first declaration of neutrality. Two days later, when the Second World War had broken out, it followed up with a declaration of complete neutrality, based on a set of rules drawn up by a group of neutrals in March the previous year. On 5 December, a few days after the Soviet Union and Finland had gone to war with each other, Stauning confirmed in parliament that Denmark had to maintain its policy of neutrality.

In the First World War, one of the most important means, and ends, of pursuing such a policy had been foreign trade. Now again the government's line was to seek to balance its trade with Germany against that with Britain. After an unsuccessful attempt by a group of neutrals to cooperate in defence of their rights to trade with the belligerents, Denmark took up independent negotiations with each of the two powers. The German negotiators, adhering to the agreed interpretation of the non-aggression pact, accepted the argument that the export of Danish goods to Germany was dependent on the import of British raw materials for Danish agriculture, and therefore on the Danish export of agricultural products to Britain. With the British, who saw Danish exports to Germany as an obstacle to their economic warfare and were prepared to reduce their dependence on Danish products, it was much more difficult to reach an agreement. The negotiations went on for more than four months, the parties signing an agreement only a week before the Germans invaded Denmark. Yet, in the economic sphere, Denmark managed to maintain a balance between the two principal belligerents in the first winter of the war.

In other areas it proved more difficult to sustain such a balance. In November the Germans requested a mining of the Danish straits, which before the war they had wanted kept clear for passage even in wartime. The Danish government decided to meet what was in effect a demand, for the same reason as in 1914, namely that if it refused the Germans would lay the mines themselves and thereby violate Danish neutrality. Thus, from an early stage of the war, Denmark seemed set on a course which would render its neutrality as biased in favour of Germany as it had been in the First World War. Soon, however, signs began to appear that in this war the country might have to face a more radical challenge to its neutrality than it had encountered in the earlier one.

By the middle of January several reports indicating that both Germany and Britain might be preparing military actions against Denmark and Norway had reached the foreign ministry. The information had only little effect on the defence posture of the country. In his New Year speech the prime minister had already reminded the nation that Denmark was armed with a view to defending its neutrality, and that the character of the country and the population's aversion to war excluded the possibility of preparing effectively for a real war. Reductions in the size of the standing army continued as planned, leaving only 6,263 men in early February, though approximately 8,000 men were recruited in the course of February and March. On the diplomatic level, the growing threat led the foreign minister to initiate a Scandinavian peace appeal, his third such appeal since December. It made as little impression on the belligerents as the earlier attempts had done.

When German forces invaded Denmark in the early hours of 9 April, they met only token and sporadic resistance. The government, threatened with aerial bombardment of Copenhagen, capitulated the same morning. Since the occupation, so to speak, took place in a peaceful manner and the Germans presented it as an act of protection against an imminent British attack on Denmark and Norway, promising not to use Danish territory as a base in the war with its enemies and to respect the territorial integrity and political sovereignty of the country, the government was able to maintain that Denmark had retained its non-belligerent status. However, the new situation did affect both the diplomatic links and the foreign trade of the country. While Denmark could maintain diplomatic relations with the neutrals and with Germany's allies, it had to break them with Britain and France. Similarly, it could continue its trade with the neutrals and Germany's allies but not with the Western powers.

Though neither of the two major opposition parties wanted to share the responsibility for the foreign and defence policy pursued in the 1930s or to become too closely identified with the decisions made by the king, the principal ministers and the service chiefs within hours of the invasion, both the Liberals and the Conservatives agreed to be represented in a coalition government. Still with Stauning as prime minister and Munch as foreign minister, the new government assumed the responsibility for protecting the population, social structure and political system of a country under occupation. The way it went about it became known to its supporters as the policy of negotiation, the term cooperation then being used to refer to relations among the political parties represented in the government. The negotiations with the authorities of the occupying power, usually the minister representing the foreign ministry in Berlin, were conducted through the Danish foreign ministry.

Three months later a reconstruction of the government took place. In accordance with the wishes of the Conservatives, the unpopular foreign minister Munch was removed from the post he had occupied since 1929. His place was taken by Erik Scavenius, the man who as foreign minister in a Radical Liberal government had helped to see Denmark through the First World War. Strongly supported by the king and well respected by Stauning, he was recognized as an expert in handling the Germans. Like so many other observers, in Denmark and elsewhere, he had been so impressed with the early victories of Hitler's armies that he had come to believe that Germany would win the war. Consequently he thought it prudent, perhaps necessary, step by step to shift the line of the government from procrastinating negotiation towards deliberate cooperation with the occupying power. However, in no way an admirer of the ideology of Nazism or the style of the Hitlerite regime, Scavenius never abandoned the basic concerns of protecting Danish interests and values and retaining as much of the sovereignty of the state as possible.

After the death of Stauning in May 1942, his place as prime minister and Social Democratic leader was taken by Vilhelm Buhl, who, as minister of finance, had been critical of Scavenius's readiness to accommodate the Germans. Buhl's brief tenure of office was marked by growing difficulties with the Germans and mounting dissatisfaction in Berlin with developments in Denmark. The major problem was the beginning of sabotage and other signs of the emergence of organized resistance to the occupying power. In November Buhl resigned after strong pressure from the German authorities. A ministerial crisis was resolved when Scavenius, at German insistence, agreed to head the government and handle foreign relations. Thus it was he who, together with the new representative of the German foreign ministry Werner Best, became responsible for managing the difficult process of cooperation in a period of emerging organized resistance. Less than 10 months later this phase of Danish–German relations came to a dramatic end.

Since the autumn of 1942 Danish workers had become increasingly dissatisfied with the economic consequences of the policy pursued by the government and supported by major institutions, including the leadership of their trade unions. The Communist party, illegal since the summer of 1941, and others intent on rupturing cooperation with the occupying power had exploited such dissatisfaction and encouraged rebellious tendencies, particularly in key industries. The result had been a considerable number of strikes. In the summer of 1943, when Germany had suffered major defeats in Russia and Africa and the fortunes of war seemed to have shifted decisively in favour of the allied powers, both strikes and acts of sabotage multiplied. Disturbances in the form of stirring public meetings, hostile demonstrations and street fights with German soldiers took place in several provincial towns, notably Odense, Esbjerg and Aalborg. Though the industrial strikes and the major public disturbances may have appeared at the time as essentially spontaneous, they were often initiated by individual members of the Communist party and organized in coordination with local resistance groups. However, they enjoyed the support of sections of the public which, growing tired of the policy of cooperation, were ready to react to reports or rumours of German brutality.

When the situation seemed to be heading for breaking-point, with one town after another subjected to curfew and other repressive measures, and paralysed by mass strike, the first reaction of the government once more was to appeal to the population to maintain order and not allow control to slip out of the hands of the Danish authorities. However, in the course of the month of August the role of the government, as a buffer between the Danish population and the German authorities, rapidly became far more difficult. At a time when it already was losing authority, the government came up against German demands and pressures so extreme as to leave little room for negotiating solutions to the mounting difficulties.

The situation was becoming equally difficult for Werner Best. He had committed himself to the policy of managing the occupation of Denmark through cooperation with its government, and had staked his career on its success. The inability of the Danish government to control the situation and put an end to the disturbances caused him to lose ground in a long-standing rivalry with the military authorities in the country, who favoured a more heavy-handed way of dealing with rebellious manifestations. Soon he was called to Berlin to face his superior, Ribbentrop, and present his account of the developments in Denmark.

On 27 August he returned with an ultimatum, which he presented to Scavenius the next morning. The list of German demands included the proclamation of a general state of emergency, which prohibited any assembly of more than five persons and any kind of strike. It also imposed a strict curfew, the introduction of censorship of the press with German participation and the establishment of special courts to deal swiftly, and most severely, with breaches of regulations to maintain security and order. The ultimatum also demanded that capital punishment be introduced forthwith for acts of sabotage, attacks on German forces or individuals and possession of firearms or explosives. The German government expected an answer the same afternoon.

The cabinet and a standing committee of representatives of the old political parties met to discuss the terms of the document, and immediately agreed that the German demands were unacceptable. An answer went off, which stated that, while the government was willing to take all necessary measures to secure order, it could not agree to implement the arrangements demanded since such a course would destroy all possibilities of maintaining lasting public order. The Scavenius–Best negotiating duel was coming to an end. While Scavenius, facing a growing public dissatisfaction with the policy of the government, was in effect losing his popular mandate, Best, through a weakening of his position in the power struggle with the military occupation forces, was losing his support in Berlin. The base of the intergovernmental form of Danish–German cooperation was about to disappear.

The following night German forces carried out surprise attacks on army camps throughout the country and, often after intense exchange of fire, disarmed and interned officers and men and seized all war *matériel*. When, simultaneously, they attacked naval establishments, most of the units managed either to sink their ships or, in a few cases, to take them to neutral port in Sweden. The Germans also arrested many prominent men and women and interned them, for use as hostages in case of public disturbances.

In the early morning of 29 August, general Hermann von Hanneken, commander-in-chief of German forces in Denmark, proclaimed a state of emergency with severe restrictions, including nationwide curfew and the death penalty for strikers. He also announced that he had assumed executive power, and that the king and the government had thus ceased to function. Later the same day, the government met for the last time, and decided to tender its resignation to the king. Not till after the liberation, on 5 May 1945, did Denmark again have an active government.

Despite his difficulties in Berlin and failure in Denmark, Best remained Ribbentrop's man in Copenhagen, and continued his rivalry with von Hanneken, and later also with general Günther Pancke, chief of the German police forces in the country. Best's first concern after 29 August was to have a new government established. Through Nils Svenningsen, head of the foreign ministry, he put his case to members of the deactivated government, stating that the alternative would be direct German government of the country. An inner circle of politicians met to discuss the proposal, and found that it would not be possible now to form a lawful government. The king concurred, and only Scavenius and a few others thought that it would be wrong and irresponsible to refuse to comply.

In the course of the debate among the politicians it appeared that German rule might not be the only possible alternative. After the king and the government had ceased to function, the permanent secretaries had decided, with the approval of former ministers, to stay in office. Each of them, acting on his own responsibility, had been taking administrative decisions within his department. In the process, they had acquired certain necessary additional rights. The rest of the civil service had also stayed in place and continued their work. Thus, in September it was possible to argue that the public administration of the country could be maintained without a government, and that there would be no need for German rule. That point was made when the politicians' refusal to form a government was presented to Best.

In the end, a practice developed of maintaining the Danish–German diplomatic relationship through meetings and negotiations between Best and Svenningsen. In this way, Germany could sustain its political pressure on Denmark through its usual channel, the local representative of the German foreign ministry. And Denmark could respond to such pressure through the head of its foreign ministry, who not only enjoyed the support and cooperation of the permanent secretaries of all the other administrative departments but also received backing and some discreet guidance from members of a committee of politicians representing the old parties and the defunct government. Thus, though the relationship could no longer be intergovernmental, the practice of limited cooperation between unequal partners continued. The arrangement lasted till the end of the occupation. However, from the spring of 1944 it was complicated by increasing contact between some of the administrative heads and the leadership of the resistance movement.

Before the August crisis the principal feature of Denmark under occupation had been governmental cooperation with the occupying power. After that event it soon became active resistance. One reason for the shifting picture was simply that the continuation, through administrative channels, of the practice of cooperation was so discreet that it attracted much less attention. The real change, however, was the growing strength and determination of the resistance movement. Here several factors played a part. One was the disappearance of a government which regularly had admonished the population to maintain order and show moderation and warned against sabotage and other militant acts. Another factor was the intensification of German brutality and terror. This was marked by the attempt only weeks after the August crisis to round up Jews and send them to German camps, by the reactions to the mass strike in Copenhagen in the summer of 1944 and by the subsequent arrest and deportation of about 2,000 police officers as well as by the torture and execution of members of the resistance movement who had been arrested by German police.

A contributory cause of decisive importance for the efforts and achievements of the resistance movement in the later period of the occupation was the arrival of organizers, instructors and radio operators as well as weapons, explosives and other equipment from Britain under its Special Operations Executive (SOE) programme. Last, but not least important, was the conditioning influence of the news of German defeats on several fronts and the prospect of Hitler probably losing the war. With German armies on the retreat in major theatres and its forces stretched, it made more sense to move from passive to active resistance in Denmark. For the same reasons, such resistance now enjoyed growing public support.

Its first aim, ending governmental cooperation with the enemy authorities, having been achieved, the resistance movement was able to concentrate on the major task of offering resistance to the occupying power. The most urgent needs were to organize the movement and build up its strength. In September 1943 six men met in Copenhagen to seek some coordination of the activities of the many different resistance groups scattered across the country. Representing four major illegal organizations, namely the Communists, the right-of-centre national movement Danish Unity, the cross-party organization *Frit Danmark* and the nation-wide cultural and political association the Ring, they decided to set up what became known as Denmark's freedom council. After a lengthy struggle to gain acceptance and secure control, the council established itself as the body representing the whole movement.

Though generally distrusted by the leaders of the old political parties and the officers of the general staff of the army and other representatives of official Denmark, initially inclined to suspect that it was a front organization of the Communists, the freedom council eventually acquired an authority which went far beyond resistance circles. In a country without government, army and police, it became a central organ with considerable influence. In crises between the public and the Germans, it gradually acquired a political role. In the general strike in Copenhagen in 1944, its influence proved decisive.

After some suspicion and hesitation, the allied powers, too, came to recognize the freedom council as the body to deal with in occupied Denmark, in both military and political matters. SOE's leader in Denmark since March 1943, Flemming B. Muus, joined it almost at the outset, representing the 'free Danes' abroad. His successor, Ole Lippmann, took part in its meetings as observer and joined its command committee. When the Soviet Union, in the spring of 1944, agreed to accept a permanent representative of 'the fighting Denmark' in Moscow, he was appointed by the freedom council.

Throughout its existence, the council issued a number of proclamations and guidelines. Aimed at both members of the resistance movement and a wider public, they were marked by moderation and a sense of responsibility. The council also set up various committees to manage existing activities, including the illegal press and sabotage, and to deal with new matters arising. Soon priority had to be given to the setting up of an underground army, to support allied forces in case of an invasion or of a final battle with German forces on Danish soil.

The plans for such an army, as for similar forces in other occupied countries, had been prepared by SOE, partly with a view to keeping the Germans in uncertainty as to the location of the Anglo–American invasion, then already under preparation. The instructions reached the leadership of the resistance towards the end of 1943. SOE envisaged a force that would be armed by Britain and be under allied command. While the former arrangement was most acceptable, the latter was not. The freedom council insisted on maintaining command and control, at least up to the time when the force might become actively engaged in the war. Eventually a compromise was reached. In June 1944 the council set up its command committee, in which SOE, the council and the illegal general staffs of the professional army and navy were represented. The committee would be responsible for recruiting, organizing, equipping and, prior to direct combat, commanding the army.

The organization of the force and the allocation of weapons, most of which arrived from Britain in the last winter of the war, presented serious difficulties, some of which had not been overcome by the end of the occupation. Already from the summer of 1943 small groups of a military nature had been set up in various parts of the country, some under Communist control and others led by Danish Unity or other middle-class nationalist associations. There were signs, and a good deal of suspicion, that some such potential task forces might be arming themselves not only against the Germans in the existing situation but also against each other in an uncertain future. A basic principle of the organization of the new army was the integration of both existing and newly established groups. This was never quite achieved. While some groups remained under Communist control, others for a long time carried the stamp of Danish Unity or other such associations. Moreover, certain task forces set up by the illegal professional army in the form of six-man groups retained a degree of independence, even though they were formally under the command of the freedom council. Such divisions led to conflicts about the distribution of weapons, the professional officers in particular being concerned that arms received from Sweden or elsewhere should not end up in Communist hands. However, despite the disagreement about command and difficulties of allocation of weapons, by the end of the occupation the resistance movement had a force totalling, according to some estimates, close to 50,000 men, though far from all of them armed.

The freedom council had to prepare not only for war but also for peace. The prospect of the allied powers defeating Germany and liberating the occupied countries raised important questions about Denmark's status in relation to the allies, about its post-war political programme and about the composition of its first government after liberation. Dealing with such matters eventually involved some contact and negotiation between the council and leaders of the four old political parties. From the outset, the politicians had been nervous about the activities, plans and ultimate goals of the council. The news that the Soviet Union was prepared to establish diplomatic relations with the council by accepting Thomas Døssing, a man of leftist views, as its representative in Moscow had added to their insecurity – at a stage when it was far from clear which of the allied armies would be liberating Denmark.

Acting on their own, the politicians had taken the initiative in seeking recognition of Denmark as an ally in the coalition against Germany. While the British and the Americans had pursued the idea in the spring of 1944, the Soviet Union had rejected it. Later in the year, after Døssing's arrival in Moscow, the politicians, still on their own but enjoying British support, tried again to secure Soviet acceptance. When the Russians failed to react, it seemed clear that nothing could be achieved in Moscow without the support and participation of the freedom council. After long and difficult negotiations between the politicians and members of the council, which involved the post-war political programme and the composition of the liberation government, a joint appeal went off to the capitals of the three great powers in January 1945. It was signed by the leaders of the Social Democrats, the Radical Liberals, the Liberals and the Conservatives, and by representatives of the freedom council. The initiative led to other lengthy debates, which in Moscow were complicated by Døssing's hostile attitude to politicians associated with the coalition government. When Denmark was liberated, by British forces, the matter was still pending. However, in May 1945 Denmark received an invitation to send representatives to the San Francisco conference, where allied states would meet to set up the United Nations.

Initially, contact between the freedom council and the politicians had been more ad hoc. After the establishment of a contact committee of the council in August 1944, with two council members and two politicians, it became more continuous. In the last winter of the war the uncertainty about the post-war political situation loomed large in the relationship between the two sides. The concerns of the politicians were fairly obvious. Since 29 August 1943 they had been disturbed by the influence of the Communists in the resistance movement. With the establishment, and ever growing authority, of the freedom council they had become afraid that it might set itself up after the liberation as some kind of government, eventually perhaps under Communist control. What they wanted instead was a restoration of parliamentary democracy, with their own parties resuming the management of the political process. Thus, when those politicians in the later stages of the occupation enhanced their influence by changing course and moving closer to the resistance movement it was more with a view to securing the future position of the parties they were leading than to strengthen the resistance to the occupying power. However, they enjoyed a degree of support from Britain, which also wanted a stable and reliable government in post-war Denmark.

For a long time the members of the freedom council, generally preoccupied with resisting the Germans in the immediate situation, gave relatively little thought to post-war problems. From the outset, however, they had made it clear that the council was not pursuing party-political aims but fighting for national goals, primarily the restoration of the freedom of the country and the reintroduction of Danish democracy but also the judicial prosecution and punishment of those who had betrayed their country by helping the Germans. Later the council expressed its views on the national programme of the transitional government and the international orientation of post-war Denmark more forcefully. Severely critical of the passive and compliant response to the invasion in 1940 and strongly opposed to the negotiation and cooperation policies of the following years, the council renounced the traditions of neutrality, isolation and weakness, which it recognized as the sources of such conduct. In a document of December 1944, addressed to the political parties represented in the committee of party leaders and former ministers, it stressed that everything possible should be done to avoid a repetition of the disaster and humiliation suffered by the country: 'Denmark's future defensive forces must be brought up to the necessary dimensions, and all notions of Denmark's isolated neutrality must be abandoned after this war.' In the projected new international organization, the country must take on all duties that may be required of it.[10]

Before the debate about the composition of the liberation government had reached its conclusion a disagreement arose within the freedom council about the political programme for the post-war period. The representatives of the Communists and Danish Unity had drawn up a detailed economic and social programme and had secured the support of some other members of the council. Given that Danish Unity was politically much weaker than the Communists, the initiative could be seen as a step by the latter towards securing control of post-war politics. In a situation where it was still uncertain whether it would be British or Soviet forces that would liberate Denmark, this was a disturbing prospect. Frode Jakobsen, organizer and representative of the Ring and from the outset a central figure in the council, argued forcefully against adoption of the programme, stressing in particular the divisive effect it would have not only on the council but on the resistance movement as a whole. As a result, the matter was dropped, and did not become an issue in the negotiations with the politicians.

Only days before the liberation, an agreement was reached about the composition of the first government. The politicians, who originally had angered the council members by secretly preparing a list of ministers made up entirely of politicians from the largest parties, had to accept the council's demand for equal representation in the liberation government and exclusion of all ministers who had served in the government led by Scavenius. Though the final list of ministers did give the resistance movement numerically equal representation, most of the more influential ministries went to politicians of the four parties. And Vilhelm Buhl, the Social Democratic leader, became prime minister.

The first free general elections took place in October 1945 and resulted in a Liberal minority government. The new prime minister was Knud Kristensen, known for a remark he made during the debate about representation of the resistance in the liberation government: 'The resistance movement? Surely it says nothing about that in the Constitution.' The establishment of his government marked the restoration of the pre-war parliamentary system, again managed by the four old parties, and the end of the formal political role of the resistance movement.

The regression from limited involvement in European politics towards disengagement that marked Danish foreign policy in the centuries after 1720 was linked to the democratization of the social structure and political system of the country. In the first long period distinguished here, foreign policy was largely in the hands of aristocrats who accepted war as a fact of international life, and were prepared to play an active role in European politics. Though war, if it involved one's own state, might be a dreadful experience which should not be undertaken without good reason, war among other powers could well present not only dangers but also opportunities for non-belligerents. Neutrality could be a means of defending one's state from the dangers, but also a way of pursuing the opportunities. While in the former instance it might call for a league of neutrals, in the latter case neutrality did not preclude some form of alliance with one or more of the belligerents. The advantages of playing the European balance of power in this restrained manner were largely economic.

In the second period, from the end of the Napoleonic Wars to the conclusion of the First World War, most decision-makers in Danish foreign policy were middle-class politicians, typically more wary of war and often less able and inclined than their aristocratic predecessors to exploit opportunities it might offer third parties. Except when deemed essential for the defence or the pursuit of vital interests of one's own nation, war in the region usually appeared as a source of danger, especially to a former minor power in severely reduced circumstances and diplomatically isolated. Now neutrality, used essentially as a protection against involvement in the wars of others, came to be perceived more in terms of the rights and duties governing relations between neutrals and belligerents. While the notion of neutrality in the eighteenth century had been basically political, in the course of the nineteenth century it became much more legal.

In most of the inter-war period, the government was in the hands of political leaders who represented the broader sections of Danish society, where anti-militarist tradition and pacifist tendencies influenced attitudes to foreign affairs. In their abhorrence of war, such politicians not only found it prudent to steer clear of the power politics of the great powers but also pointless to maintain more than the most minimal armed force. In their anxiety about national security in a Europe of growing international tension, they tried to reconcile the League principle of collective security with the traditional precepts of neutrality. In the process, they developed a novel version of neutrality. While the neutrality of earlier times had been, at least in principle, impartial as between the belligerents and passive in regard to their wars, the new neutrality was more partial and active. By all means at their disposal, short of going to war themselves, the neutrals should seek to prevent or restrict war among others. The theory of such neutrality, developed largely by Georg Cohn, legal adviser to the foreign ministry, and the international lawyer Philip Jessup, rested on a new evaluation of war. On both legal and moral grounds this phenomenon of international politics was simply disqualified. Whatever the circumstances, nobody had the right to go to war. Staying out of war and endeavouring to prevent or extinguish wars between other states, it followed, was the morally superior policy. Neo-neutrality, as it became known, added a moral dimension to the tradition of neutrality – and sometimes lent a touch of self-righteousness to its champions.

Generally speaking, the Danes who in the 1940s rebelled against the long trend towards disengagement and neutrality by offering active resistance to the occupying forces of Nazi Germany did not represent a particular class of society. In the first year after the invasion, when they numbered perhaps no more than a few hundred, most seem to have come from the middle classes, especially from Danish Unity circles. In the next few years, after the German invasion of the Soviet Union and the banishment of the Communist party, a larger number of Communists took up resistance, with the result that the emerging movement came to rest on an alliance between the right-of-centre and the left sections of the Danish political spectrum. In the final two years of the occupation, after the turn in the fortunes of the German armies on the fronts, the retreat of the Danish government and the establishment of the freedom council, the movement built up its strength rapidly, in the process broadening its social base on both the right and the left. Though the four old political parties remained under-represented in the movement, many young Conservatives and left-wing Social Democrats joined the resistance at that stage. Throughout the years of resistance, the typical freedom fighter, as the members became known, was a man in his twenties living in a town.

In the later years of occupation, and especially towards the end of the war, the resistance movement gained fairly broad support. Shocked by the invasion, humiliated by governmental policies, provoked by German atrocities and, of course, encouraged by allied victories and German retreats in major theatres of war, a large number of people from most walks of life eventually came round to accepting the resistance and offering at least moral support. The series of events denoted by 9 April, the date of the invasion of Denmark, had been an experience traumatic enough, it seemed, to lead a large and representative section of the population to question the wisdom and morality of traditional Danish foreign policy. On the eve of liberation there were signs that the nation might be moving towards a moral and political turning-point in its international conduct.

2
1940–45: From cooperation to resistance

While Danish reactions to German occupation showed a broad development from cooperation to resistance, the more detailed picture of political thought and action during those five years presented considerable complexity. Almost from the beginning and to the very end of the occupation there were instances of both cooperation and resistance. Often the two were mixed, with public bodies, private institutions – as well as groups and individuals – each finding their own, often shifting, balance between cooperating with and resisting the authorities of the occupying power. Moreover, there were different types and degrees of the two kinds of reaction.

Rather than attempting a chronological sketch of the whole complex and chequered development, it will be more useful here to construct a spectrum of reactions, ranging from wholehearted support of the occupying power to armed resistance. Such a structure may be divided into three segments, namely support, cooperation and opposition, and each of them divided into two parts, allowing for differences of nature and degree within each of the three broad kinds of reaction. Within each of the six subsections it will be possible to present a number of significant instances of particular types of reaction, discuss their motivations and indicate their influence.

2.1 Support

First a few distinctions between support and cooperation, its contiguous segment in the spectrum, will be to the point. Whereas cooperation usually implies a degree of mutuality between the parties, support, as the word will be used here, typically denotes a more subsidiary role for the supporting party. While cooperation generally rests on a measure of common ground between the parties, support is more likely to spring from some kind of identification with the party receiving the support. The most active form of support can be described as collaboration, an activity which may be defined as requiring a more complete commitment than mere cooperation.

Danish supportive reactions to German occupation will be considered under two headings, wholehearted support and opportunistic service. The former type was largely ideologically motivated, the latter much more economically conditioned. The former came from ethnic organizations, political parties and uniformed corps of various kinds, the latter more from private companies and individuals. Though there were instances of both types throughout the period, such support was by far the least common of all the Danish reactions to German occupation distinguished here.

Wholehearted support

The two foremost institutional sources of the more devoted type of support for the occupying forces in Denmark, and the Nazi regime in Germany, were the organizations of the German minority in North Schleswig and Denmark's National Socialist Labour Party (DNSAP). The Germans in North Schleswig, since 1920 again part of Denmark, numbered about 30,000 during the occupation. In the general election in April 1939 they had gained about 15,000 votes, which had given them just one seat in the Danish parliament. Thoroughly Nazified well before the war, they had set up a number of Nazistic organizations and arranged various provocative uniformed demonstrations. Their ultimate goal had been another shift of the Danish–German border. Their masters in Berlin, however, had failed to support them in that enterprise, and had made no move to change their line after the invasion.

Always ready to comply with directives issued by the Nazi authorities in Germany, the minority organizations concentrated their efforts during the occupation on serving German interests in economic and cultural matters. They also responded positively to calls for young people to report for military service, with the result that a total of about 2,000 joined the armed forces of Germany, of whom more than a third were killed in action. Moreover, the German minority set up a home guard and an anti-sabotage guard of its own. On the grounds of the absence of so many of their men, as soldiers or workers in Germany, the minority authorities declared themselves unwilling to let their members vote in the general and local elections of 1943. In the general election, however, the Germans in North Schleswig appear to have cast their votes for DNSAP rather than abstain.

DNSAP was established in 1930 but not represented in parliament till after the election in 1939, where it received 31,000 votes, i.e. 1.8 per cent, and gained three seats. Under its leader Frits Clausen, a physician by profession, it became a faithful imitation of the German Nazi party in both name and style. Its members wore the swastika and greeted each other with raised arm. The programme was taken from Hitler's Germany, including anti-Semitism, and Mussolini's Italy, especially the idea of the corporate state. Its membership rose from approximately 5,000 at the outbreak of the war to about 21,000 in the spring of 1943. Yet, in the general election in March that year it received only 43,000 votes, i.e. 2.1 per cent, which again gave it three seats. By the end of the occupation the party, by then under a new leader, still had about 12,000 members, most of the new ones having come from the working class.

With substantial financial support from German sources, for the party as well as for its chief organ *Fædrelandet* (The Fatherland), DNSAP always steered close to the German authorities. In Copenhagen and other towns, it arranged challenging meetings, provocative demonstrations and uniformed marches, which led to violent clashes with anti-Nazi spectators and Danish police. With its offensive programme and aggressive propaganda, and a leader who struck most Danes as a rather comical figure, the party failed to attract public support outside its own narrow circles. Indeed the chief effect of its pro-German image and bombastic efforts seems to have been to convince the Danish population that to be a Nazi was to be a traitor.

Nor did the party command significant forces of its own. Its storm troopers, numbering only 1 or 2,000 men, had no weapons other than spades. At no stage of the occupation was the party, acting on its own, in a position to bring about a coup. However, DNSAP was not always alone. In the summer of 1940 it entered into tentative cooperation with *Landbrugernes Sammenslutning* (LS), an extremist agrarian association, and its close associate *Bondepartiet*, the Farmers' party with four seats in parliament. With many members who were attracted by Nazi ideology, both of those organizations were against the coalition government and campaigned for a non-party caretaker government on good terms with Germany. In an apparent attempt to prepare the way for a government headed by Frits Clausen, spokesmen of the two organizations tried unsuccessfully to achieve their anti-parliamentary goal by putting pressure on the king.

When DNSAP, despite its unpopularity, weakness and lack of parliamentary support, for some years remained a threat to the political system and national reputation of Denmark it was because of German political support. Already at the earliest stage of the occupation several highly-placed German officials supported the idea of pressing the king to accept a Nazi government. In October 1940, when plans for a Nazi takeover were under debate among German authorities, a delegation from the foreign ministry in Berlin visited Copenhagen and had meetings with Frits Clausen and other Nazi leaders. In February–March 1942, we now know, Hitler stated that he in due course wanted Clausen to replace the Danish king, an idea which he brought up again later that year. Subsequently, however, German interest in such plans waned. After the poor showing of the party in the elections of March 1943 economic support from German sources ceased. In the spring of 1944 Clausen had to retire as leader of the party. A year later, after the liberation, the party went into liquidation.

Though DNSAP never achieved its ultimate goal of governmental power under German protection, it did find some ways of assisting the Nazi bid for European domination. It procured political intelligence for the occupying power and played a leading role in the recruitment of Danes for German military service. In 1940 Heinrich Himmler's Waffen-SS started recruiting in Denmark together with DNSAP and the German minority in North Schleswig. The following year the party collaborated in the recruitment for a new unit, known as Frikorps Danmark.

Established on Himmler's initiative in June 1941, after the launching of the German attack on the Soviet Union, Frikorps Danmark was conceived as a purely Danish unit under Danish flag but attached to the SS. Volunteers were invited to join the crusade against Bolshevism. Initially the unit was under the command of a Danish officer who was anti-Communist but not pro-Nazi. After training in Germany and Poland, Frikorps Danmark fought on the Eastern Front in 1942–43, and suffered substantial losses. On leave in Denmark in October 1942, its soldiers joined civilian Nazis in violent and provocative disturbances.

No doubt some of the Danish volunteers were adventurers, others men escaping severe unemployment in Denmark. A number were army officers frustrated by the defence policy of the pre-war government and the feeble reaction to the German invasion. But most seem to have been ideologically motivated, whether primarily pro-Nazi or more anti-Communist. After the Winter War, in which many young Danes volunteered to help Finland against the Soviet Union, some must have seen Hitler's invasion of Russia as an opportunity to again take up the battle against Bolshevism. Others, however, were fanatical Nazis.

In Denmark, most people soon came to regard all the volunteers simply as traitors. Yet, the establishment and existence of the corps presented a problem for the government. While avoiding a formal recognition of Frikorps Danmark, it gave in to German pressure by allowing Danish officers so inclined to take leave of absence and join the corps. The total number of Danish citizens, including minority Germans, serving with German forces in the war has been estimated as about 7,000.

There were also a few corps of Danes who had volunteered to serve in the armed or the police forces of the occupying power on Danish soil. The most notorious was the Schalburg Corps, called after a DNSAP youth leader who had become the second commandant of Frikorps Danmark and had been killed in action, and led by another officer from that corps. First established, by Himmler, in April 1943 under the name of *Germansk Korps*, its original purposes were to recruit and train soldiers for the Waffen-SS and to prepare the ground in Denmark for the Greater Germanic *Reich*. It had a military and a civilian and political section as well as a number of more specialized departments, including an intelligence service and terror department. Its foremost functions turned out to be to combat the resistance movement and terrorize the public. In addition to creating a large number of violent incidents, its members informed for the German police. During the mass strike in Copenhagen in 1944 one of the demands of the freedom council was to have the Schalburg Corps withdrawn from the country. After a good deal of reorganization, it was abolished three months before the liberation because of insufficient intake. A number of minor bodies of Danes working for the Germans included the Sommer Corps. Called after its founder, a former commander of the Schalburg Corps, it took on the guarding of German airports and factories working for the Germans. After the war about 700 members of the Schalburg Corps were prosecuted and given heavy sentences. Ten, including its first commandant, were executed.

After the arrest of the police officers in September 1944, an auxiliary police unit was set up in Copenhagen under the name of Hipo (an abbreviation of *Hilfspolizei*). Made up of about 550 uniformed Danes, it was under German control. Its function was to combat illegal activity. Recruited partly from within the Schalburg Corps, it became a branch of the civilian intelligence service of that organization. Patrolling the streets of Copenhagen, its members, sometimes working together with

Danish terrorist gangs, became notorious for shooting people at random and carrying out explosions and other acts of terror, and for arresting suspects and torturing prisoners. Up to, and including, the days of liberation Hipo men contributed to the horrors and the insecurity of life in a city without a proper police force. After the war they received prison sentences averaging 11 years.

Finally, a form of collaboration encouraged and organized by German or pro-German bodies but performed by Danish individuals must be mentioned, namely informing. Infiltration by informers was already a problem in the earlier stages of resistance but became more serious after August 1943, when the Gestapo operated independently and built up its own network of information gathering. For the resistance movement, the dangers presented by informing were so great that the freedom council decided to permit the liquidation of known informers. Approximately 400 people were shot, most towards the end of the occupation and nearly 10 per cent of them women. While it is conceivable that some informers, at least in the early years of resistance, were misled by ministerial admonishments against engaging in sabotage or by professional officiousness of members of the Danish police force, others no doubt informed mainly for monetary reward. Many, however, were motivated by ideological convictions, whether pro-German Nazism or anti-communism.

The sources of wholehearted support for the occupying power and its Nazi programme which have been presented here were of little significance in terms of direct effect on public opinion in Denmark. Motivated largely by ideological fanaticism, of one kind or another, and embodied through small, marginal parties and groups or in novel, militant corps and units, they failed to attract the larger public or influence the established institutions and organizations of the country. Far from helping to build bridges between the authorities and political programme of the occupying power and the ministries and policy of the Danish government, they rather served to emphasize the difference, at least in principle, between resolute collaboration and unavoidable cooperation with the Germans. The goals and means, character and behaviour of most Nazi activists and many members of the various auxiliary military and police units undoubtedly helped to develop and shape an enemy image of both the Germans and their locally recruited henchmen. Thus, paradoxically, the ultimate effect of such pro-German reactions to the occupation may have been to help prepare the way for popular acceptance of the resistance movement in the later years of the occupation.

Opportunistic service

If the wholehearted sort of pro-German activity helped to accentuate the distinction between collaboration and cooperation, the type of support that was motivated largely by considerations of expediency rather tended to blur that dividing line. Rarely inspired by pro-Nazi sympathies, activity of this kind might be seen as falling within a grey area between supposedly patriotic and decidedly unpatriotic behaviour. The companies, groups or individuals who, for economic advantage or out of need, provided certain services for the occupying power stood somewhere in between officials engaged in governmentally approved forms of cooperation with the Germans and the parties involved in blatant collaboration. Occasionally their predicament was, in certain respects, similar to that of public bodies which had to deal with the German authorities, in the sense that both might be acting from a combination of need and advantage. However, while the public bodies in principle were motivated by considerations of national interest and political necessity, the non-governmental parties were usually moved by more private calculations. Often the latter had more choice when deciding whether or not to provide the service required, and hence more responsibility for the decisions taken. What we are dealing with here are types of parties who, often in politically confusing and economically difficult situations, allowed themselves to take advantage of a particular constellation of circumstances and draw substantial benefits from serving the occupying power in some way or other.

The foremost instances of such support were those of the so-called *værnemagere* (a pun on the Danish word for *Wehrmacht*), companies which benefited unduly from carrying out work for the occupying power or producing goods for German importers. Almost immediately after the invasion the German authorities announced that they intended to build new airports in Jutland and were prepared to have the work done by their own companies, using either German workers or a conscripted Danish labour force. As a lesser evil, the government preferred to prevail upon Danish contractors to carry out the work with Danish workers. That solution, which prevented the arrival in Denmark of a large number of German workers, gave employment to many Danes without work and secured a modest degree of Danish control of the whole enterprise, was accepted by the Germans. It also became the model for the construction of many of the various German fortifications established on Danish soil during the following years.

In the same period, a growing number of Danish industrial firms entered into business relations with Germany, exporting manufactured goods, mainly in return for coal and raw materials. While accepting such business as not only unavoidable but also essential for the economy of the country, the Danish authorities endeavoured to control prices and profits, maintain the balance between export of goods and import of raw materials, prevent a distortion of traditional Danish industry and to exclude the supply of goods which constituted a direct contribution to German war efforts. However, official attempts to maintain some control of the companies involved, whether contractors or exporters, were not always successful.

For a contractor to respond to Danish ministerial pressure to take on major projects for the Germans was from the outset deemed a patriotic act by those who knew the circumstances. And for a manufacturer to give in to German demands and start exporting to Germany was also considered acceptable, provided it was done as far as possible within the guidelines indicated by the Danish government. But to charge hugely excessive payment for the services rendered or set abnormally high prices for the goods exported was not regarded as respectable practice. Nor was it in order for a manufacturer himself to institute the relationship with the Germans, or to change his line of manufacture in order to suit German needs. All such acts were deemed unpatriotic, particularly when seen in retrospect. Since the costs of constructing German fortifications on Danish soil were charged to a special account with the Danish National Bank and the excess of the value of Danish exports over that of imports from Germany was charged to a clearing account with the same bank, and since both of those accounts were guaranteed by the Danish state, any party exploiting the opportunities offered by dealing with the Germans was in effect doing so at the expense of the Danish nation. Having become increasingly unpopular in the course of the war, a substantial number of *værnemagere* were arrested and tried after the liberation. Under laws introduced retrospectively in response to the wishes of the freedom council, only relatively few were imprisoned and had their profits confiscated. Many were able to plead in their defence that the government or the civil servants had prompted them to collaborate with the Germans.

Another type of service, again motivated much more by financial need or advantage than by ideological convictions or sympathies, also came about as a result of German pressures. In the spring of 1940, when Denmark and Germany were negotiating a trade agreement, the Germans decided to make additional supplies of coal, which were essential for Danish industry, dependent on workers from Denmark helping to man the mines. Instead, the Danish negotiators agreed to provide labour for other kinds of work in Germany. Thus Denmark not only avoided conscription of workers for service abroad but also eased its unemployment problem, which was particularly severe in that year. While nobody may have been downright compelled, some workers were pressurized and many encouraged by the Danish employment service to take jobs with German employers. The number of people who escaped unemployment in this manner, or simply found better-paid work abroad, culminated in 1941, when about 36,600 left for Germany and another 4,000 took jobs for the Germans in Norway. Many of those in Germany apparently ended up working in the armaments industry. The people who took work in Germany usually transferred part of their wages to Denmark over the clearing account, thereby in effect adding to the financial burden of their country. After the war, only those who had served as uniformed guards were prosecuted.

Finally two other sets of individuals may be mentioned briefly, under the heading of opportunistic service to the occupying forces, namely those informers who committed their deeds simply or mainly for monetary reward and the women who associated with German soldiers. While some of the former were retained by the German police, others worked on an ad hoc basis, collecting a modest reward for each case. Perhaps the women may be divided along similar lines, with some involved in a close relationship and others having only casual relations.

As in other countries in north-western Europe deemed co-racialist, the German authorities permitted sexual relations between their soldiers and willing local women. The number of Danish women who failed to follow the unofficial rule of cold-shouldering all Germans must have been fairly substantial, because about 5,500 children were registered as Danish–German during the occupation. The fraternization caused some friction between the Danish and the German authorities charged with managing it. It also made the women highly unpopular with the general public. Usually referred to as 'field-mattresses', some of them were hunted down by youthful crowds and publicly humiliated, typically by having their hair cut very short and their clothes stripped off. After the liberation about 300 women who had had relations with German soldiers were convicted of informing.

Though support for the occupying power took many different forms, in general it remained insignificant in terms of both the number of people involved and the degree of political influence exerted.

The number engaged in any kind of outright collaboration never exceeded a few per cent of the population. In the course of the war, many people grew increasingly hostile towards those who had chosen, or agreed, to support or serve the Germans, even towards those who had been requested or encouraged by Danish authorities to do so. The only real threat presented by collaboration was that of a Nazi takeover of government with German support. During the first two years of the occupation that risk was a decisive consideration for the Danish political system.

Above all, the Danish government was not directly involved in any of the kinds of collaboration distinguished here. When individual ministers or government agencies prevailed upon contractors to undertake projects or put pressure on unemployed workers to accept work for the Germans, they usually did so in order to avoid more onerous arrangements proposed by the Germans. As they saw it, they were acting out of necessity or in the national interest. Thus, it is not under the heading of support for, but of cooperation with German authorities that such attitudes and behaviour must be considered.

2.2 Cooperation

As distinct from collaboration, typically driven by ideological commitment or opportunistic calculation, cooperation was in principle motivated by patriotic considerations. For those in positions of responsibility, the overriding concern was to avoid the installation of a Nazi government, or direct rule by the occupying power, and to maintain a democratic government able to protect the population and institutions of the country. In a situation of military occupation by an overwhelming power, this might be achieved only through some form of political interaction with the authorities of the occupying power. From an early stage of the occupation the nature and degree of such interaction became a subject of some disagreement among the political leaders and other influential people. While some found it necessary or prudent deliberately to enter into limited cooperation with the occupying authorities, others thought it possible and wiser not to go beyond protracted negotiation and minimal concessions. The former searched for common ground between the parties. The latter strove for minimal involvement with the adversary.

Willing cooperation

The foremost exponent of deliberate cooperation with the German authorities was Erik Scavenius. Decidedly a man of the realist tradition of thought about international politics, he enjoyed the advantages but also shared some of the weaknesses of that approach to the theory and practice of politics among nations. At an early stage of his diplomatic career, before the First World War, when he was serving in Berlin and taking an interest in North Schleswig, he had made certain observations and reached some conclusions about the nature of international relations. While people might be moved by national sentiments and liberal ideas, policy, he had noticed, was based more on constitutional doctrines and legal rights. However, the actual outcome of an international conflict, he had found, was determined essentially by military power. In the same years, again according to his memoirs, he had given some thought to the foreign and security policy of Denmark, and had developed certain ideas about its role and place in international politics which later were to guide him as foreign minister. To avoid becoming embroiled in the wars of other states, he had concluded, Denmark must seek to balance between those great powers whose political interaction was decisive for its fate. Second, as a result of its geographical location, Denmark had to accept its dependence on the power dominating North Germany, since 1871 the German Empire, and adjust its foreign policy accordingly.[1]

The same points were made, in a more polemical form, in a book based on an account prepared by Scavenius in 1944 in defence of Danish policy towards Germany before and during the occupation. In the preface, the author was sarcastic about the opinion, held by a large section of the public, that relations with foreign countries must be governed by emotion rather than intellect. The decisive factors in the formulation of Danish foreign policy, he maintained, were the European balance of power and Denmark's position in relation to the nearest great powers. As a continuation of the North German plain with no significant physical obstacles and with only limited natural resources and armed forces, Denmark was without military options against Germany. Whether one liked it or not, that was the power-political basis on which the country had to formulate its policy and manage its relations with Germany. As in the First World War, Scavenius's conduct of foreign relations was motivated not only by a deep sense of responsibility and a clear intellectual commitment but also by power-political convictions marked by a degree of geopolitical determinism.[2]

No sooner had he decided, after strong pressure from Munch in particular, to accept the post of foreign minister in the Stauning government formed in July 1940 than Scavenius put his stamp on Danish conduct of relations with Germany. Critical of the passive and procrastinating tactics of his predecessor, which he thought too dangerous in a situation where military victories had boosted the self-confidence and determination of Hitler's regime, he believed that it was wiser for Denmark to demonstrate its willingness to cooperate with Germany in various fields. In a declaration approved by Stauning and issued on 8 July, Scavenius surveyed the foreign policy of Denmark since the First World War and pointed out that it had always followed a line favourable to the great neighbour to the south. The crucial passage came at the end:

> With the great German victories, which have struck the world with surprise and admiration, a new time has dawned for Europe which will involve a reorganization politically and economically under German leadership. Here it will be Denmark's task to find its place in a necessary and mutual active cooperation with Greater Germany. The Danish people trusts that it will be able to retain its independence in the new European order, and hopes to find understanding for its peculiarity and for its traditionally peaceful political and social development.[3]

In its humble style, which many Danes found offensive, that declaration revealed Scavenius's lack of feeling for, or indifference to, public opinion. More important, the expectation that Germany would win the war and remain the dominant power in Europe, on which his projection for Denmark's future role rested, proved a serious misjudgement. It was of course an opinion shared by many people in the first year of hostilities, not only in Denmark but in most parts of Continental Europe. For Scavenius, of a pessimistic temperament and long in the habit of focusing on the military dimension of power, it seemed a safe assumption on which to base his conduct of relations with the occupying power. However, though stylistically unfortunate and, ultimately, politically unsound, Scavenius's statement of intent was in no way treacherous. His decision to seek cooperation with Germany was motivated by reason-of-state considerations. In 1940 he was convinced that the course he was proposing was the safest, perhaps the only, way of maintaining the independence of his country and protecting the interests of its people in post-war Europe. More immediately, he saw it as the best way of warding off a Nazi rule of Denmark.

When the declaration of 8 July reached Berlin, German officials were given to understand that Denmark was prepared to discuss future economic cooperation even before a European peace settlement had been accomplished. Before the end of the month they proposed a customs and monetary union between the two countries. Despite the highly disturbing implications of such a project, Scavenius thought it advisable to enter into negotiations. When the Germans presented a preliminary framework agreement which was totally unacceptable to the Danes, Scavenius still wanted to continue negotiations and proceeded to draw up a counter proposal. Here, however, he met strong opposition from most of his fellow ministers, the committee of parliamentary representatives and the king as well as from the big trade organizations. Fortunately, the German proposal met some resistance from trade interests within Germany itself, which made it possible eventually to discontinue the negotiations. Thus Denmark avoided becoming a founding member of an abortive *Neuropa*.

Other controversial goodwill measures sponsored or approved by Scavenius met with less determined opposition from his colleagues. On the initiative of the foreign ministry, a Danish–German Society was established in July, with Peter Knutzen, director general of the state railways, as chairman. Such a society could be justified on the grounds that it would be desirable for German officials and officers serving in Denmark to meet Danes other than the Nazi or pro-German set they usually encountered. The following summer the government tolerated the formation of Frikorps Danmark and allowed Danish officers so inclined to join and fight among German units on the Eastern front.

More controversial was the accession to the Anti-Comintern Pact, which Germany and Japan had concluded on 25 November 1936 and revived after the German attack on the Soviet Union in June 1941. At very short notice, the German minister made it clear that Denmark was expected to join a small group of countries, including Finland, which would meet in Berlin in November to celebrate the anniversary and renew the pact. Scavenius was immediately of the opinion that Denmark had to accept the invitation, but met strong opposition from most other ministers and the committee of parliamentary representatives. In response to rapidly increasing German pressure, the king, the government and the parliamentary representatives soon settled for a conditional accession to the pact. Though Scavenius had to struggle to uphold the agreed qualifications, he reached Berlin in time dutifully to represent Denmark at the ceremony. However, on the day of the celebrations a few hundred students demonstrated in Copenhagen against the decision to accede to the pact. They appealed to the king to reject outright all attempts to interfere in the country's domestic affairs and attacked Scavenius and his policy towards Germany.

A year later, the so-called telegram crisis was resolved only when Scavenius agreed to German demands that he head a new government in which he would remain in charge of foreign affairs. The crisis blew up when Hitler, already dissatisfied with developments in Denmark and upset by reports of widespread anti-German feeling in the country, became furious on receiving a rather curt acknowledgement of his customary message of birthday congratulations to the Danish king. The diplomats were recalled, and the fairly accommodating and tactful commanding officer of the German forces in Denmark was replaced by general von Hanneken, a much more authoritarian type. After a month of anxious uncertainty about Hitler's intentions for Denmark, Scavenius was called to Berlin for a long meeting with Ribbentrop. The German foreign minister insisted on having the anti-German Buhl government replaced by one which included not only representatives of the trade unions but also ministers with pro-Nazi sympathies. Scavenius rejected the latter condition as well as a suggestion that he should take the part of prime minister himself.

Back in Copenhagen, he argued that the only way out of the crisis would be to accept Ribbentrop's proposal for a change of government as a basis for negotiation. The so-called political ministers and the party leaders insisted on having the German demands reduced substantially. In particular, they wanted to retain Buhl as prime minister. After a confrontation with Scavenius, they gave way and started looking for a suitable person to lead a new government. When they failed to find a willing and acceptable candidate Werner Best, newly arrived as Germany's permanent minister in Denmark, decided that the only acceptable solution was to have Scavenius in that post. After intense debate among ministers and parliamentary representatives, and a helpful contribution from the crown prince on behalf of the king, it was agreed to accept Scavenius as prime minister, despite the suspicions he had aroused, among Conservative and Liberal leaders in particular, and the unpopularity he was likely to incur in the country as the choice of the Germans. Round him, as prime minister as well as foreign minister, a new government was formed, with many of the old ministers retained. Having had Scavenius at the helm for well over two years, the decision-makers did not dare disrupt the established relationship with the occupying power.

During the following 10 months, till the rebellion in August 1943, Scavenius maintained the policy of willing but limited cooperation with

Germany. Engaged in a constant duel of negotiation with Best, who for reasons of his own wanted the Danish government to stay in power, he dealt with one imminent danger after another as best as he could, while all along playing for time. Thus he acted as a shield between the occupying power and the Danish population. Though becoming ever more unpopular with a growing section of the public, he enjoyed the explicit or tacit support of most ministers and parliamentary representatives, practically all national and local authorities and the leading trade organizations as well as of the Danish radio and the bulk of the legitimate press.

The outstanding result of the Danish policy of willing cooperation in this period was the parliamentary elections in March 1943. According to the country's constitution, regular elections were due by the beginning of April. The political leaders assumed that the occupying power, which in 1941 had ruled out municipal elections in order to avoid civil disturbances, would demand a postponement. However, they found that the new plenipotentiary, Werner Best, preferred to go ahead and, moreover, was able to secure the support of his masters in Berlin. The politicians, though well aware of the risks and difficulties involved, on balance preferred to have the elections forthwith. Their main reason was that a parliament resting on a breach of constitutional law would lack formal legitimacy. This would weaken the political system, and could even serve as a pretext for the occupying power imposing a government that would lack parliamentary cover. Ultimately, the proclaimed Danish sovereignty was at stake.

The German authorities gave their consent on three conditions: there would be some restraint on the election campaign; no criticism of the occupying power; and some protection for the German minority in the country. The themes of the campaign became democracy and national solidarity, instead of disagreements among the governing parties. The day of the elections, 23 March, was celebrated as a national holiday. The turnout was 89.5 per cent, the highest ever recorded, with 95 per cent of the votes supporting the parties of the coalition.

Though the party leaders had been careful to distance themselves from Scavenius in the conduct of their campaigns, the result of the elections was seen as a victory for the policy of cooperation. Moreover, it spelt the end of DNSAP, which again secured only three seats. With the DKP banned, Communists had to be excluded from the elections.

Among Scavenius's ministerial colleagues, some of his staunchest supporters were men without party-political attachments. One was Gunnar Larsen, a young and prominent industrialist who joined the ministry formed by Stauning in July 1940 and remained minister of public works till the end of the occupation. In matters of foreign affairs, he identified with the policy of active cooperation with the occupying power. His first task was to lead the delegation that went to Germany to negotiate a customs and monetary union. Several later projects initiated or managed by him included the setting up of a committee in the autumn of 1941 to explore the economic possibilities for Danish industry and trade in the Soviet territories then occupied by German forces. A few other Danish–German enterprises of his turned out to be equally fruitless.

Larsen defended several of his major public-works projects in terms of their potential for reducing unemployment, which since the early 1930s had been one of the most important political and economic problems of the country. Some of his governmental colleagues, however, suspected that he, a successful businessman with an international horizon, was not blind to other potential advantages of such projects, perhaps including some affecting his private business interests. His relations with the professional politicians were further complicated by a general feeling that, like Scavenius, he was less than enthusiastic about the parliamentary system and its tedious procedures. In the illegal press, he was attacked not only for the nature of his policies but also for a tendency to confuse political concerns with private economic interests. Though educated at Massachusetts Institute of Technology, and personally a man of British and American sympathies and standards, Larsen was widely deemed to be pro-German.

His position as Scavenius's right arm, his close contacts with German officials and his numerous efforts to strengthen Danish–German bonds made Larsen one of the most unpopular men of the occupation years. After the liberation he was imprisoned, charged with collaborating with the Germans and giving financial support to Danish Nazi circles, but was eventually acquitted. In his defence, he was able to state that he had worked for the British Secret Service since April 1940 and had made a large sum of money available for organized resistance in the spring of 1943. The Supreme Court accepted that his payments to Nazi groups had been motivated by national considerations. However, though legally exonerated, public criticism of his person continued in the post-war years and made it impossible for him to remain in Denmark.

Not having been a member or representative of a political party, Larsen had no one to share the responsibility for the policies he had pursued and help defend him against the acrimonious and vengeful attacks his critics directed against him in the post-liberation period. Another non-professional minister found himself in much the same situation in 1945. As commissioner of police since 1938, Eigil Thune Jacobsen was, from the outset of the occupation, saddled with the responsibility for maintaining law and order in the country. It was a task that he carried out with conviction and determination, letting the police deal firmly with anti-German manifestations as well as Nazi disturbances. Identifying with the policy of the government, he accepted the principle that Danish authorities should punish persons caught challenging or resisting the occupation forces. In some cases it might be necessary to impose severe sentences, and thus prevent the Germans from intervening and imposing harsher measures on the country. Personally, he was particularly opposed to violent and disruptive actions of the type usually associated with Communist campaigns. Having established and maintained close professional contacts with the police authorities in Vienna and Berlin since the early 1930s, Thune Jacobsen was well placed to handle relations with the German police in Denmark in the first year of the occupation. He was also an obvious choice for membership of the board of the newly established Danish–German Society.

When the Germans, in the summer of 1941, demanded the resignation of the minister of justice the leaders of the Social Democratic party pressed Thune Jacobsen to take over the post. The first task of the new minister was to prepare a law prohibiting Communist associations and activities. In response to a German demand made immediately after the invasion of the Soviet Union, internment of leading Communists throughout the country had already been set in motion before the change of minister. The new law, of 22 August 1941, provided for the arrest and punishment of persons guilty of Communist activity or agitation, and for the detention of persons whose conduct indicated that they might engage in such activity and become a threat to the security of the state or its relations with foreign powers. The law was administered jointly by the ministry and a parliamentary committee. Thune Jacobsen was also responsible for the preparation of a law, passed in December 1942, to provide protection against industrial sabotage. As minister, his basic concern was to retain the administration of justice in Danish hands. To achieve this, he thought, it was necessary to calm relations between the population and the occupying power and to continue the policy of cooperation. Even as late as 28 August 1943 he hoped to avoid a final rupture of the intergovernmental relationship with Germany.

The orders he gave to the police in the initial period, and the laws he introduced and influence he exercised on the judiciary as minister, made Thune Jacobsen a hated figure in resistance circles. Soon after the liberation he was arrested, but immediately released as a result of an intervention by Frode Jakobsen. He hoped to clear his name through a process of impeachment but was not given the opportunity. Thus, he never provided a formal proof of certain claims he made in his defence, namely that he had worked for the British Secret Service and had been passing information to London about the police and sabotage in Denmark, which had been one of the reasons why he had had to escape to Sweden in October 1944.

Among the professional politicians, Scavenius found his most loyal supporters in the Social Democratic party. Foremost among them was Thorvald Stauning, who as prime minister till his death in May 1942 totally identified with the policy of negotiating with the Germans, making concessions when necessary and cooperating as required. It was a policy which followed naturally from the course he and Munch, as leaders of the Social Democratic and Radical Liberal coalition government, had pursued towards Germany in the 1930s and which, in his view, became imperative in the circumstances of the first years of the occupation. Like Scavenius, he apparently expected Germany to win the war and found it necessary for Denmark to prepare itself for German domination of Europe in the post-war world. His most important contribution to the political process was to maintain a degree of parliamentary backing for Scavenius's dealings with the Germans. Time and again he defended the policy and measures of his foreign minister in the committee of leading politicians set up in the summer of 1940, to represent the old political parties and provide vicarious parliamentary control, and secured its backing for the government's handling of relations with the occupying power.

Other Social Democratic leaders in support of the policy of cooperation included Alsing Andersen, Hans Hedtoft-Hansen and H.C. Hansen. Andersen was minister of defence in the pre-war government and remained in office till July 1940, and thus shared the responsibility for the extremely weak military preparedness of the country in 1940 and the early decision to cease fighting on 9 April. In the later part of 1942 he served as minister of finance. His most notorious act, however, was to put his name to a circular which, as acting chairman of the Social Democratic party, he issued to its representatives throughout the country on 2 September 1943. It was not only an aggrieved defence of the government's occupation policy, which had saved the country from the disasters of war and could well have continued doing so till the end of hostilities, but also a bitter attack on the resistance movement, that 'coalition of chauvinists and Communists which irresponsibly and secretly has sought to throw suspicion on the ends and means of cooperation and bring about a different mentality in sections of the public.'

That circular, which correctly expressed the party's attitude to the events of August 1943, and may have been drafted by Hedtoft-Hansen, became a lasting embarrassment for Andersen.[4] Carrying the formal responsibility for its appearance, he was strongly criticized in some of the illegal press. In subsequent years, when the attitude of the public to cooperation and resistance had changed markedly, the leaders of the party failed to acknowledge their responsibility for the circular, preferring instead to treat it rather as a mistake committed by Andersen. When Hedtoft-Hansen, in 1947, appointed him minister of finance he lasted only two days, his past once again catching up with him.

Hedtoft-Hansen and H.C. Hansen, both younger than Andersen, had no ministerial responsibilities during the occupation but, as members of parliament, held high posts in the leadership of the Social Democratic party. Since the 1930s they had been known for their inveterate anti-Nazi and anti-Communist attitudes. Though, early in 1941, the Germans forced them to resign their honorary posts in the party, both remained part of its informal leadership throughout the war. At all stages they were convinced that the policy of cooperation was both justified and necessary. Like Vilhelm Buhl, leader of the party after the death of Stauning, they were highly sceptical about the resistance movement and its leadership, the self-appointed nature of which they found difficult to reconcile with their democratic convictions. They also suspected that the Communists dominated its activities. In an apparent attempt to secure some control of its efforts, each established contact with members of the movement and, eventually, with the freedom council. Both became ministers in the liberation government and each of them eventually became prime minister, Hedtoft in 1947 and H.C. Hansen in 1955.

The state organs and public bodies of the country largely supported the policy of willing cooperation, especially in the first three or four years of the occupation. Since the most obvious alternatives to the existing order were government by the Nazi party and its sympathizers and military rule by the occupying power, official Denmark found it necessary to accommodate the Germans and avoid provocations. King Christian X set the tone from the very beginning. In the morning of 9 April, after the order to cease fighting had reached the units of the armed forces, the government prepared a proclamation which called for calm and restraint by the public and maintenance of law and order throughout the country. The king added his personal appeal for correct and dignified behaviour, explaining that any rash act or remark could have the most serious consequences. As it did for members of the public, caution became the first principle of official dealings with the Germans.

Though the king was cast in several roles in the course of the occupation, in his constitutional acts and public utterances he managed to back his government and support its policies. In the initial period he quickly became the focus of a public swell of patriotic feelings and expressions. His daily, unaccompanied ride on horseback through the streets of Copenhagen strengthened his bond with the people and helped make him the foremost symbol of national unity in trying circumstances. Soon, however, he also became a bold example of how to deal with the Germans on personal levels. Numerous stories about the king – some true, others apocryphal – went round, most of them involving some kind of snub to representatives of the occupying power.[5] In British propaganda directed against Danish politicians involved in cooperation with the Germans, the king was sometimes presented as an alternative rallying point for patriotic efforts. However, though the king may have been attracted to some such roles, he usually made sure to consult the political leaders and secure their support for his interventions.

In the first summer of the occupation there was some uncertainty among politicians about the king's commitment to the parliamentary system of government. Their fears culminated when the so-called Højgaard circle, a group of prominent men with rightist views, in November 1940 put pressure on the king to dismiss the Stauning government and, with or without parliamentary approval, appoint a ministry of politically independent people, drawn mainly from trade and industry and led by prince Axel, a cousin of the king. Such a government, it was argued, would not only protect the country against a Nazi take-over but could also secure some advantages from the Germans which were beyond the reach of the existing government. The king rejected the proposal, and let Stauning assure the parliament that he had no intention of acting without its approval.

After the telegram crisis and the riding accident in October 1942 and subsequent prolonged illness of the king, he gave loyal, if not always enthusiastic, support to Scavenius in the critical period of 1943. In May he marked his return to official duties with a broadcast address in which he spoke against sabotage. Aware that such an admonition now ran counter to the trend of public opinion, he had long resisted it, but eventually agreed because both Scavenius and Best wanted it. During the rebellion some months later he was again reluctant to associate himself with an appeal for law and order, which went out on 21 August, and gave in only after a long argument. Yet, despite his qualms, the king did not disown the policy of cooperation. Indeed, when the rupture of formal relations with the Germans finally came, on 29 August, he remarked that it had happened too soon. After the August crisis the king, like the government, was constitutionally out of action without having abdicated. Regarding himself as a prisoner, Christian X remained in this state of suspension till the end of the occupation but kept in touch with Scavenius indirectly.

In the state administration, the department responsible for formulating and carrying out the policy of cooperation, before as well as after the August rebellion, was the foreign ministry. Immediately after the invasion it was agreed that relations with the German authorities in the country should be conducted mainly through that ministry. Such an arrangement made it possible to maintain the fiction that occupied Demark remained a sovereign state, able to handle relations with its belligerent neighbour through normal diplomatic channels. Thus the policy and practice of cooperating with the occupying power acquired a formal, albeit legalistic, base which was convenient or acceptable to each of the parties. It survived the deactivation of the Danish government and lingered on, in its make-believe existence, till the collapse of the occupying power. Its function was to help the government and the ministry in their efforts to protect the independence of Denmark in domestic affairs.

The central figure in the ministry was Nils Svenningsen. At the time of the invasion head of the department handling political and legal matters, he had identified with Munch's policy towards Germany in the late 1930s and accepted the geopolitical dependence of Denmark on a powerful Germany. In the spring of 1941 he was appointed head of the ministry. As such, he became Scavenius's most loyal and reliable helper in the conduct of relations with the German authorities in Copenhagen and Berlin. He entirely accepted the policy of willing but limited cooperation. Drafting most of Scavenius's statements, he helped to formulate the policy and took responsibility for putting it into practice. In diplomatic crises with the Germans, as well as in recurrent issues between Scavenius and the politicians, he invariably gave his minister full support. After August 1943, when he became chief negotiator in relations with the German authorities, he faithfully continued the policy of protecting the remains of Danish sovereignty by engaging in restrained cooperation with the Germans. This meant close and continual negotiations with Best under discreet supervision by the political leaders.

Never having any doubts himself about the necessity for such cooperation and its moral and political righteousness, Svenningsen resented anything that stood in his way. He could not accept any breaches of loyalty to the ministry by diplomats and diplomatic staff serving abroad during the occupation. Thus, he never forgave Henrik Kauffmann, the

Danish envoy in Washington, who immediately after the invasion and occupation, declared his legation independent of the government in Copenhagen and a year later, in the name of the king, signed an important agreement with the United States for the defence of Greenland. Nor did Svenningsen ever accept, or even understand, the motivations behind sabotage and other militant efforts of the resistance movement. Seeking solutions through established diplomatic channels was for him the only way. Through steadfast negotiation and expedient compromises he kept the dialogue with Best going till the end of the war, thus helping to ward off German intervention by military means. After the liberation Svenningsen was attacked for collaboration and sent into exile, as envoy to Sweden. In 1951, however, he was recalled to Copenhagen, where he again ended up as head of the foreign ministry, under the government of H.C. Hansen.

Military matters were not managed by the foreign ministry but dealt with through direct contact between the Danish and the German armed forces. For occupied Denmark it was important to maintain its army and navy, not only because they were visible symbols of its claimed sovereignty but also because they might be needed to quell internal disturbances, whether by Danish Nazis or, after June 1941, by Communists. Within a few weeks of the invasion agreements were reached with the Germans about the conditions on which the army could be retained in the new situation. Many barracks and installations had to be vacated to make room for the German troops; narrow rules for exercise and training were laid down for the army; and all weapons and explosives were put under German control. Later other agreements were negotiated to limit the manpower of the army, and frequent demands were made for the handing over of substantial parts of its war materials. For von Hanneken, who assumed command of the German troops in the autumn of 1942, the goal soon became the elimination of the Danish army and navy. This, however, did not come to pass till 29 August 1943.

The pivotal figure in the conduct of the army's relations with the occupying power was Ebbe Gørtz. As chief of the general staff and senior liaison officer to the German military authorities, he managed the negotiations of the conditions imposed on 9 April. Promoted to lieutenant general and commander-in-chief in the autumn of 1941, he saw the army through the crises of the next few years. After the internment of officers and men in the autumn of 1943, he set up the so-called small general staff, which under the auspices of the leading politicians took charge of the army's illegal activities and preparations during the rest of the occupation. His concerns throughout were to protect the army and ensure that its officers and men did not upset the orderly relations with the German authorities that had been developed by the politicians responsible. Within the given limitations, he sought to train as many soldiers as possible and to maintain discipline throughout the army. When, on 29 August German troops attacked army barracks and other places of duty throughout the country and many units did not resist, or fought only briefly, and did not destroy their stock of weapons, they were following orders issued by him. Firmly believing the role of the army to be that of a loyal and obedient tool of the responsible government, Gørtz accepted the policy of cooperation and the many compromises and concessions it entailed.

Gørtz was against officers independently engaging in illegal activities, on the grounds that their professional loyalty to the government should always have priority. This was also his position after the setting-up of the small general staff, which he, in the absence of an acting government, saw as subordinate to the political leaders, Buhl in particular. That attitude made him unpopular with the resistance movement, and led to frictions with those who looked to the freedom council, rather than the politicians, for leadership. However, Gørtz retained the confidence of the Social Democratic leaders, with some of whom he had developed close relations in the earlier stages of the occupation. In October 1944 the allied powers appointed him leader designate of the Danish resistance forces in case of an allied invasion of Denmark. Thus he ended up as commander-in-chief of the forces of the resistance movement mobilized on 5 May 1945. In the post-war years he managed the reconstruction of the army and its reorganization for NATO membership. However, still under attack for his inflexible attitude during the occupation, he decided to decline when he, in 1950, was invited to apply for the new post of chief of defence.

The major organizations of the economic life of the country, which in its foreign trade had become highly dependent on Germany, fully supported the policy of cooperating with the occupying power. Since both the Association of Trade Unions (DsF) and the Danish Organization of Employers (DA) needed to keep the production flowing, they shared an interest in accommodating various German requirements and avoiding any disturbing rupture of the Danish–German diplomatic relationship. For the former organization, the most pressing problem was the high and rising rate of unemployment, which in the first winter of the occupation reached 36 per cent with unskilled labour particularly hard hit. This was the basic reason why the Association accepted the German demand for manpower, and encouraged, eventually pressed, unemployed members to take work in Germany and thereby reduce the demands on its unemployment fund. Axel Olsen, chairman of the Union of Unskilled Labourers (DAF), was particularly willing to supply Danish manpower to Germany, on the principle that to look after his men was more important than anything else. Nor did he have great difficulty accepting the idea of a customs and monetary union with Germany proposed in the summer of 1940.

Another concern of the Danish labour movement was the challenge of the Communists, who competed for the loyalty of its members. Before their party became illegal, they continually attacked and criticized the Social Democratic party and the trade union leaders. After June 1941, the DsF took measures to suppress the influence of Communists within its organization. From late 1942, however, the problem was exacerbated by the growing number of strikes and acts of sabotage which appeared to be organized mainly by Communists. In the summer of 1943 rampant demonstrations and sporadic rebellions added to the fear of a Communist challenge to the leadership of the labour movement. Spokesmen of the Social Democratic party and the trade unions responded by defending the national policy of cooperating with the occupying power, warning against the dangers for the labour movement of a rupture in relations with the Germans and stressing the need to keep their organizations intact. Danish democracy itself, the DsF chairman Eiler Jensen warned, could be at stake.

In the summer of 1944 the DsF joined the DA and a number of leading politicians in an appeal to call off the mass strike in Copenhagen. Later the same year, when most of the departmental heads of the state administration were considering resigning in protest against the German arrest of the Danish police, the two organizations again joined forces, and put pressure on the civil servants to stay in office and continue the negotiation and cooperation with the occupying power. The trade union movement maintained that line till the end of the occupation. Throughout the war the overriding concern of the Social Democratic labour movement was to keep its political and economic organizations intact.

The DA, from May 1941 under the chairmanship of T.K. Thomsen, played a complementary part in supporting the policy and promoting the practice of cooperating with the German authorities. As chairman of the Organization of Contractors and director of one of the country's largest such companies, Thomsen was from the outset of the occupation deeply involved in several major German projects carried out on Danish soil by Danish companies and workers, and with the approval of the government. Later he took the lead in condemning sabotage and opposing strikes, as a result of which he and his organization attracted much criticism in the illegal press. At the same time, however, the DA donated large sums of money to a relief fund set up in 1943 to support various activities of the resistance movement.

By and large, the policy of cooperation, as developed by the political and promoted by the economic establishment of the country, enjoyed the support of the press. Immediately after the invasion, the occupying power banned news detrimental to its military interests as well anti-German propaganda, but left it to the Danish government to carry out the censorship. This became the responsibility of the press bureau of the foreign ministry. Since that office also maintained the contact to the German press attaché, it became the link between the occupying power and the Danish press. In practice, the system that emerged was one of self-censorship, though with frequent German complaints, requests and warnings.

That this procedure worked well enough to survive the first few years of the occupation was not only a consequence of German threats and interventions, which in a number of cases took the form of removal of anti-German journalists or editors. It was also because nearly all legal Danish newspapers were organs of one or other of the old political parties, and as such were disinclined to publish material detrimental to the established relationship between the coalition government and the occupying power. Thus, as late as the autumn of 1942 the press loyally backed the government in its condemnation of the growing anti-German sabotage. Later that year and in 1943, when Germany suffered setbacks in several theatres of war and the Danish population grew more critical of the policy of always accommodating the Germans, it became more difficult for the press to toe the line. Presumably motivated not least by a concern not to lose their readers, most newspapers now found ways of keeping their more discerning readership informed of developments both at home and abroad.

The period of self-censorship came to an end after 29 August, when the Germans took over the censoring themselves. Now both military, political and economic copy had to be passed to German censors, through the press bureau. Moreover, the Germans regularly supplied propaganda material which had to be published in full. If in the first couple of years the press on the whole had supported the governmental line towards the Germans and in the period leading up to 29 August to some extent had followed the rapidly changing political feelings and public attitudes of its readers, after that date it lost what remained of the traditional freedom of the press.

To the extent that the press in the summer of 1943 managed to minister to sections of a public growing tired of governmental policy and turning towards some form of opposition to the Germans and, at the same time, made sure to continue its support of the official line of cooperation, the press could be said to have been playing a double game. Of the various persons and organizations presented here as practitioners, advocates or supporters of willing cooperation, perhaps the one who came closest to such double-dealing was Christian X, who at several crucial stages seemed to be torn between demonstrating his sympathy with popular anti-German feelings and backing his government. When the DA donated substantial sums to a relief fund set up for various illegal ends it might be seen more as a case of hedging one's bets. When Gunnar Larsen and Thune Jacobsen after the liberation claimed to have assisted British intelligence-gathering it had the taste more of an attempt at retrospective self-justification than of a revelation of a purposeful double game. And when Hedtoft-Hansen and H.C. Hansen established contact with the resistance movement as well as when general Gørtz set up the small general staff of the army and later took command of the military forces of the resistance movement, the basic concern appears to have been to secure some control of the activities of that movement and to make sure that the political leaders, the Social Democrats in particular, had as firm a hand as possible on political developments and military actions during the rest of the occupation and immediately after liberation.

For the men responsible for developing the policy of cooperation and conducting the relations with the occupying power there could be no double-dealing. Guided by a political realism which tended to take the form of geopolitical determinism, and in the cases of Stauning and Scavenius misled by the expectation that Germany would win the war and dominate post-war Europe, they felt compelled to accommodate the Germans, and emboldened to do it in a proactive way. Recognizing that the success of their policy depended on German confidence in Danish integrity, both Scavenius and Svenningsen negotiated in good faith and endeavoured to honour the agreements reached.

While the basic concern of ministers, political leaders and diplomats who identified with the policy of cooperation was to maintain what remained of the legal sovereignty and political independence of Denmark, the guiding principle of the leaders of the Association of Trade Unions was to look after the economic and social interests of their members and protect the organizations of the Danish labour movement. While the former set, concerned with present and future needs of the state and nation, took a broader view of the interests at stake, the latter focused more narrowly on the welfare of a large section of the population. Neither group acted under the influence of Nazi sympathies or pro-German feelings; both were acting in a self-protective mode when they willingly engaged in limited cooperation and carefully steered clear of anti-German activities.

Reluctant negotiation

Those who recognized that some interaction between the Danish and the German authorities was unavoidable but preferred to keep it to a minimum were moved by much the same fears and concerns. As aware as those who felt compelled to engage in deliberate cooperation of the risk of a Nazi take-over or a German military rule and of the need to protect Danish institutions and political traditions, they tried to follow the principle of least contact and negotiation with the occupying power. In practice, that usually meant handling only particular matters which required attention or simply dealing with disputes in Danish–German relations as they arose.

However, though the approach was reluctant and procrastinating, it inevitably led to one concession after another, and thus threatened to take the Danish negotiators on to a slippery slope. While often presented as an alternative policy, this line of conduct turned out to be more a way of exercising some restraint on those who found it necessary or expedient to engage the country in various forms of willing cooperation. Ultimately, the course of reluctant negotiation and minimal concessions survived because it was shielded by the established policy of continuous contact and active cooperation. Yet it allowed many politicians and public servants to maintain some dignity in trying circumstances, especially in the first years of the occupation when there was little active resistance to the occupying power.

The first minister to attempt a pragmatic policy of limited contact and minimal concessions was P. Munch, who remained foreign minister for the first three months of the occupation. The German invasion and occupation meant the failure of Danish foreign and defence policy, the purpose of which had been to keep the country out of war. However, since the fighting by Danish forces in the morning of 9 April had been only brief and minimal and since the Germans immediately had described their occupation as a peaceful and protective measure, and had undertaken to respect the territorial integrity and political independence of the occupied country, it was possible for the Danish government to describe the situation that had arisen as a case of peace occupation (*occupatio pacifica*). Munch, in his answer to a German note of 9 April, presented a formal protest against the violation of Danish neutrality, but also expressed his government's willingness to manage relations within the country with due regard to the existing situation.

Having arranged for most official contact with the Germans to be through the foreign ministry, Munch stuck to his pragmatic policy of dealing with matters case by case as they arose. In this manner he helped to establish the principle that matters at issue were settled through negotiation, rather than through naked imposition by the occupying power. At a time when the Danish government was highly nervous about German intentions, and far from sure that its democratic form could be maintained, this seemed an important point. However, a series of concessions made in response to German pressure underlined the inequality between the occupier and the occupied and undermined the notion of Danish sovereignty. The latter effect of his policy and diplomatic style was reinforced by developments on the international scene, where the rapid victories of the German armies in the summer of 1940 made Hitler's Germany seem almost invincible.

In the governmental crisis in early July, Munch gave way to Scavenius in the foreign ministry. By now a tired and disillusioned man, he was still unpopular with the old opposition parties – especially the Conservatives, who held him responsible for the policies that had led to invasion and capitulation – and well aware that the German minister found him too uncooperative. After retiring, he took one of the two Radical Liberal seats in the committee of parliamentary representatives of the old political parties, where he became a useful mediator in a series of disagreements between Scavenius and the party leaders.

Vilhelm Buhl, minister of finance for the first two years of the occupation and, after Stauning's death in May 1942, prime minister for six months and leader of the Social Democrats, was critical of Scavenius's policy towards the Germans. He could not support the 'active negotiation policy', according to which Denmark quickly offered concessions deemed likely in due course to be demanded anyway, and believed that the negotiators should give way only when compelled to do so. Thus, in the earlier years he tended to act as a brake on Scavenius's endeavours. In particular, he opposed the proposed customs and monetary union, the setting up of a committee to explore possibilities of Danish participation in the development of areas of the Soviet Union occupied by German forces and the accession to the Anti-Comintern Pact.

As prime minister, Buhl's situation became more difficult, marked as it was by the beginning of sabotage and growing tension with the German authorities. In September 1942 he broadcast a notorious speech in which he made a heartfelt appeal to the public to support the fight against those engaged in sabotage. His political concerns were to avoid a rupture of relations with the German representative and to maintain public support for his government's policy of reluctant cooperation. An unchecked growth of sabotage and other anti-German acts, he feared, would jeopardize the continuance of Danish jurisdiction and consequently endanger public support for governmental policy. The Germans had already threatened court-martial jurisdiction and the death penalty for acts of sabotage.

The so-called telegram crisis, which broke out later the same month, saw the end of Buhl's ministry. In Berlin, where his record both as minister of finance and as prime minister was well known, he was regarded as the main stumbling block to the development of a satisfactory relationship with the Danish state. When Best arrived in Copenhagen he was determined to have him replaced. While the political leaders, initially inclined to reject the German demand, were looking for a suitable person to replace him, Buhl decided to step down. Like Munch, he joined the committee of parliamentary representatives of the coalition parties, of which he soon became the unofficial leader. Though he tended to keep a distance from Scavenius's government, at a crucial stage of the August crisis of 1943 he supported his party's endeavours to uphold the policy of cooperation and sponsored the broadcast call for law and order. However, a week later, after the receipt of the German ultimatum of 28 August, he was the first politician to speak up and decisively reject it. In the debate that followed in September he also rejected as impossible all ideas of forming a new parliamentary government. In contrast with Scavenius, he always kept an eye on public opinion and displayed a keen sense of what was possible and prudent in any given domestic political situation.

It was inevitable that Buhl, as the country's most influential politician, should establish contact with the freedom council in the last year of the occupation. But, like other Social Democratic leaders, he did it more to secure some control of the resistance movement than to support its efforts. Highly suspicious of the self-appointed leaders of the resistance and afraid that the movement might present a threat to the political system of the country, he relied on the illegal general staff of the army and the officers and on the Danish brigade, set up in Sweden largely under Social Democratic auspices, to protect the traditional order. From the last winter of the war he became increasingly preoccupied with the risk that the resistance movement, through its growing popularity and its allied support, should emerge as the only body that had played a part in the defeat of the Germans and the liberation of Denmark, and thus obscure the standing and role of the official organs of the country.

However, Buhl enjoyed the support of the politicians, who saw him as the most suitable candidate for the post of prime minister in the liberation government. After a good deal of misgiving, the freedom council accepted him too. His post-war career, first as prime minister of the liberation government for six months and from 1947 as minister in Hedtoft's government, marked the restoration of the pre-war Danish political system and the reinstatement of 'the old politicians'.

Throughout the occupation, Buhl's performance was a balancing act between too much and too little cooperation with the Germans. His political calculations and deft manoeuvring were motivated not so much by a patriotic urge to oppose the occupying power or a will to support the allied cause in the struggle against Nazism as by essentially domestic considerations. His concerns were to protect the traditional political system and established social order against the German onslaught and, once the disturbance of major war in Europe was over, return to the old ways of party politics in a democratic country gifted with powerful Social Democratic organizations.

Buhl and Munch, who had both been ministers in the Social Democratic and Radical Liberal coalition government of the pre-invasion years, found it relatively easy to accept a degree of cooperation with the occupying power. For the leaders of the two major opposition parties, the Liberals and the Conservatives, it was more difficult. Knud Kristensen, prominent in the Liberal party and minister of the interior from July 1940 to November 1942, had been very reluctant to join the broader coalition government formed in the summer of 1940, initially insisting on merely observer status for his party's representatives. He had accepted the establishment of a committee of parliamentary representatives only on certain conditions, namely a revision of social services and a tightening of the rules for unemployment benefits, both parts of the economic programme of the Liberal party.

As minister, he often infuriated Scavenius by opposing his policy of cooperation with Germany and criticizing his diplomatic conduct. In particular, he rejected the proposed customs and monetary union. While acknowledging that such a union could lead to higher German prices for Danish exports, which he suspected might tempt many, he stressed that the decisive consideration must be national independence. In the summer of 1941 he took the leading part in an unsuccessful attempt to replace Scavenius, attacking him for never wanting to say no to the Germans and calling for a different policy. In the telegram crisis the following year Kristensen, now chairman of his party, maintained till a late stage his opposition to Scavenius becoming prime minister. When Scavenius did form a new government he refused to serve under him, but did not object to his party keeping its representation in the government.

Like Munch and Buhl before him, Kristensen joined the committee of parliamentary representatives after his resignation, and thus helped to maintain parliamentary backing for, and control of, Scavenius's government. In the later period of the occupation he did not go out of his way to establish contact with the resistance movement, whose efforts he dismissed as attempts to engage in 'private foreign policy'. When he, towards the end of the war, heard about the plans to have members of the freedom council represent the resistance movement in the liberation government he was not enthusiastic. However, in that government he again took the post of minister of the interior. In October 1945, following the first post-war parliamentary election, he became prime minister in a Liberal minority government.

John Christmas Møller, chairman of the Conservative party in the 1930s, minister without portfolio immediately after the invasion and minister of trade, shipping and industry for three months from 8 July 1940, had a much more positive attitude to the resistance movement. Resenting the practically immediate capitulation on 9 April, he reacted by delivering outspoken anti-German speeches at political meetings, which soon attracted the attention of the German authorities and led to his resignation as minister. Nor would the Germans accept him as member of the committee of parliamentary representatives. After further public statements of anti-German character, including remarks about 'the enemy' being in this country, the Germans demanded, in January 1941, that he give up all his posts, including membership of parliament. Politically isolated, he soon found himself in contact with prominent individuals who were disposed to engage in illegal activities against the occupying power. One was Frode Jakobsen, Social Democratic maverick and founder of the resistance organization the Ring. Another was Aksel Larsen, the Communist leader, with whom he started an illegal paper, *Frit Danmark*. This period came to an end in the spring of 1942, when Christmas Møller, after receipt of an invitation from London, illegally left the country for Sweden and, together with his wife and son, flew to Scotland.

When Christmas Møller, despite his opposition to the foreign and defence policy of the Stauning-Munch government in the 1930s and his indignation at the capitulation on 9 April, accepted a ministerial post in Stauning's government he did it in the compatriotic spirit that marked Danish political life in the period after the invasion. He saw the need for some negotiation with the occupying power, especially in regard to economic matters, but believed it should be conducted on the basis of the Danish–German exchange of notes immediately after the invasion, in which Danish sovereignty in domestic affairs had been acknowledged. In principle, he was sceptical about the pragmatic approach of dealing with matters as they cropped up because he thought it might lead the government on to a slippery slope. In practice, however, he accepted as unavoidable a number of cases where the government yielded to German demands which showed little respect for Danish sovereignty, but were backed by superior power. What he could not accept were voluntary concessions. In particular, he rejected the proposed customs and monetary union, seeing it as a deliberate signing away of national independence in a number of fundamental areas, which would be effective not only during but also after the war. Here he took a strong stand, staking his ministerial post on the outcome of the negotiations.

In contrast with Buhl, for whom the occupation was a Danish–German matter to be managed largely in the context of domestic political considerations, Christmas Møller was very aware of the wider international dimensions of the situation and conduct of his country. Given the minimal fighting and immediate capitulation on 9 April, he was concerned about the impression that the free world, and the allied powers in particular, might gain of the attitude and policy of the Danish government towards the occupying power. Anxious that Denmark should not be seen as collaborating with Germany, he wanted it understood that the country had retained a degree of independence, and was prepared to do its utmost to resist German diplomatic pressure. Hence, he was angry with Kauffmann in Washington for having declared himself independent of the government he was representing on the grounds that it was no longer free but controlled by the German occupier. While the government should give in to German pressure only when palpably forced to do so, the diplomats serving it abroad, he insisted, should remain loyal.

Christmas Møller's experience as minister demonstrated the difficulty of reconciling the principle of limited contact and minimal concessions with the practice of dealing with a forceful occupying power. In London, where he was most of the time till the end of the occupation, he was able to devote his efforts to encouraging the activities of the resistance movement in his BBC talks to Denmark and to rallying Danes in Britain and other allied countries. Towards the end of the war he engaged in some delicate and complex political manoeuvring, which led him to the post of foreign minister in the liberation government, where he represented the free Danes abroad.

The secondary ranks of the leadership of the four major political parties as well as most ordinary members of parliament, none of them personally involved in dealings with the Germans, on the whole preferred protracted negotiation and reluctant concessions to willing cooperation with the occupying power. After August 1943, when relations with the German authorities were managed by the permanent heads of the state administration, there was again a tendency for dissatisfaction with the policy of cooperation to be more marked among those less directly exposed to German pressure. Thus, it was Nils Svenningsen, the chief negotiator, and Eivind Larsen, a departmental head in the justice ministry responsible for matters relating to the police and jurisdiction, who negotiated the details of cooperation, and other departmental heads who occasionally opposed particular proposals put forward in response to German demands.

A major question from the autumn of 1943 related to the role of the Danish police in the fight against sabotage. The Germans wanted their assistance in return for an undertaking that any saboteur caught would be dealt with under Danish jurisdiction. A proposal prepared by the justice ministry met strong opposition when presented to a meeting of the departmental heads in January 1944. The arguments advanced against it were that the Germans could not be trusted to honour their undertaking, that an arrangement possibly requiring Danish police to open fire against saboteurs could lead to civil war, and that the proposed form of cooperation might compromise Denmark's reputation among the allied powers. However, Svenningsen and Larsen got their way, and the justice ministry prepared a proposal for the Germans, who failed to respond.

Four months later the matter came up again. An expansion of sabotage against railways and several attacks on armament factories led Best to demand that the Danish police take over the guarding of a large number of industrial concerns. Svenningsen again wanted to comply; but the majority of civil servants, this time including Larsen, were against it, as were the professional organizations of the police. The result was a refusal of the German demand. But the mass strike in Copenhagen later the same month, which was accompanied by some spectacular acts of sabotage, brought the issue to the fore once more. This time the departmental heads, supported by the politicians, agreed on a compromise proposal for the solution of the problem. Best found it acceptable, and a system of limited cooperation went into force.

Only two months later, however, general Pancke, head of the SS and German police in Denmark, attacked the police stations and rounded up nearly 2,000 policemen and sent them to concentration camps in Germany. That meant the end of Danish jurisdiction, and was a fundamental blow to the system of administrative management of relations with the occupying power. Buhl, and some other politicians, thought that the departmental heads should retire and break off relations with the Germans. Most of the heads as well as the freedom council took the same line. However, both the trade union movement and the employers' association, with the support of some politicians, appealed to the heads to remain at their posts. Svenningsen, determined to continue the existing system, succeeded in preventing a break with the German authorities. Thus, the policy and practice of negotiation and cooperation, whether willing or reluctant, stayed in force till the end of the occupation. When the large organizations in a major crisis took the side of Svenningsen and colleagues against other colleagues and a number of politicians on the opposite side, the pattern emerging had much in common with that typical of earlier years, when Scavenius, together with his most faithful colleagues, usually could rely on the support of the central administration and various major organizations against the political leaders. What had changed was public opinion. In the first years after the invasion the nation, rallying in support of the king and the coalition government, could accept the policy of accommodating the occupying power and the practice of making concessions of the sort which either could be deemed necessary or could be seen as practical, perhaps even advantageous for Danish interests. In the last year of the occupation, a considerable section of the population had long since come round to the view that it was not always necessary to give way to German demands, and usually not in the Danish interest to do so. An increasing number of people had also decided that it was both politically justified and morally right to resist the occupying power, even with arms.

2.3 Opposition

The third section of the spectrum of Danish reactions to German occupation presented here is characterized by opposition to the occupying power and its local representatives and servants. Here the most obvious distinction is between passive and active opposition. While the more passive forms predominated in the first period of the occupation, the decidedly active, and more obvious, manifestations came to the fore in the later years, with the rise and organization of the resistance movement.

Most of those engaged in some form of passive opposition supported, or at least implicitly accepted, the policy of limited cooperation with the Germans pursued by official Denmark. Others, however, were less satisfied with that policy, and more inclined to regard passive opposition as a preparation for increasingly active resistance to the occupying power. While the reactions of the former, generally to be found at the broader levels of society, typically were spontaneous and emotional, the efforts of the latter, often involving particular categories of people, were usually more organized and purposive. To some extent, it was also a difference between those who were plainly pro-national and some who were more anti-German.

Passive opposition

The state of shock and perplexity of the Danish people immediately after the invasion on 9 April was soon followed by a wave of nationalism stronger than anything experienced in the inter-war period. The nationalism of 1940 had a negative as well as a positive side, but in both of its aspects found only a rather feeble expression in terms of public behaviour and practical politics. The negative side, taking the form of fairly mild anti-German feelings, led to the popular practice of cold-shouldering the Germans in Denmark. Resolved to ignore them, people would look the other way when meeting one of the soldiers in the street. At the same time a large number of heartening stories about Danish–German personal exchanges, for example relating a snub by the king or a bold answer by a delivery boy, went round, many no doubt invented.

The positive side of the new nationalism took the form mainly of an intense cultivation of national identity. The focus of the movement was the king, who became the symbol of the Danish nation. Despite his rather reserved nature and less than democratic style, he soon gained enormous popularity, which reached a peak with his seventieth birthday in September 1940. To mark the occasion, silver and gold badges, designed with the Danish flag and crown, the king's monogram and the year 1870 and 1940, were produced for sale, and worn by very many people throughout the occupation.

Some other demonstrations of national unity in the first summer of the occupation took more unusual forms. One was what became known as *alsang*, community singing of patriotic songs in the open air. It started in Aalborg with 1,500 participants, and quickly spread to other parts of the country. Within two months it was possible to arrange simultaneous and coordinated rallies throughout the country with one sixth of the total population singing along. The meetings that day finished off with telegraphic greetings to the king. Attempts the following year at *algang*, brisk community hikes in the country, were physically more demanding and did not rouse quite the same degree of patriotic passion.

The nationalist feelings also found more intellectual expressions at this early stage of the occupation. Throughout the country well-attended meetings with lectures and talks, typically about Danish history or Danish identity, were arranged. Here the foremost sources of inspiration were the writings of N.F.S. Grundtvig, the nineteenth-century clergyman who devoted his life to awaken the people of Denmark to an awareness of its identity and, through a monumental religious and historical quest of Danishness, became a formative influence on the Danish mind in modern times. At Copenhagen University Hal Koch, professor of ecclesiastic history, delivered a series of lectures on Grundtvig which attracted large audiences. About the same time the Royal Theatre showed a play about Grundtvig's youth written by Kaj Munk, a clergyman and dramatist who since 9 April was moved by uncompromisingly anti-German feelings. In their different ways, both Koch and Munk became vehicles of the new nationalism.

A more organic manifestation of the gush of national feelings in 1940 was the establishment of *Dansk Ungdomssamvirke* (DU), an organization set up to facilitate cooperation among the various youth associations of the country. Conceived as a national and cultural body, it acquired also a political programme when Hal Koch became chairman of its council. In a Europe where the democratic form of politics was challenged by contending political systems, by Nazism from the right and communism from the left, he thought it vitally important to protect Danish traditions and values by guiding and educating the youth of the country. The result was a large number of meetings and events for young people in many parts of the country which were intended to go beyond emotional appeals on the theme of the thousand-year-old Denmark and also address the challenges and risks of the existing political situation of the country. The ultimate concern of the leadership of the organization at that stage of the war was to protect the nation against future attempts by a victorious Germany to Nazify Denmark.

In the following years, when the danger of a Nazi take-over of the government became increasingly unlikely, DU acquired the additional function of serving as a channel for disseminating news about Danish–German governmental and administrative relations. In its earlier as well as in its later phase the organization, which in its composition itself reflected the parliamentary and governmental cooperation of the four old political parties, supported the established policy of accommodating the occupying power.

The forms of passive opposition considered so far could be described as politically self-protective and nationally introspective. Though essentially reactions to invasion and occupation, their opposition to German forces and Nazi ideas stopped short of antagonism. For some people, however, a commitment to king, government and parliament, with its implied acceptance of the policy of cooperation with the occupying power, was not enough. Though the immediate political situation might preclude more active forms of opposition, sections of the population found it possible to combine passive opposition with preparing for active resistance at a later stage. Here three initiatives proved important, namely the setting up of clubs for cross-country sports in most major towns, the creation of a nearly nation-wide ring of political study circles and the preparation of the Communist party for illegal activities.

The idea of a civilian movement for cross-country sports, which were already part of the training of army officers, arose among officers and found support among people with a positive attitude to national defence. It could be a way of training young men in cross-country racing and map-reading as well as in close combat and perhaps shooting. A council, composed mainly of officers, was set up in the summer of 1940, and contact was established with circles which might be willing to start such clubs. In the autumn of 1941 the Danish Cross-Country Sports Union was established, later to be attached to the Danish Rifle, Gymnastics and Sports Association. Moved by the idea of laying the foundations of a better Denmark, the leadership of the Union attached importance to inculcating members with patriotism and willingness to defend their country and native soil. Soon the movement built up 30 branches, starting with major cities and the garrison towns. For many members, involvement in cross-country activities led directly to active resistance. Indeed, some branches of the movement were set up as cover for the training of illegal groups.

In November 1941 a group of academics and intellectuals formed the Danish Study Ring, which after August 1943 became known simply as the Ring (*Ringen*). The original purpose was to build a defence for Danishness and democracy by setting up cross-party study circles round the country. Largely through the efforts of its manager Frode Jakobsen, several dozen such circles and individual contacts were organized. In Copenhagen, a further dozen groups, each made up of members of a particular profession, as well as some groups for Social Democrats only were set up. In the first year or two the leadership of the organization limited its activities to providing confidential information about governmental policy and the occupying power and publishing relevant pamphlets, eventually also producing a regular publication with political news and comments.

For Jakobsen, who before the occupation had majored in German at Copenhagen University, travelled in Germany and there established contact with anti-Nazi circles, that programme was not enough. As a maverick Social Democrat belonging to the left wing of the party, he was in conflict with its leaders about the policy of accommodating the Germans, and more minded than any of them to engage in active resistance. From an early stage he clearly saw the organization he had built up as a potentially illegal body, eventually engaged in anti-German activities. In the course of 1942 a disagreement developed between him and the chairman, the historian Erik Møller, who wanted the organization to stick to its educational programme. When Møller retired, early in 1943, the Ring rapidly moved towards illegal activity with Jakobsen as its most influential leader. In the later period of the occupation it expanded immensely, establishing itself as a corner-stone of the resistance, with Jakobsen as its powerful representative in the freedom council.

Denmark's Communist Party, which at the outbreak of the war had less than 8,000 members and only three seats in parliament, found itself in a complicated position when Germany invaded and occupied Denmark. Since 1933 Nazi Germany had demonstrated, in words as well as in action, its hostility to communism. Yet, as recently as August 1939 the Soviet Union, for a while allowing strategic and diplomatic considerations to override the ideological and political conflict dividing Europe, had signed a pact with its potential enemy. The situation that resulted was one which called for particular circumspection on the part of a Communist party in a small country contiguous to Germany. On the day of the occupation, when two of its leaders, including the chairman Aksel Larsen, happened to be in Moscow for consultation with the executive committee of the Comintern, the political committee of the Danish party met to discuss the situation. The issue was whether to provoke the occupying power to ban the party and drive it into illegal existence or, as the majority urged, to endeavour to maintain its legality. The following day telegraphic directives arrived from Moscow, instructing the party to seek to retain legal status as long as possible, while at the same time preparing for eventual illegality. This was the course the party took.

Deeming the war to be a struggle among imperialist powers for the resources of the world, the party could not support any of the sides but only strive for peace. The first few months it directed its critical comments mainly at the Western powers, especially Britain, but later presented a more balanced view in its reporting on the progress of the war. In domestic politics, where the long-term aim of the Communists was the overthrow of the capitalist system, the party opposed the formation of a coalition government of the old political parties and cautiously dissociated itself from the policy of accommodating the occupying power. In parliament it failed to support various measures introduced in response to German pressure, and devoted most of its efforts to attacking the social and economic legislation of the government for being detrimental to the standard of living of the workers and the many unemployed. In defending the interests of those groups, the spokesmen of the party concentrated their attack, in parliament as well as in the Communist press, on the Social Democratic party and the leadership of the trade unions. As a result, the party strengthened its position among the working classes and attracted some new members.

In its attempt to prepare for illegal existence and activity, the Communist party took some steps to decentralize its structure and set up an alternative organization, with unknown leaders, cover addresses and secret lodgings. It also began to make arrangements for the printing of illegal publications. However, it was not till well after the German attack on the Soviet Union in June 1941, and the subsequent arrest and internment of about 150 leading Communists and the banning of the party, that the reorganization was completed. After an initial period of collapse and chaos, a leadership was set up, consisting of Aksel Larsen, the deputy chairman Alfred Jensen, the party secretary Thorkild Holst and Børge Houmann who was responsible for the finances of the party and for its publishing activities. In the provinces, too, efforts were made to decentralize the organization of the party. A leadership of three persons was established in most towns and secret cells were set up at lower levels, on the principle of no horizontal links and only minimal vertical contact. Printing and distribution of publications were also reorganized, so as to facilitate the printing of local papers and thus avoid the hazard of bulk posting of illegal materials.

With the Soviet Union now an ally of the Western powers in the war against the Nazi and fascist powers and the Communist party banned by both the German and the Danish authorities, its members were both freer and more motivated to engage in active opposition to the occupying power. Guided by Moscow, the party adopted the revived tactical principle of popular front, which required Communists to join non-Communists in the struggle against the Nazi enemy. That meant giving priority to the goal of national liberation and letting the ultimate aim of social revolution recede into the background. Thus, for a while, the national fight was allowed to eclipse the class struggle. Soon Communists established themselves as among the leaders of anti-German resistance, in practically all its forms. Sometimes, as in various strikes and demonstrations in August 1943, ordinary party members, perhaps led by a shop steward, acted more or less independently of their leaders, possibly initiating events which turned out to be of some importance. The influence of the party and its members in the emerging resistance movement was manifested in the composition of the freedom council set up in September 1943. Two of the six founding members were Communists, namely Børge Houmann and Mogens Fog, the latter representing the cross-party illegal paper *Frit Danmark*, which started on Communist initiative as an exercise in popular front.

In so far as the more self-protective and introspective forms of passive opposition mentioned here were at all meant as anti-German demonstrations, they were on the mild side. As largely emotional expressions of attachment to Danish qualities, values and institutions, they carried only little risks of provoking the Germans in the country. They could be seen as merely innocuous reactions of placid people to a precarious situation. People who were more resistance-minded than those who went to *alsang* and similar events tended to dismiss such manifestations of the national awakening as mostly cases of sentimental stir, or even to discredit them as ignoble substitutes for more practical and courageous activities. Yet it seems possible that the exploration and cultivation of Danishness in those early years may have led some individuals towards more active opposition to the German menace, at a later stage. Perhaps more important, the collective engrossment in the study and enjoyment of Danish history and identity in the first summer of the occupation may have helped prepare the way for the growing public support for armed resistance three or four years later. If so, it might be seen as a preparatory stage in the political education of a people conditioned by generations of neutrality to steer clear of international power politics and schooled for decades in Radical Liberal pacifism and Social Democratic anti-militarism.

The three organizations introduced here as representing those who wanted to go beyond pro-Danish sentiment and start preparing for anti-German action showed that there were groups of individuals and sections of the population who did not need to go through such a learning process. Each organization attracted particular groups and types of people and developed its own programme of preparations for future activities. As the war in Europe took its course and the political situation in Denmark developed, with international as well as national conditions becoming more conducive to active resistance, all of them, or at least many of their members, became ready to join groups or individuals already engaged in anti-German activities.

Active opposition

The last of the six subsections of the broad spectrum of Danish reactions to German occupation, too, presented so many different forms that some distinction will be required. The most obvious one is between unarmed and armed, or at least militant, types of active opposition. The former were in force from the very beginning, or from a relatively early stage, of the occupation and lasted till the liberation of the country. Among them were the most direct and substantial of Danish contributions to the allied efforts to defeat Hitler's forces and conquer Nazi Germany. The more warlike kinds of opposition, however, depended much more on the fortunes of the allied powers in the war and on the development of public opinion in Denmark. Thus, armed opposition only rarely established itself as a significant influence in Danish–German relations till the last few years of the occupation.

In the first years, before a resistance movement emerged and became organized, and throughout the rest of the occupation Denmark contributed to the allied cause in three ways: by shipping, with intelligence and through propaganda. The most important contribution was that of the merchant navy. It became involved in the hostilities between the great powers soon after the outbreak of war in September 1939, and in the following seven months, when Denmark was still neutral and unoccupied, lost 29 ships and 362 sailors, nearly all victims of attacks by German torpedo-boats in the North Sea.

The invasion caught the shipping companies, as the rest of the country, by surprise. Two thirds of their tonnage and more than half of their crews were on the high seas or in foreign ports. Two of the largest companies, J. Lauritzen's and A.P. Møller's, ordered their captains to seek neutral port and follow the instructions of their authorized representatives in New York. A few months later A.P. Møller's son, Mærsk McKinney Møller, moved to New York to take control of the Mærsk fleet. East Asiatic Company, operating through its subsidiary in London, managed to arrange for the transfer to British service of the right of disposal for 12 of its large ships. Some ships on the high seas belonging to other companies received conflicting instructions from various authorities, which left the decision-making to the captains, most of whom consulted their officers and crew. Of 60 or 70 ships on which the crews were free to decide, about one half chose a British and the other half a neutral port. Most of the approximately 230 Danish ships in allied (mostly British) or neutral ports in the summer of 1940 ended up in allied service.

Danish ships which had reached Britain, or some part of the British Empire, were formally treated as prizes and put under British flag, and their crews encouraged to stay aboard and continue their service. About 90 per cent of the sailors agreed to do so. Like the officers, they eventually formed a trade union. Their leader became Børge Møller, an able seaman who had been trade union representative in Antwerp and had escaped to London after the German invasion of Belgium. Their base was Newcastle-on-Tyne, where they signed on and enjoyed various facilities. In the course of the war, about 3,000 Danish sailors attended their centre there. Many of them also joined the association of 'free Danes' in Great Britain.

In the summer of 1941 the United States, responding to British pressure, seized 40 Danish ships which had been laid up in American ports, and later put them back in service with Danish captains. Since most of the original crew had left and signed on Norwegian, American or British ships, many of the officers and men of those ships were foreigners. Many of the ships, now flying the flag of Panama and bearing new names, crossed the Atlantic with supplies for British forces in the Middle East. Within only a few months seven of them were torpedoed. Once the United States had joined the war, in December 1941, the demand for experienced officers and men to man the many new ships being launched increased rapidly. In the end, there were as many Danes sailing for America as for Britain.

Danish ships and sailors played a part in most kinds of war transport on the oceans of the world. While large ships sailed in convoys along the English and Scottish coasts during the crucial 1940–41 stage of the war, small steamers carried goods to various ports of the British Isles. There were Danish contingents in the transatlantic convoys at the time when German submarines still had the upper hand in naval warfare.

About 25 Danish ships, now again carrying their own flag, took part in operation Overlord, the allied invasion of Normandy in 1944. In the war in the Pacific region, A.P. Møller's large ships were useful in carrying American troops to the Far East, each taking a few thousand soldiers at a time.

The deployment of the home fleet of the merchant navy was regulated by a Danish–German agreement reached within weeks of the invasion. In addition to carrying goods to and from Denmark and between harbours within the country, Danish ships should provide transport and carry cargoes, such as iron ore, for the Germans at their expense. However, since they frequently called at German and Swedish ports, such ships were occasionally able illegally to take individual Jewish refugees, allied airmen and resistance fighters with them to neutral Sweden. Some ships also played an important role in ferrying illegal post and other materials between the resistance movement in Denmark and its representatives and contacts in Sweden. Total losses incurred by Danish shipping in the course of the Second World War have been estimated as 192 ships and approximately 2,000 sailors.

However, the most memorable episode in Danish shipping during the Second World War did not involve large ships of the merchant navy sailing on distant oceans but small boats of all kinds navigating in home waters. Within two weeks in October 1943 a large number of boats, ranging in size from rowing to fishing boats, set out from more than two dozen Danish harbours and moorings to ferry persecuted Jews across the Sound to safety in neutral Sweden. Arriving at more than a dozen diverse points on the Swedish coast, the skippers managed to save about 95 per cent of all Jews in Denmark. This achievement, as we now know, was not merely a manifestation of Danish solidarity and individual bravery but also a result of German hesitation and personal discretion.

During the first few years of the occupation the so-called Jewish question had not become an issue in relations with the occupying power. The Danish government had categorically denied its existence and resisted all pressures for discriminating legislation. The German minister Cecil von Renthe-Fink had taken much the same line, for the reason that anti-Semitic initiatives might spoil the good relations with Denmark and thus stand in the way of what mattered most, namely upholding the image of Denmark as a model protectorate and maintaining its export of foodstuff to Germany. The relatively small number of Jews in Denmark may well have made it easier for his superiors to accept such arguments and postpone the pursuit of racial policies in that country.

Werner Best, the high-ranking SS officer who succeeded Renthe-Fink in November 1942, initially followed the moderate line laid down by his predecessor. However, following the dramatic events of August 1943, when demonstrations, strikes and sabotage led to martial law, diplomatic crisis and the retreat of the Danish government, it very soon became more difficult for him to maintain such a course. In a weakened position in relation to both the top leadership in Berlin and the new head of the armed forces in Denmark, Best seems to have started a double game of his own. On 8 September he sent a telegram to the foreign ministry in Berlin, which passed it on to Hitler. Formally the message called for action against the Jews in Denmark, but also listed quite a few reservations and objections to such an initiative. Whether Best had received confidential information about an impending order, as he insisted after the war, or simply expected it and wanted to turn the situation to his own advantage is not clear. But Hitler's order for action in Denmark followed on 17 September, with allocation of extra police forces for the task.

For handling the situation in Denmark after despatch of his telegram, Best relied heavily on Georg Ferdinand Duckwitz, a fellow diplomat responsible for shipping, who previously had spent some years in Denmark, learnt the language and established contact with many people in business and political circles. He, and a few other Germans, went to Berlin in an attempt to avert the action under preparation. Duckwitz even travelled to Stockholm in order to persuade the Swedes to accept the Danish Jews. In the meantime Best denied rumours of an impending action and, in his meetings with the permanent head of the ministry of foreign affairs, asserted that a recent day-time robbery in the office of the Jewish community and a subsequent seizure by the German police of the membership archives had nothing to do with any such action.

However, on 28 September Duckwitz turned up at a meeting in Copenhagen of Social Democratic politicians and confirmed to friends among the younger leaders of the party that a raid was imminent and urged that all Jews be warned and offered shelter. There are indications that this decisive warning was given in tacit understanding with Best, who, though a man of anti-Semitic convictions, did not particularly want a manhunt across the country. Duckwitz's message was passed on to C.B. Henriques, head of the Jewish community, the same night and was read out at the morning service in the synagogue the next day.

The Jewish community was far from ready to deal with the situation. It was dominated by long-established, fully integrated and socially distinguished families of conservative views, confident that the governmental policy and administrative practice of cooperating with the occupying power would protect them against the imposition of anti-Semitic measures. There were no emergency plans for safeguarding the less influential and poorer members, including more recent arrivals on Danish soil. Ideas of mass escape or underground existence had been rejected on the grounds that such solutions would require too much help from non-Jewish members of the population. In a situation of alarming rumours and urgent warnings, the representatives of the community focused instead on a few desperate and rather unwise alternatives broached by the departmental heads and themselves.

In the evening of 1 October, a Friday, trucks with German police soldiers, accompanied by members of the Danish Schalburg Corps, drove round Copenhagen and arrested Jews. Though the soldiers, according to reports, were brutal and rough in their treatment of people, they followed orders not to break into locked houses and flats. In the course of three hours they made only 202 arrests, the overwhelming majority of the Jewish population in the capital having already left their homes. Another 82 Jews were arrested in Jutland and on Funen. Later a further 197 Jews were arrested while trying to escape. All 481 Danish Jews were immediately sent to Theresienstadt, initially a ghetto for Czech Jews established 60 kilometres north of Prague. In a message of 5 October to his masters in Berlin, Best could declare Denmark 'judenrein'. Himmler and other superiors were less than enthusiastic about the meagre result of the action.

Though for propaganda purposes presented as a model town, Theresienstadt had become a transit camp where Jews stayed for some months until moved to Auschwitz or some other extermination camp further east. However, according to agreement reached on 2 November between Best and Adolf Eichmann, who was in charge of the administrative side of the final solution of the Jews of Europe, those from Denmark were allowed to remain in Theresienstadt. It was also agreed that they could have a visit by representatives of Danish authorities and receive food parcels and clothes from Denmark.

Moreover, they were in good company. Theresienstadt had also become a camp for privileged Jews from the *Altreich*, many of them prominent scientists or artists. A rich cultural life, organized by the Jewish ghetto administration, helped the inmates to cope with the material deprivations and uncertain future in the later period of the war. Shortly before the final collapse of Nazi Germany the Jews from Denmark were evacuated and brought back to Denmark on the 'white buses', sent to rescue surviving concentration camp inmates under a joint Swedish Norwegian–Danish initiative. By then 52 of them had died, mainly from old age and illness.

The Jews not arrested in October 1943 also underwent a harrowing experience. Immediately after the start of the German police raid in Denmark the Swedish government lodged a protest in Berlin and broadcast a message offering to accept escaping Jews. With the help of non-Jewish Danish citizens, 7,056 Jews and 686 non-Jewish relatives reached the Swedish coast unharmed. This mass escape in the earlier weeks of October was not an operation organized by the emerging resistance movement, though groups and members here and there no doubt played a part. Rather, the help provided was a case of improvised reactions of a very large number of local individuals, backed by a united public opinion outraged by the Nazi provocation. The reactions were also encouraged by the stand taken by national authorities. On 2 October most of official Denmark, including the king, the politicians, the trade organizations and unions and various other institutions, lodged protests against the Nazi initiative. The following day, a Sunday, a pastoral letter from bishop Fuglsang-Damgaard, sharply criticizing the action and calling on people to help the victims, was read out in the churches of the country.

Most of the escaping Jews made for the east or north coasts of Zealand, primarily Gilleleje, and other major islands, where they hoped to secure passage to Sweden. At all stages, they were able to rely not only on neighbours, friends and acquaintances but also on strangers for secret help with transport, shelter and a place on a boat. Many owners of the larger boats, risking boat, livelihood and perhaps their freedom if caught by German police, charged for their services. But all involved, whether on land or sea, accepted the risks incurred.

Few of the helpers could have known that those risks were not quite so great as generally assumed. At this stage, too, there was a degree of tacit and passive coordination of German measures. While pursuit of Jews not yet arrested was left to a modest number of Gestapo soldiers, surveillance of the Sound by German police units was suspended during the month of October. Thus, the greatest threat to the escaping Jews may have been Danish Nazis and informers. Yet, only a very small number were caught.

Apart from a few who drowned or committed suicide, the rest, including some European Jews who had escaped to Denmark in the 1930s, settled down in Sweden for the duration of the war. There they established themselves as an influential section of the community of nearly 20,000 Danish refugees living in Sweden by the end of the war.

Some of the Jewish men and youths joined the Danish Brigade set up there in November 1943 with a view to deployment in Denmark at the end of the occupation.

For the Nazi masters of the occupying power, the relocation of nearly all Jews in Denmark to safety in Sweden represented a compromise. It served their purpose of preparing Denmark for a future Nazification, but excluded well over 7,000 Jews from their projected final solution of the racial problem. For the Danes, the successful exodus turned out to be the most laudable result of the dual interaction marking relations with the German authorities, limited cooperation and restrained resistance. Achieved at a time when the emphasis in Danish reactions to the German presence was shifting from cooperation towards resistance, it was also of political significance. The story of the events in October, which took place only weeks after the drama in the last days of August, helped to enhance the reputation of Denmark abroad, not least in the United States, and prepare the way for acceptance as an ally in the war.

The second major Danish contribution to the allied cause, the gathering and transmitting of intelligence, started at an early stage of the occupation and continued till the German forces in north-western Europe capitulated and Denmark was liberated. The work was initiated and, till the autumn of 1943, carried out by a small group of army and navy officers, assisted by a few well-placed civilians. In the course of the war, approximately 18,000 pages of information were passed to the allied powers, mostly to London via Stockholm. The material supplied dealt mainly with the troops and authorities of the occupying power but included also occasional information about political and social developments within Denmark deemed of interest to Britain and its allies.

In 1940 the Danish intelligence services were run by half a dozen officers of the army and the navy, supported by two fairly basic networks of military and civilian informants stretched across the country. After the invasion the flow of intelligence to the general staff of the two services continued, but was of little use to the Danish authorities after the government's decision to capitulate. It was not till later in the year that the intelligence officers, at heart anglophile, managed to establish contact with Britain. It went through Ebbe Munck, a journalist with good contacts in both Denmark and England who in the autumn managed to be appointed Stockholm correspondent of *Berlingske Tidende*, a leading Danish daily. Among his acquaintances in Copenhagen was major Volmer Gyth, one of the intelligence officers in the general staff of the army. Before Munck's departure it was arranged for the intelligence reports to be smuggled out by couriers and delivered to him in Stockholm, and there passed on to the British legation.

In Stockholm, Munck was soon approached by Charles Hambro, who represented the newly-established sabotage organization Special Operations Executive (SOE). The connection was strengthened when that organization set up an advanced headquarters for the Nordic countries in the Swedish capital. The result was that most Danish intelligence reports ended up in SOE's headquarters in London. There they were passed on to Secret Intelligence Service (SIS), SOE's potential rival, on the condition that British activities in Denmark were left to SOE. However, the Danish officers, for a long time apparently unaware of the existence of SOE, were under the impression that their connection to London through Munck was with SIS directly.

Confident that the supply of military and political intelligence was the most important contribution Denmark could make to the allied cause in the existing situation, the officers were opposed to any form of anti-German activities in Denmark likely to stand in the way of their collecting and transmitting information for London. Thus, they turned against the growing sabotage in 1942 as well as the later anti-German demonstrations, all of which they recognized as destabilizing threats to the coalition government and its policy of cooperation, which provided the cover for their secret, illegal and dangerous activities. Unaware of the rivalries and disagreements among organizations and ministries in London and not conversant with changes in British policy towards Denmark and other occupied countries, the officers tended to assume that their own priorities were in harmony with those of London. Since this was not always the case, their reactions to sabotage and other disturbing activities not only led them into conflict with the emerging resistance movement but also seriously complicated their interaction with SOE.

In the autumn of 1942, after the priorities of SOE had shifted from building up secret armies in the occupied countries to organizing sabotage against the occupying power, the Danish intelligence officers' relations with that organization reached crisis point. Some of the senior SOE officers, general Colin Gubbins in particular, having developed suspicions about the commitment and reliability of the Danish officers, the organization decided to test their loyalty to the allied cause and willingness to engage in active resistance by calling for some spectacular acts of sabotage to be carried out by the Danish army. The reactions of the Danes revealed that their concern was not merely to secure optimal conditions for the continuation of their intelligence work but also to keep the Danish army intact – ready, as they liked to think, for deployment some great day in the distant future. Here their position was in accordance with the programme of the army's general staff and in harmony with the policy of their government.

The confrontation lasted more than six months and was never quite resolved. It soured relations between the parties and affected their cooperation. While the Danish officers, perhaps inclined to overestimate the importance for the British of the intelligence provided, felt unappreciated and distrusted, the more activist among the SOE officers, for long sceptical about the need for complete peace and quiet in Denmark, reached a low opinion of the military morality and professional judgement of the Danish officers.

The events of 29 August 1943 broke up the League, as the senior intelligence officers called themselves. One was arrested and sent to Germany for the rest of the war and another temporarily interned in Denmark. Three went underground and ended up in Sweden, from where two of them, with the help of others and some support from the Swedish intelligence service, set out to restore the Danish service. This involved re-establishing a network of contacts across the country. The man entrusted with that task was lieutenant Svend Truelsen, a reservist of the Royal Life Guards who had been attached to the general staff and trained in intelligence work, and was now employed by the Agricultural Council. In a short time he managed to reorganize and develop a highly efficient network across the country, for both the army and the navy. While the network of informants in Copenhagen was expanded, the organization in the provinces was decentralized. Moreover, a direct telegraphic connection with London was set up.

In the course of this work, Truelsen established and maintained contact with members of Denmark's freedom council, but declined a request to set up an independent intelligence service for the council. However, his connection with the resistance movement led him into conflict with the so-called small general staff, set up by younger officers of the army's general staff during their internment in the aftermath of the events of August 1943. That body owed its existence not least to a prevailing nervousness within the Danish establishment, especially among the Social Democratic leaders, about Communist influence in the resistance movement and plans for the post-liberation situation. Hence it was determined to keep contact with the resistance movement to a minimum, and eager to secure control of the reorganized intelligence service. To this end, one of its members, major Svend Schjødt-Eriksen, assumed formal responsibility for the domestic part of the service, which in principle included information about Communist activities in the country.

Schjødt-Eriksen belonged to a small group of younger officers who, out of frustration with the events of April 1940 and the defence policy of the country, had decided to join DNSAP in the summer of 1940. Only a passive member, he had left the party after some months, and later developed close relations with the Social Democratic leaders. The result of the struggle that ensued between him and Truelsen for control of the intelligence organization was that the latter in May 1944, by then hotly pursued by the Germans, had to escape to Sweden. As Gyth had done before him, he soon moved on to London, where he spent the rest of the war. However, while Gyth was largely ignored by SOE, Truelsen was appointed major and attached to its head office with responsibility for intelligence work. Subsequently he joined the Danish section, where he managed and organized intelligence work and participated in the planning of SOE actions in Denmark, notably the bombing by the Royal Air Force of three Gestapo headquarters.

After the departure of Truelsen, major F.B. Larsen took over the management of the intelligence service in Denmark. Like his predecessor, he guarded its independence of the small general staff. After Larsen's arrest, in September 1944, by the Germans – who never realized whom they had caught – Schjødt-Eriksen assumed overall management of the service. By then, however, it was so decentralized that each region or section functioned more or less independently. The collection, transmission and presentation of intelligence were carried on efficiently till the end of the war. If the information produced turned out to be of relatively minor importance to the allied powers, it was because Denmark belonged to an area of low priority in the conduct of the war. However, towards the end of hostilities in western Europe, when at one stage it looked as if Denmark might become a theatre of war, the up-to-date and comprehensive information supplied by the Danish intelligence service was appreciated in the headquarters of the armies commanded by general Montgomery.

The third major unarmed form of active opposition was the propaganda that the illegal press directed against the Danish authorities and the occupying power. To the extent that the allied powers disapproved of the coalition government and its accommodating policy towards the occupying power and wanted the Danes to make a stand and resist the Germans, an illegal press that campaigned against the government and called for resistance was in effect supporting the allied cause. That such a press did not emerge till well into the second year of the occupation was partly because the allied powers themselves for a long time were not willing or ready to encourage the Danes to turn against their government and start resisting, but mainly for the reason that the political situation within Denmark itself was only then becoming conducive to the emergence of an illegal press.

In Britain, Denmark did not enjoy much respect in the period after 9 April 1940. At war with Germany since September, and now involved with the Norwegians in their fight against the invading forces of the German army, the British tended to overlook that Danish reactions to Nazi Germany before, during and after the invasion, were in harmony with the policy pursued by Britain itself practically up to the German invasion of Poland. Nor did they perhaps appreciate that the Danish policy of appeasement had been sealed in 1937, when the Foreign Office had indicated to the Danes that they could not expect British military support in case of German aggression against their country. If the British now censured the Danes for nonchalant conduct on 9 April and the following months it may have been mainly out of fear that the country might end up as vassal of Hitler's *Reich*.

The policy that Britain later that year developed towards Denmark was to encourage the government to stand firm against German demands and pressures. In its propaganda, it made a distinction between the king and the government, building up the former while criticizing the latter. The criticism, however, was directed more at Scavenius and the other ministers without party-political attachments than at the party leaders in the government. In 1942, after the beginning of sabotage in Denmark, the propaganda switched aim, focusing the attack on collaborators among the public while leaving the government in peace. The immediate reason was still to protect the flow of information from the Danish intelligence officers. A more long-term consideration for the Foreign Office was to keep the Danish political structure intact in order to smooth a future transition from occupation to liberation and secure goodwill and cooperation from post-war governments. Thus Britain tried to balance between the existing government and the emerging resistance movement.

It was not till the spring and summer of 1943 that British propaganda towards Denmark again hardened. The entire government and its accommodating policy now came under attack, while those engaged in active resistance received some encouragement. However, while calling for a stepping up of sabotage and other forms of resistance, the British still did not want the government to collapse and the German authorities to assume complete control of the country. Their aim was to encourage passive resistance by the public and militant efforts by the growing resistance movement, all within the existing political structure of the country. Thus, British propaganda was still conditioned by the political considerations of the Foreign Office on the one hand and motivated by the military ambitions of SOE on the other.

American policy, diplomacy and propaganda towards Denmark in the earlier years of the occupation, too, went through several stages. The first one lasted from April 1940 to April the following year, when the United States signed its agreement with Henrik Kauffmann about the defence of Greenland. The second stage came to an end with Japan's attack on Pearl Harbor and the United States' entry into the war in December 1941, which led to the closing of the American legation in Copenhagen the following month. The third stage concluded with the public rebellion in August 1943 and the retreat of the Danish government. Though the relationship between the two states was continuously complicated by Kauffmann's declaration of independence of his government at the outset of the occupation and the partial acceptance by the United States of his unprecedented diplomatic status, the Washington administration endeavoured to stay on reasonably good terms with the government in Copenhagen throughout the whole period. Its reasons for pursuing that policy towards Denmark, however, varied from stage to stage.

The first year, when the outcome of the war in Europe was uncertain, the United States had good reasons to stay on cordial terms with Denmark. Any peace settlement which established Germany in a dominant position on the Continent and left a formally independent and neutral Denmark within a German sphere of influence would present a situation in which it might be in American, as well as in Danish, interest to maintain friendly relations between the two neutrals. Though the US administration was disturbed by a series of apparently voluntary concessions by the Danish government to the occupying power, it was sufficiently well informed to know that such acts were not motivated by Nazi sympathies or pro-German inclinations and to appreciate the reasons and calculations governing Danish conduct. Kauffmann's campaign, which presented Denmark to the American public as a hostage to German power and its policy as forced upon the government, also helped the administration to tolerate Danish management of relations with the occupying power.

The second stage in US–Danish relations, up to December 1941, was marked by the agreement for the defence of Greenland. Signed by Kauffmann on behalf of a 'free Denmark', it inevitably burdened

American relations with the legitimate government of the country. Since the administration already then recognized the importance of also being able to maintain its military presence on Greenland after the end of the war, it was eager to limit any damage done by the independent envoy and by its open implicit acceptance of his diplomatic status in Washington. To mend relations with Copenhagen, president Roosevelt wrote a letter to the king, assuring him that the United States still recognized Danish sovereignty over Greenland and had merely taken charge of its defence.

After Pearl Harbor and the entry into the war, it became in some respects easier for the American administration to distance itself from the Danish government and start reconsidering Danish conduct of relations with the occupying power. Kauffmann's personal accession, again on behalf of the 'free Denmark', to the Declaration of the United Nations on 2 January 1942 and other activist initiatives encouraged such a development. A certain amount of discreet competition with Britain in the sponsorship of a Danish resistance movement, and even in the projection of post-war spheres of influence on the European Continent, was a further incentive to begin to think of Denmark as a potential ally in the war. Yet, the policy and diplomacy of the administration remained ambiguous. Continuously well informed, mainly by its legation in Stockholm, about conditions and developments in Denmark, it understood and, in the period leading up to the events of August 1943, even came to respect Scavenius and his policy. Thus, at no stage of the first several years of the occupation did the American political authorities initiate or encourage a propaganda campaign directed against the Danish government and its policy of limited cooperation with the occupying power.

Till well into the occupation, the Soviet Union had reasons of its own not to engage in or encourage anti-German propaganda against the Danish government. Having signed a non-aggression pact with Germany in August 1939, with a secret additional protocol which divided eastern and central Europe into a Soviet and a German sphere of interest, the Soviet government was inclined to regard Denmark as belonging to the German sphere. When Germany invaded Denmark the Soviet envoy in Copenhagen referred to the event as the 'arrival' of German forces, and enjoined the Danish Communists to avoid critical comments on the occupation. Instead they should blame the British and French imperialists for the war, and the Social Democrats for letting Denmark become involved. Diplomatic relations between the Soviet Union and Denmark continued, with the Danish side seeking to expand trade between them and the Soviet representatives focusing their concern more on the strategic importance of Denmark, at the entrance to, and exit from, the Baltic.

The German attack on the Soviet Union in June 1941 immediately led to a breaking off of diplomatic relations between Copenhagen and Moscow. In the following period till the dissolution of Comintern in May 1943, the only significant political relations between the two countries were between the headquarters of that organization and the Danish Communist party. Here contact seems periodically to have been via the Swedish Communist party and intermittently by radio. After August 1943 the party had its own representative in Stockholm, Alvilda Larsen, and through her presumably regular contact with the Russians. On a broader and more public level, there was continuous contact during the war through Radio Moscow, which broadcast news and propaganda and issued orders and directives to the Communist parties of the occupied countries. During the last year of the occupation the resistance movement had its own representative in Moscow, Thomas Døssing who acted as envoy of the freedom council.

As an ally of the Western powers, the Soviet Union presented a new interpretation of the war. No longer a war of imperialist powers, it was a joint struggle for liberation from Nazi and fascist domination. In a speech broadcast on 3 July 1941 Stalin appealed for a united front of peoples in defence of freedom, thus reviving the tactical dogma of popular front enunciated by the Comintern congress in 1935. Shortly after, Moscow called upon the Communist parties in occupied countries to organize resistance through strikes, rebellions and guerrilla warfare.

Denmark, however, seems to have been of only marginal importance to the Russians, even in the later years of the war. Though still concerned about the future strategic importance of the Danish straits, they do not appear to have included this country in their plans for an expanded sphere of Soviet influence in the post-war world. Nor do they seem to have developed an active interest in the political life of the country. Though critical of the close cooperation of the government and administration with the occupying power and resentful of the anti-Soviet policy of the parliament and political leaders in 1941, the Russians did not go out of their way to encourage and support the Danish resistance movement, as a whole. Not too impressed with some of the people who represented it abroad, they thought it lacked efficient leadership and a political programme, and was far from being a mass movement. Thus, for a long time the Russian attitude to Danish resistance remained uncertain and hesitant. When the Soviet authorities eventually accepted a representative in Moscow of the 'fighting Denmark', they used him as a willing tool for their own purposes but did little to facilitate his ordinary work.

Yet, despite the late arrival of the Soviet Union as an allied power, its limited interest in Denmark, sceptical attitude to Danish resistance and minimal support for the movement, this power became a greater ideological inspiration and political influence than the Western allies for some more resistance-minded sections of the Danish public in the two years leading up to the events of August 1943. This was so particularly in the sphere of illegal publications and anti-government and anti-German propaganda. Here it was those who looked to Moscow, rather than to London, for inspiration and guidance who seized the initiative. At both local and national levels, it was Communists, whether party members or sympathizers, who took the lead in setting up an illegal press. Spearheading the counter-offensive against the German propaganda machine, this press played an important part in shattering the image of occupied Denmark as a model protectorate of governmental cooperation and social order promoted by Nazi Germany.

Whatever the attitudes of Britain, the United States and the Soviet Union to Danish politics, it was largely because of the situation within Denmark itself that a year or two went by before propaganda against the coalition government and the German authorities got under way. Till the autumn of 1941 the general public saw little need for an illegal press which could publish uncensored news and influence public opinion. Conditioned by generations of neutrality in foreign policy and affected by anti-militarist attitudes and pacifist ideas, it was at that early stage quite willing to accept the policy of cooperation forced upon the government by the prime minister and the king. Once they had adapted to the situation of an occupied country, most people were able to put up with a radio and press which, though restricted by governmental guidelines and German control, did provide daily information about Danish relations with the German authorities and the progress of the war. Those who wanted uncensored facts and opinions could read the Swedish newspapers, provided they understood the language, or tune in to the BBC, which broadcast in Danish from the beginning of the occupation. Listening to the BBC was not expressly forbidden, though many Danes thought it was.

The turning-point was the banning of the Communist party after the German attack on the Soviet Union. With its leading members arrested and interned or living underground, the party needed an illegal press to present its views and further its cause. Its first such publication, the pamphlet *Danske Toner*, came in September 1941. It contained the speech against the bill to ban the party that Aksel Larsen, its leader, had been unable to make in parliament. The following month the first issue of the monthly *Politiske Maanedsbreve* appeared in duplicated form. Renamed *Land og Folk* in March 1942, and eventually properly printed, it became the foremost illegal paper of the country, appearing in numerous local editions and maintaining a print run of 120–130,000 in the last few years of the occupation. From May 1943 to the end of the occupation the party also published *Nyt fra Sovjetunionen*. Moreover, a large number of illegal papers, of various sizes and varying regularity, were published by local Communist groups during the later years of the war. Always attaching great importance to propaganda, the Communists dominated the illegal press up to August 1943 and went on to play a major part in this form of resistance till the end of the war.

From the autumn of 1941 a few non-Communist groups, too, were formed for the purpose of publishing illegal papers. One of the first was a small group in Copenhagen which started *De frie Danske*. Its first number, appearing in December, was a protest against the Anti-Comintern Pact and a plea for the government to refuse future demands by the enemy. From January 1942 Frode Jakobsen's Ring published *Det politiske*. In August the same year the first number of *Studenternes Efterretningstjeneste* appeared. It was published by a group of Conservative students in Copenhagen, who the previous November had set up a group under the same name in connection with the demonstration against the Anti-Comintern Pact. It became a fortnightly, which by the spring of 1944 reached a print run in excess of 100,000.

The most important development in the illegal press of 1942, however, was the emergence of *Frit Danmark*. That paper, as well as the organization by the same name, owed their origins to plans, developed by the Communist party the previous autumn, for a broad, cross-party illegal forum. The project took concrete form when Christmas Møller, leader of the Conservatives, joined forces with Aksel Larsen with a view to creating an organ which could serve as a mouthpiece for a national rally of those ready to oppose the policy of the government and resist the occupying power. A cross-party editorial committee was set up, and the first issue published in April. From an early stage, the driving force behind the paper was Børge Houmann, who also edited *Land og Folk* and other Communist publications. Moreover, for its printing and distribution *Frit Danmark* had to rely on the facilities and networks already organized by the Communist party. Thus, *Frit Danmark*, the paper together with the organization, may be seen as a cover organization of the Communist party, set up in accordance with the tactical slogan of national front against the enemy. However, the paper had a non-Communist co-editor throughout its existence, in the earlier period Ole Kiilerich and later

Kate Fleron, both Conservatives. Thus, from another point of view, *Frit Danmark* may be deemed a successful exercise in cross-party cooperation, with both sides of the political spectrum represented, each in rough proportion to the degree of its ideological commitment to the anti-Nazi cause and the level of its organizational preparedness for active resistance in 1942.

In a deliberate attempt to create a counterweight to the dominating influence of the Communists in the illegal press, several new papers were launched in the earlier part of 1943. One was *Danske Tidende*, which came out in January with Conservative and Social Democratic sponsorship. Another was *Hjemmefronten*, set up by Kiilerich and other Conservative Youth (KU) members and launched the following month. Despite raids, arrests and imprisonment, all the illegal papers mentioned here managed to maintain publication up to May 1945. Moreover, a large number of new publications appeared after August 1943, with the result that more than 250 different papers were in circulation in 1944–45.

In the same period a few illegal news services were set up to provide reliable information to editors, of both illegal and legal sections of the press, as well as to the world press. One was *Information*, a service instituted and, till his arrest in October 1944, run by Børge Outze, then a journalist working for the national newspaper *Nationaltidende*. This service prepared daily reports on the sort of news and information that could not be published legally and distributed them to a small circle of interested parties. The list of subscribers eventually included also editors of Communist papers, who since January 1943 had had their own news service, *Ugens Nyt* edited by Houmann. Via Sweden, *Information* also managed to keep other countries informed about developments within Denmark.

After the events on 29 August 1943 a number of Danish journalists stationed in Stockholm, finding themselves cut off from the legal papers they represented, decided to set up a central news service of their own, which they named *Dansk Pressetjeneste*. Its aim was to collect news from Denmark and pass it on to the world press, and thus help popularize the Danish resistance movement. Led by Erik Seidenfaden, the service eventually had a staff of about 50, with its own correspondents in the major Danish ports of shipment. News for the BBC's Danish section was sent telegraphically, and used selectively in broadcasts to Denmark. During the mass strike in Copenhagen in the summer of 1944 the service succeeded in keeping the attention of the press of the free world for several days.

The establishment of the freedom council affected the illegal press in several ways. First, the council became a source of illegal publications of its own. Within a month of its formation it published the pamphlet *Naar Danmark atter er frit* (Once Denmark again is free), its programme for the immediate post-war situation. Representing a compromise between the different views of influential members of the council, the pamphlet served to allay the widespread fear among the public of the Communist section of the resistance and to moderate the revengefulness of parts of the illegal press. Written mainly by Mogens Fog, it became an important historical document. Later followed a long line of directives which, striking the public as wise and responsible, enhanced the authority of the freedom council. Statements and instructions were usually published in *Information*, which thus became the mouthpiece of the freedom council. Several members of the council, Houmann and Fog in particular, wrote frequently for *Frit Danmark*, the political line of which was to the left of the council's.

Another way in which the freedom council exerted influence on the illegal press was through the setting up of a press committee. It started as an attempt to pacify certain right-of-centre illegal organizations and papers, including *Studenternes Efterretningstjeneste*, *Danske Tidende* and *Hjemmefronten*, which initially were inclined to disown the freedom council as a self-appointed body dominated by the Communist party and Danish Unity at the expense of less extremist sections of the resistance. In the winter of 1943–44 Arne Sørensen, leader of Danish Unity and member of the freedom council, took up negotiations with its opponents in the illegal press, with a view to forming a link between them and the council. In February the press committee was established, with representatives from both sides. Soon Outze from *Information* joined too. Though the freedom council failed to dominate the views and positions espoused by the illegal press and the press failed to control the decisions and statements made by the council, the weekly meetings of the committee did help to coordinate the efforts of the parties involved, especially in some crucial situations.

A retrospective study of the political contents of the bulk of the illegal press, from the autumn of 1941 to the spring of 1945, revealed some common features as well as a broad development. The minimal shared programme of the press in the first year, up to the autumn of 1942, was to expose breaches of faith by the occupying power and to oppose acts of deliberate cooperation by the government. In the following period, up to August 1943, there was broad agreement about supporting and encouraging sabotage and criticizing and opposing the government, which was maintaining its policy of cooperation and carrying on a campaign against sabotage. There was also solid support for a hate campaign against collaborators, Nazis, informers and women having relations with German soldiers. In the last year of the occupation, well after the emergence of the freedom council and the establishment of its press committee, the illegal press reached a broad consensus in support of intensified sabotage, recurrent anti-German demonstrations and resolute liquidation of informers. When the freedom council, in the summer of 1944, found itself in disagreement with the politicians about the phasing out of the mass strike in Copenhagen, it enjoyed the solid backing of the illegal press. One reason why this press eventually could identify with the freedom council was that SOE had accepted the council as representing the leadership of Danish resistance and British propaganda had promoted it accordingly.

The overall trends in the illegal press were a hardening of opposition to the policy of cooperation pursued by the coalition government and the central administration and an intensification of propaganda against the occupying power and its collaborators. Seen from one point of view, this pattern simply reflected political developments within the country, in relations between the public and the government and administration as well as in interaction with the authorities of the occupying power, both of which ultimately were conditioned by the course of the war among the great powers. Yet, the illegal press itself obviously had some influence on those political developments in occupied Denmark.

In a situation in which the legal media of the country were prevented from carrying negative information about the occupying power and encouraged to support the accommodating policy of the government, even an emergent and sectarian illegal press which exposed the conduct of the Germans and criticized the policy of the government must have played some part in strengthening anti-German sentiments and weakening support for governmental policy at least in some sections of society. In a later situation, in which a broader and more representative illegal press promoted sabotage and opposed the government, such a press seems likely to have had a significant role in helping to educate a wider public and preparing the ground for various forms of resistance. In the final situation, which arose after the retreat of the government and the establishment of the freedom council, a fully-fledged illegal press soon became an integral part of the resistance movement, serving as an essential means of communication at critical stages and a useful forum for debate about long-term aims. From an international perspective, the contribution of the Danish illegal press can be seen as a local supplement to the diverse and intermittent propaganda drives of the allied powers.

Militant resistance

The last part of the spectrum of Danish reactions to German occupation presented here comprises various sorts of militant activity, each apt to lead to violent confrontations, namely sabotage and liquidations, demonstrations and strikes, organizing a resistance army, and serving with the forces of an allied power. Engaging in sabotage and executing informers was generally the closest members of the resistance movement came to actually fighting the Germans in the country. Participating in anti-German demonstrations and strikes was often the defiant reactions of sections of a public provoked by German reprisals following a wave of sabotage. Setting up a secret army ready to support allied forces in battles on Danish soil was part of the resistance movement's preparations for a situation which, as it turned out, never arose. Enrolling in the armed forces of an allied power, whether in a regular unit or in the special forces of SOE, was the choice of Danes eager to join the fight against Nazi Germany and its allies.

In the first few years of the occupation there was not much sabotage. Nearly everybody was against it. Official Denmark, from the government to the police and the law courts, condemned it and punished perpetrators severely. The press and public opinion denounced it as irresponsible and dangerous, liable to provoke the Germans and upset the precarious relations with the occupying power. The allied powers refrained from encouraging it. Even SOE, cautioned by the Foreign Office and besieged by the Danish intelligence officers, for a long time held back. Above all, there was no organized movement in the country to plan and carry out sabotage. Thus, the acts that did take place during the first year or two were, on the whole, not only few but also casual, minor and insignificant.

The first real sabotage group to come to the attention of the public was the Churchill Club in Aalborg. Formed early in 1942, it was made up mainly of high-school students in the 15–17 age group, all from respectable middle-class homes. In April and May they carried out about 25 relatively minor acts of sabotage directed against the Germans, including arson and vandalism as well as some thefts of weapons. After arrest and imprisonment, a few of them, using the blade of a hacksaw, managed to leave and return to their cell at night-time and thus for many weeks continue their sabotage in the town. Two of the older ones were sentenced by a German court martial to 10 and 15 years and sent to gaol in Germany. The others ended up in a Danish prison, where they were allowed to continue their high-school studies. While the name of the group indicated the pro-British orientation of its members, their actions, together with their conduct in court, constituted a challenge to their parents' cautious and timid generation.

It was not till well into 1942 that the first signs of more organized forms of sabotage appeared. Here, too, it was Communists who took the lead. After a straw poll round major places of work, the party decided to organize sabotage against industrial production of military importance for Germany. The first result was a series of fires across the country in the summer months. The Germans reacted by demanding greater efforts by Danish authorities to prevent such incidents and threatening to resort to German courts martial. The government's response was a broadcast address on 2 September, in which prime minister Buhl deemed sabotage an act against the national interest, appealed to the public to assist the police in its investigations and warned about the risk of loss of Danish jurisdiction in such matters. Only a few days later, Christmas Møller made his speech over the BBC in which he, ignoring the British censors, strongly urged the nation to engage in sabotage against the enemy. At that stage, the Danish population, still rightly suspecting sabotage to be largely the work of Communists and gangs of youths, was overwhelmingly opposed to it.

During the following winter the Communists continued their offensive, now also using explosives. The first successful railway sabotage, again carried out by a Communist group, took place north of Copenhagen in November. However, it was not till January 1943 that sabotage became a regular illegal activity. For a long time it remained largely the work of Communist groups. Yet, by the spring SOE, now with a new leader in Denmark and more men in the field, was beginning to establish some management and control of those actions. As instructors and organizers, the SOE men helped to strengthen existing groups and set up new ones, mainly in the larger provincial towns. They also introduced new materials, especially plastic explosives. About the same time non-socialist sabotage groups and organizations were formed, mostly in Copenhagen. Usually having better connections with the established authorities, not least with the police in parts of Copenhagen, such groups provided a counterpart to the Communist organizations, thus helping to make sabotage more acceptable to the public. The result of those developments was marked intensification of sabotage in the summer of 1943, which provoked the German authorities and helped to touch off the interaction between German threats and reprisals and Danish demonstrations and strikes, a process which culminated in the events of August.

After the retreat of the government and the introduction of German police in Denmark acts of sabotage grew, in size as well as in number. The major targets were large concerns linked with the armaments industry, such as Riffelsyndikatet and Globus, and shipyards building ships for German use. But many smaller factories or repair shops which, directly or indirectly, worked for German bodies as well as numerous retail shops were also destroyed. And railway sabotage, mainly in Jutland, grew steadily. However, the earlier months of 1944 showed a decline in both industrial and railway sabotage, mainly as a result of an SOE call for a pause in such activities. The subsequent retreat of the German armies across Europe and the approach of the allied forces, giving rise to the expectation that the war would soon be finished, greatly encouraged selective forms of sabotage. In common with other activities of the resistance movement, sabotage now attracted ever broader support from the public.

Sabotage, at the level of intensity reached during the last two years of the occupation, required efficient organization, not only of the planning and carrying out of the various acts but also of communication with England and reception of instructors, explosives and weapons from abroad. The first large sabotage organization had its roots in the efforts of a score of Communists in Copenhagen in the summer of 1942. The Danish police eventually arrested so many of them that the Communist party in the course of the winter decided to broaden the membership of the organization and, in the name of popular front, include also non-Communists. As a private joke, the new groups, made up mainly of students, were referred to as bourgeois partisans or BOPA, which later became the name of the whole organization. Over its less than three years of existence, BOPA had nearly 400 members, of whom 175 remained at the end of the occupation. About 40 had been killed and most of the rest either arrested or driven to escape to Sweden. Despite the many arrests and casualties, the organization retained its dual composition, most of its members being either mechanics or students, and stayed largely under Communist control.

The leader of BOPA in 1944–45 was Børge Thing, code-named Brandt. Under his leadership, the organization carried out many minor and some large and well-planned actions, all in the Copenhagen area.

A few amounted to regular partisan attacks, carried out in daylight against well-guarded industrial concerns and involving exchange of fire and throwing of bombs. The organization also performed about 30 liquidations of informers. In the last weeks before the German capitulation BOPA was attached directly to the freedom council as an elite group, ready to engage in military action if required. After a final parade in the summer of 1945 the organization was disbanded.

The other large sabotage organization operating in the Copenhagen area was *Holger Danske*, called after the mythical Ogier the Dane. With the cross-country sports movement and the illegal paper *De frie Danske* among its sources of origin and with later links to Danish Unity and the Ring, it established itself as a non-socialist counterpart of BOPA. But Holger Danske was larger, looser, more democratic and less disciplined. Repeatedly plagued by casualties and arrests, it had to be rebuilt or reorganized several times during its two years of existence. First set up in April 1943 with Josef Søndergaard, code-named Tom, as the central figure, the group relied initially on BOPA for instruction and explosives but within a few months established contact with SOE. During the summer of that year it carried out, partly with British materials, a number of actions. One of them, namely the blowing up of the central public building Forum, was so spectacular that most of the members of the group, including the seriously injured Søndergaard, had to escape to Sweden.

The organization was rebuilt by Jens Lillelund, who through a connection in Danish Unity was able to establish contact with SOE agents in the country as well as with the freedom council. From October five sabotage groups were in existence, one made up of cornets and another of naval cadets and students. The latter group, led by a teacher Svend Otto Nielsen known as John, carried out a number of acts of industrial sabotage, relying on teams which combined bombing experts and marksmen. In the course of the winter, however, practically all the groups were uncovered, many of its leaders and members being arrested or forced to escape. Lillelund and Nielsen were denounced by a female informer. While the former got away, the latter was seriously wounded and arrested by German police, and later executed. Lillelund's successor, and briefly Danish Unity's representative in the freedom council, Jørgen Staffeldt died in a German concentration camp.

The rebuilding of the organization started in the spring of 1944, after a dissatisfied BOPA member had broken away and taken two groups with him, and subsequently attached himself and his men to Holger Danske. New groups were recruited, and Lillelund was recalled from Sweden. He soon arranged for Holger Danske to be linked to Frode Jakobsen's Ring, instead of to Danish Unity, which strengthened the organization's representation in the freedom council. Sabotage activities, which the groups had started again in the early part of the summer, were resumed late in the autumn, after a lengthy lull following the general strike in Copenhagen.

However, in its revived form, Holger Danske was more than a sabotage organization. From the summer of 1944 it saw itself also as a military unit preparing to play a part in a final encounter with the forces of the occupying power and its uniformed collaborators. In the meantime members of the organization carried out a large number of liquidations in the Copenhagen area, perhaps nearly 200, mainly of known informers but in some cases also of persons whose behaviour or company made them obvious security risks. Some groups organized ruthless attacks on armed units of Danish guards and others serving the German authorities, such as the hated Sommer Corps. Not all such executions and attacks had the approval of the leadership of the organization, or the sanction of the freedom council. Like some acts of sabotage, they were occasionally carried out by local groups, or even individual members, without authorizations from above. Throughout its existence Holger Danske lost 64 men, some killed in action and other executed by the Germans, but it still had about 350 members by the end of the occupation.

The major activities of the two largest sabotage organizations were usually directed against industrial concerns and shipyards in or near the capital which, in one way or another, served the interests of the occupying power. In the provinces, sabotage was much more against railways. Since the aim of such sabotage was to delay and harass German transports, most of it by far took place in Jutland. It was usually there that the occupying power moved men and equipment to and from Germany and, especially in the last year of the war, from Norway to Germany. Troops and armaments moving southwards might be needed on one of the fronts. The selection of targets and timing of actions depended largely on reports about planned German movements received from contacts within the Danish State Railways (DSB).

Till late in the summer of 1943 railway sabotage, in Jutland and elsewhere in the country, was essentially the work of Communist groups. By the autumn of that year, however, groups operating within the ambit of SOE were making their presence felt. The most remarkable action took place in November, when the railway bridges over the Gudenaa, a small river in North Jutland, were blasted and the line disrupted for 12 days. After the pause in the first half of 1944 railway sabotage grew significantly. In response to orders issued by allied headquarters after the invasion of Normandy in June, the resistance movement stepped up its efforts to sabotage the transport of German troops to and from Denmark. The effect, however, was not particularly impressive. Six months later, after the launch of the German Ardennes offensive, London demanded faster and more powerful sabotage. Lieutenant colonel Vagn Bennike, then leader of the resistance in Jutland, responded by introducing a system of coded signals, transmitted by the BBC in its Danish broadcasts, for ordering collective discharge of sabotage at several points of the railway system. This soon led to a marked improvement in the effectiveness of Danish efforts. Though a retrospective analysis has shown that the delays caused by railway sabotage were on the whole fairly minimal, this form of resistance did cause the occupying power considerable inconvenience. In the last winter of the war it had to allocate many thousands of troops to guarding the railway tracks.

Historians have calculated the total number of proper acts of industrial and other non-railway sabotage to be in the region of 2,800 and that of railway sabotage to exceed 1,500. Though obviously a hostile activity directed, instantly or ultimately, at the occupying power, such sabotage, like most isolated efforts in a great war, may well have been less effective in military terms than most of those closely involved with it at the time believed it to be. However, sabotage should also be seen in terms of its psychological and political, and even its diplomatic, impact in the later years of the occupation. For people humiliated by the capitulation in 1940 and frustrated by the accommodating attitude to the Germans of Danish authorities in subsequent years sabotage served as a release, not only for freedom fighters actively involved but also for more passive members of the public. As a forthright act of defiance of the enemy in the country, it was an explicit indication of anti-German attitudes and anti-Nazi convictions.

Politically, sabotage – together with its two concomitants, demonstrations and strikes – constituted a challenge to both the German and the Danish authorities. It rocked the rationale behind the German notion of peace occupation and the policy of negotiating agreements with the occupied country; and it undermined the Danish fiction of sovereignty and the policy of maintaining law and order in the country while cooperating with the occupying power. Diplomatically, sabotage was a friendly greeting to the Soviet Union from the fighting Denmark, and an explicit demonstration to the British and American allies of Danish will to play an active part in the struggle against Nazi Germany. Thus sabotage, together with the industrial strikes and public protests of 1943 and 1944, helped prepare the way for the Danish bid for allied status in the later period of the occupation.

From the spring and summer of 1943, when the sabotage groups were growing increasingly dependent on SOE for guidance about targets and timing and for supply of instructors and material, rapid and efficient contact with London was becoming essential. Already the first parachute drops of agents – of lieutenant Thomas Sneum in September 1941, representing SIS, and of the ill-fated SOE captain C.J. Bruhn in December the same year – had included a radio telegraphist with relevant equipment. Others followed with later drops. But there were problems, to do with the equipment as well as with the telegraphists themselves. The senders, large and heavy, were often lost or damaged in the drop. For the telegraphists, not all of them sufficiently trained by their British instructors, the efficient German detector vans were frequently more than a match.

Most of those problems were solved when L.A. Duus Hansen, Bang & Olufsen's chief engineer, became involved. Several of the early agents had turned to him for technical advice and spare parts, as a result of which he had become familiar with the English equipment and the code system. Himself a trained telegraphist, he offered to take over some of the sending. From the spring of 1943 the Danish intelligence officers, whose contact with London so far had been essentially by letter, used him for urgent military messages. A few months later, after several unsuccessful attempts by SOE to send more telegraphists and equipment to Denmark, Duus Hansen suggested that Danish-trained telegraphists and Danish-built senders be used henceforth. Though not in accordance with established SOE rules of security, his proposal was eventually accepted by London. From the autumn of 1943 Duus Hansen was the leader of all Danish radio communication with the free world.

Duus Hansen's main contributions were technical and organizational. He constructed new and more practical types of senders, some of which were as light as 1.5 kg (only one tenth of the weight of the British type) and small enough to fit into a briefcase (instead of a suitcase). They could also be used as receivers. Suitable for both AC and DC, they could even be run from the battery of a car, which made it possible to outwit the German detector vans by frequent and rapid changes of location. The advantages of the new transmitters were so obvious that the British introduced them in other countries where SOE was active.

Duus Hansen also found a number of proficient and reliable telegraphists who were able to learn the British codes and ready to start serving areas of the country which had been without adequate contact with London. His brother H.K. Duus Hansen, who as a veterinary surgeon had a suitably ambulant profession, started sending from Funen in March 1944. After some serious initial misfortunes, other telegraphists managed to establish continual sending from parts of Jutland from July the same year. On Zealand, which had had permanent radio contact with London since September 1943, automatic high-speed transmitters able to send eight to ten times faster than by hand were introduced in the summer of 1944. While Copenhagen acquired five such instruments, Jutland got only two. The organization also ran a workshop for the manufacture of transmitters.

Under Duus Hansen's leadership the security system was greatly improved. As a rule, each telegraphist had more than one transmitter at his disposal and many places to send from. He also had a team of trained and armed guards to transport transmitters from place to place and to warn him when the Germans approached. Yet the struggle with the German detection system, constantly being refined, continued till the end of the occupation, sometimes with tragic results. To avoid straining the direct radio link to London more than necessary, Duus Hansen established a wireless telephone connection with Sweden across the Sound, and later a high-speed (UHF) connection which allowed him to transmit to London using Malmø as relay. The Germans failed to discover those means of communication. Thus, after a slow and difficult start, Denmark ended up with a highly efficient system of wireless communication, which both technically and organizationally became recognized as exemplary.

The reception on the ground of agents, equipment, explosives and arms, too, was marked by first dedicated and heroic performances by outstanding individuals and then by growing organization, at both local and national levels. The first proper reception, with a team on the ground, took place in the night of 12 March 1943 near Mariager in Jutland. Here a Royal Air Force aircraft, having already dropped the new SOE leader Flemming B. Muus and three other agents elsewhere in the country, delivered six containers. The team was led by Flemming Juncker, a landed proprietor with links to Danish Unity who since 1941 had been involved in active resistance and had become leader of the emerging movement in Jutland, and by Ole Geisler, captain in SOE who only the previous month had been parachuted into Denmark as leader of a team of four agents.

The containers received were transported on a horse-drawn carriage by Marius Fiil, owner of the Hvidsten Inn. Round him and his inn a group was formed for the reception of future drops on a local site. In the course of the spring and summer five drops were received there. Since they included not only weapons and explosives but also seven SOE agents, the Hvidsten group played a significant part in the subsequent expansion of this organization's work in Denmark. Within a year, however, almost the entire group was arrested by the Gestapo. Eight of its members, including Marius Fiil and two close family members, were executed and others imprisoned, several in Germany.

In the course of the summer of 1943 a further half dozen drops took place in Jutland and on Funen and Zealand, with the new SOE agents now helping local groups to arrange reception of the containers and packages and distribution of their contents. From August of that year till the following summer only a few drops took place, mainly because the British and the Americans, fighting the Germans in Italy and busy preparing the invasion of Normandy, had higher priorities than arming the Danes, but also because the resistance movement was undergoing nation-wide organization. In accordance with SOE directives received by Muus, the country was to be divided into six regions, each to have its own organizer with direct radio link to England and its own military groups for future action. Those plans affected also the arrangements for receiving and distributing weapons.

Jutland was nominally divided into three regions. For a long time, however, Juncker maintained a degree of overall authority in that part of the country. In March 1944, after a wave of arrests of members of his organization, he made Anton Toldstrup leader of reception. Toldstrup, an active member of the cross-country sports movement who had links to Danish Unity, immediately organized reception groups in north and mid Jutland (regions 1 and 2). His energy and efficiency soon secured him a place in the unofficial leadership of resistance in Jutland. When Juncker the following month had to escape to Sweden – from where he continued to London, to become SOE's organizer of despatches to Denmark – he left the movement in Jutland in the hands of Vagn Bennike and Toldstrup. When drops started in August, and rapidly reached substantial proportions, the latter was still in charge of receptions. Subsequently, however, he took over the leadership of region 1 at the request of Bennike. This arrangement led to a bitter feud between the army officer and the civilian resistance leader, in which the latter enjoyed the support of London. In the last months of the occupation Toldstrup again concentrated on the organization of reception.

On Funen (region 4) the leader of reception and distribution became Erik Frandsen, an engineer and instructor in the local cross-country association who, as member of the leadership of resistance in Odense, had been responsible for sabotage. During the last seven months of the occupation the organization he built up managed to take delivery of about 30 drops, with approximately 700 containers, practically without losses. On Zealand and Lolland-Falster (region 5) Stig Jensen, editor and former lieutenant with friends in Danish Unity, became reception chief in the autumn of 1944. A veteran of Danish resistance and one of SOE's first contacts in the country, he built up an organization which reflected his concern with security. Insisting on using only people not involved in other forms of resistance, he separated reception from transport and distribution and kept contact between groups to a bare minimum. The efficiency of his organization was decisive for meeting the needs for weapons and ammunition of the large resistance organizations in the Copenhagen area (region 6), in the months before German capitulation.

Altogether about 620 tons of weapons, explosives and other British or American materials were delivered to Denmark by air, most of it small arms. The great majority of the missions were carried out by the RAF on behalf of SOE, some of the flights crewed by Poles. At the later stage of hostilities, when SOE cooperated with the Office of Strategic Services (OSS), its American counterpart, under the joint name of Special Forces, American aircraft, too, carried out missions to Denmark. A further few hundred tons were transferred to Danish fishing boats on the high seas or smuggled in via Sweden. While the Danish side of the former traffic was handled by Toldstrup's organization, the latter operation was initiated by Ebbe Munck and carried out with the tacit consent of the Swedish authorities. In the later period of the occupation the supply of weapons was meant not so much for current operations of the resistance movement as for use by the illegal army then being set up to be available in case of an allied invasion of Denmark.

Hand in hand with sabotage, as concurrent militant activities directed against both Danish and German authorities, went demonstrations and strikes. In the first few years of the occupation, when the public largely supported the policy of cooperation and put up with the German presence in the country and many workers feared having to join the legion of the unemployed, there were very few industrial strikes and public demonstrations. Any such manifestations of dissatisfaction that did appear were usually minor and economically motivated, reflecting the severe effects of the war on the daily lives of wage earners in particular. It was not till early 1943 that illegal strikes and demonstrations became more numerous and serious, and began to take on a decidedly anti-government and anti-German character.

One reason for this development was the efforts of Communists, more of the men on the shop floor than of the party leaders, to exploit growing feelings of discontent and restlessness among workers in key industries and turn them against Social Democratic and trade union leaders, who generally were staunch supporters of the coalition government and its policy of cooperation with the German authorities. Another reason was a more general change in public attitudes to that policy and to the German presence in the country, a change which no doubt was conditioned by spectacular defeats of German armies in Russia and Italy and optimistic rumours of an early collapse of the Axis. A third factor in that development was the wave of sabotage that was building up in the earlier part of 1943. While significant acts of such nature might spur on the workers to challenge the Danish authorities and spite the occupying power, German reprisals to the sabotage could provoke industrial strikes and public demonstrations.

Odense presented the first notable case of sabotage leading to strike. One of the last days in July an SOE group carried out sabotage against a mine vessel at the local shipyard. When the Germans responded by placing armed guards on board the ship the workers immediately went on a sit-down strike, arguing tongue-in-cheek that 'the rifles could go off'. The strike quickly spread to other places of work within the town's iron industry, with about 3,000 men walking out, and lasted more than a week. By then, however, the unrest had spread to Esbjerg on the west coast of Jutland, where a Communist group had set fire to the fish warehouses and scuffles between German soldiers and local people had broken out during the fire-fighting. When the German commandant imposed a curfew the street disturbances spread, and a strike, organized by Communist shop stewards, closed down the engineering industry of the town. After some inconclusive negotiations between Social Democratic representatives of the trade union, who were against the strike, and the Communist strike leaders, a large meeting of workers called for a general strike until the Germans lifted the state of emergency. On 11 August the entire town closed down, which remained the situation till the Germans agreed to end the curfew.

After the victory of the protest movement in Esbjerg the disturbances spread to Funen, where Odense again became the focus of confrontation with the Germans and their collaborators. It started with Danes, including some soldiers, going on the attack in the streets. After a few days of restraint, the German commandant sent out patrols to quell the disturbances. This led to bloody street fights with more than a dozen Danish casualties. The next morning, on 18 August, a call for a general strike went out. Within a few hours the town was in open revolt. The following days were marked by demonstrations in the street, rallies of workers, assaults on the properties of collaborators and punishment of women associating with Germans as well as by continual clashes with members of the Schalburg Corps and German patrols. In one incident a German officer who happened to be passing through the country was handled so roughly that it nearly became a case of mob lynching.

In response to intense German pressure, the local police force was rapidly reinforced from other parts of the country to help deal with the situation in the streets. With a view to stopping the strike and putting an end to the Communist agitation, the trade union leaders and the Social Democratic mayor negotiated an agreement with the Germans, but failed to secure the acceptance of the workers. The strike, organized and directed by Communists and goaded on by a series of acts of sabotage carried out by local groups, continued. At this point the situation seemed critical enough for Paul Kanstein, SS officer responsible for the internal administration of the country, Nils Svenningsen from the foreign ministry and Johannes Kjærbøl, minister of labour, to travel to Funen and help bring about a solution. The local negotiators, helped by the support from Copenhagen but opposed by a strike committee dominated by Communists, reached another deal with the Germans, who again agreed to keep their soldiers off the streets for the next few days. The strike was called off on 23 August and work resumed the following day. Since the occupying power had accepted a compromise, the strike was regarded as a victory for the protest movement.

In the meantime the movement had spread to the smaller towns on Funen and a few on Zealand and to Jutland, mainly to towns in its eastern and northern parts. There the development in Aalborg, Denmark's fourth largest town, became particularly dramatic. The occasion that touched off demonstrations and strike was the death of a young saboteur killed in a shoot-out between a resistance group and German soldiers. When the funeral on 23 August was advanced by some hours in order to avoid violent demonstrations and German military intervention, the town went on a strike immediately. Demonstrations in the town centre led to violent clashes, in which German soldiers used tanks and carbines to suppress the activists and killed several people. After more casualties the following day, the strike was intensified, and now specifically linked to a demand for the withdrawal of troops from the streets. When the Social Democratic trade union leaders negotiated a deal with the German commandant, a meeting of shop stewards in which unskilled workers and Communists were strongly represented rejected it. A mass meeting led to more violent clashes, in which the Germans, on the orders of general von Hanneken, deployed armed patrols and imposed a state of emergency. The situation remained deadlocked till 29 August, when the national emergency eclipsed the resistance in Aalborg.

The events of the month leading up to 29 August gave rise to several myths. One was that the occupying power deliberately provoked the rebellion to prepare the way for a more forceful policy in Denmark. On the contrary, in town after town the German commandant exercised a degree of restraint to avoid exacerbating the conflict, or gave way to help bringing it to an end. Preoccupied with the possibility of an allied invasion, the German authorities had little interest in upsetting the established political and diplomatic balance in the country. Nor can London be held responsible for bringing about or abetting the rebellion. Neither the Foreign Office nor the masters of SOE wanted a popular revolt at that stage of the war, especially not one instigated or led by Communists. Nor can the events of August be attributed to the strategies or tactics of the Communist party as such. The leaderships in Copenhagen and the major provincial towns could hardly be enthusiastic about unpredictable events which disclosed the identities of local leaders and, by challenging the Social Democrats, compromised the Communist tactics of united front. Not even the idea, so popular with Danish authorities at the time, of itinerant Communist trouble-makers travelling from town to town and touching off disturbances seems well founded.

After thorough research at grass-roots level, Danish historians have shown that the August rebellions, in the 17 provincial capitals and market towns in which they occurred, were primarily the work of local industrial workers. Often instigated by Communist shop stewards, who seem largely to have been acting on their own initiative, and sometimes coordinated with local resistance groups, calls for strikes and demonstrations drew a quick response from workers whose dissatisfaction and anger had reached flash-point. Occasionally well-timed acts of sabotage followed by German or pro-German measures of retaliation helped to consolidate their support. However, it was not only workers who were ready for actions of protest. At that stage of the war and the occupation many other people, too, were becoming increasingly frustrated by the political and social situation, and more inclined to challenge the authority of the occupier. Thus, in town after town salaried employees, employers, shopkeepers and professionals responded to the call for strike, quickly turning it into a general strike, or town strike as it was also described. This sudden and simultaneous emergence in many provincial towns of a fairly broad-based protest movement weakened the authority of the Danish government and undermined its policy of cooperation.

The combination of strikes and demonstrations that erupted in Copenhagen the following summer was even more dramatic. By then not only the international but also the national political situation had changed markedly. The elated optimism which already in the summer of 1943 had superseded the general pessimism which had prostrated the nation in the first years after the invasion had now been reinforced through the allied invasion of Normandy in June. One effect was a widespread conviction that the war in Europe was reaching its end, which was matched by a growing desire to show some defiance of the Germans still in the country.

An important difference in the domestic situation from the summer of 1943 was that there was no longer a working government, with responsible ministers ready to call for law and order when tension with the occupying power threatened to reach crisis point. The pressure on the population of the German military and police forces was now more direct. The wave of sabotage in June which, as mentioned above, included some spectacular and successful attacks in Copenhagen, led to a sharp increase in that pressure. The retaliatory measures included the execution of eight members of the resistance, the introduction of military courts on Zealand and a number of devastating acts by members of the Schalburg Corps, including the blowing up of the Tivoli concert hall. Provoked by such measures, the workers in Copenhagen, still dissatisfied with their economic deal but, in a situation close to full employment, now no longer so cowed by the spectre of unemployment, were ready to react to any further acts of punishment meted out by the occupying power.

On 26 June the German authorities proclaimed a curfew for Copenhagen, from eight o'clock in the evening to five in the morning, partly to punish its inhabitants and partly to facilitate the fight against sabotage. The blacksmiths at Burmeister & Wain (B&W), which was the biggest workplace and had a notoriously red labour force, reacted immediately by leaving work at 12 noon, on the pretext that they had to get some fresh air and look after their allotments before the curfew set in. The next few days the 'go-home-early strikes' spread to other parts of the machine industry, largely through the Communist network, as well as to other industries and workplaces. By the 28th more than half the workforce left work early. At that stage the Germans gave way and postponed the curfew by three hours. Many, perhaps half, of the striking workers responded by resuming work full time.

Hand in hand with those strikes went a street rebellion, taking the form of demonstrations, erection of barricades and lighting of fires, initially in the working-class areas but later also in other parts of the town. In the course of the four days it lasted 15 Danes were killed and about 100 wounded in fights with the German patrols. While the Danes saw the demonstrations rather as defensive measures, directed against the Schalburg Corps and German terror, the Germans, seeking to enforce their curfew and quell the demonstrations, were engaged in a battle to regain control of a rebellious city apparently bent on challenging the occupying power.

A few days later events in Copenhagen took a more serious turn. It started with rumours of a fatality incurred in connection with the overturning of some tram cars, which led the tramway employers to refuse to take out their cars the next morning. With people reduced to walking or cycling, the streets emptied and an air of suspense set in. The more decisive event was the announcement in the morning papers that eight members of the Hvidsten resistance group had been executed. The factories, metropolitan train services, telephone exchanges and department stores closed down immediately, with salaried employees and shopkeepers following soon after. By the afternoon only dairies, hospitals, fire services and power stations remained open. In the evening the Germans turned off the gas, water and electricity supplies of the capital in an attempt to force its inhabitants to give in.

The next day, 1 July, the occupying power proclaimed a state of military emergency in Copenhagen. It drew armoured troops and artillery to the town and deployed fighter aircraft over the rebellious quarters to demonstrate German power. Taking up key positions in various parts of the city, it bombarded the barricades with cannons. The next day the rebellion was crushed, the Danes having incurred losses of 60 persons killed and about 350 wounded in only a few days of fighting.

There is no evidence of a general plan or a central organization of the rebellion. While the Communist leadership warned against an open challenge of the occupying power, all the big resistance organizations ordered their members to refrain from taking part. If there was a degree of organization it seems to have been at the local rather than at any higher level. The list of casualties indicated that it was mainly young workers who bore the brunt of the battles. It was also youths who, at the height of the crisis, took the lead in attacking and punishing collaborators, Nazis and female friends of Germans, as it was youthful groups who, ignoring the warnings of the Communist leaders and the freedom council, vandalized and looted a number of food stores and tobacconist's shops – not all of which belonged to collaborators.

For the Danish police, those days presented a particularly difficult situation. While most of them privately may have sympathized with the national protest movement, their task and orders were to maintain law and order. This meant not only preventing or forcefully dealing with cases of vandalism and attacks on persons but also taking action against the building of barricades, in so far as this could be done without becoming involved in actual battles between German patrols and rebels. Since the police made many arrests and occasionally used their truncheons or fired warning shots, many of the activists were inclined to treat them as being with the enemy. On the other hand, the German authorities were dissatisfied with the performance of the police, which became an issue in Danish–German negotiations during the strike.

Though the street rebellion had been crushed, the strike continued for a few days more. After the imposition of the state of emergency the freedom council had intervened by proclaiming the strike to be continued till the Germans had lifted the restrictions imposed and had withdrawn the Schalburg Corps from the streets. The following day spokesmen representing the Danish authorities and organizations and the politicians, all of whom were inclined to be afraid of the Communists and nervous of the freedom council, sent out an appeal for resumption of work the next day, which had been approved by the German authorities. The freedom council, recognizing this as a proposal for unconditional capitulation, distributed handbills opposing it and calling for a continuation of the strike. Despite very strong pressure from the municipal authorities, the strike continued the following day and, moreover, began to spread, with sympathy strikes breaking out across Zealand. At this point Werner Best agreed to lift the emergency and keep the Schalburg Corps and German patrols off the streets. The same evening the leading politicians and organizational representatives made a second appeal to the public, this time over the wireless, calling on the strikers to avoid catastrophe and resume work the next day, 4 July. However, the freedom council, demonstrating its authority, declared the strike on for yet another day. A very large proportion of the strikers chose to follow the instructions of the council and ignore the appeal of the politicians and organizations.

In the allied world, the whole event was hailed as a victory for Copenhagen over the occupying power. Spread over 10 days and involving about 700 casualties, it became the foremost confrontation between the Danish public and the German authorities. That it turned out to be a success for the protest movement was partly a consequence of German self-restraint. While the police forces of the occupying power resorted to torture, executions and terror in the fight against sabotage and its military forces used cannons to suppress street rebellions, the political representative of Germany eventually decided to compromise to put an end to strikes. He seems to have recognized that the practical circumstances of the ostensible peace occupation of the country still required a degree of cooperation with the Danish authorities, if the production and export of goods essential for Germany had to continue. At that stage of the war, there may also have been other reasons for not allowing a further deterioration of the political and social order of the country.

Whatever the nature of Best's reasons for making a few concessions at a crucial stage, the conclusion of the crisis indicated that industrial strike, especially when managed by the freedom council, remained a useful weapon for the resistance movement. It was used again several times during the next month or two. In the middle of August the freedom council set off three-day strikes across the country in protest against the shooting of 11 members of the resistance movement, said by the Germans to have been trying to escape from custody. A month later railway workers near the Danish–German border went on strike in protest against the deportation to German concentration camps of 195 internees from the Frøslev camp, which the German police had set up for Danish prisoners who should remain in Denmark. When the strike started to spread to other parts of the country the freedom council assumed control. Only a few days later, when German soldiers attacked the police stations across the country and disarmed and arrested, and eventually deported, about 2,000 policemen, the freedom council again proclaimed a strike of limited duration. Perhaps the most important result of the waves of strikes in the summer and autumn of 1944 was to consolidate the authority of the freedom council in conflicts between the Danish public and the German authorities, and to strengthen its hand in the rivalry with the politicians of the old parties.

The initiative for the setting up of a properly organized resistance army, which went on throughout the last 18 months of the occupation, came from London. The considerations motivating the British were partly of a military and partly of a political nature. In the later stages of the war, it was important for the allied powers to have in Denmark, as in other occupied countries, a substantial body of men ready and able to assist the allied forces if and when the need arose. In the earlier months of 1944, it was also essential to leave the Germans in uncertainty as to the location of the projected Anglo-American invasion of the Continent, and hence expedient to create the impression that Denmark, too, was being prepared for the arrival of invading forces.

The political considerations of the British related ultimately to the post-war situation of Denmark. Having come to regard that country as an important part of a future British sphere of influence on the Continent, they were concerned that the transition from occupation and resistance to liberation and restoration of democratic government should come as smoothly as possible, and at an early stage lead to stability in domestic affairs and pro-British orientation in foreign relations. Hence they were worried by the tension and issues between the Communist and the more rightist wings of the resistance movement as well as by the conflict between resistance leaders and certain remains of official Denmark, in particular the general staff of the army and the more prominent politicians of the defunct coalition government. A substantial army recruited across party-political divisions, officered by both professional soldiers and resistance fighters and ultimately under British or allied control, it was thought, could help deal with such difficulties and prevent a disorderly and violent transition followed by lasting political instability.

When Muus, the resident SOE chief, returned to Denmark in December 1943 he was under orders to organize a nation-wide underground army divided into six regions, each with a separate structure and own leadership. The deadline was 1 March 1944. The freedom council set up a military committee to carry out the plans. In practice, however, the committee limited its activities to Copenhagen and the eastern parts of the country, while leaving the organization of the three regions of Jutland in the hands of Flemming Juncker.

The leadership of each region was intended to consist of three persons, namely a member of the Communist party, a member of Danish Unity and one who belonged to neither, together with an officer to provide military expertise. In practice, however, it often proved difficult to follow this pattern, especially in the Jutland regions where Juncker in effect set up a joint leadership round himself and his two helpers, Anton Toldstrup and Vagn Bennike. After his departure for Sweden and England a bitter rivalry, as we have seen, developed between Toldstrup and Bennike, in which the resistance leader, who had proved an outstandingly efficient reception chief, had the support of SOE and the officer had the backing of the illegal general staff of the army.

The general tendencies in the regions were for the leadership to grow larger and for the professional officers to become more influential. After the arrest of the police in September 1944, a representative of the illegal remnants of the police was in several cases attached to the regional leaderships. In the following months liaison officers from SOE, too, were added. From the end of the year representatives of the other two major resistance organizations, *Frit Danmark* and the Ring, were also among the leaders. While the professional officers originally were intended to act as guides and instructors, by the end of the war, the chief of each of the seven regions (including the island of Bornholm organized as a new region in September 1944) was an officer.

The regions were divided into sections, towns, districts, counties, etc., each with its own leaders. As a result of pertinacious German efforts to roll up sections of the resistance army and arrest its members, it frequently became necessary to replace leaders, whether at local or at regional levels. Thus, region 3 (southern Jutland) was totally uncovered twice in 1944, while region 6 (Copenhagen) needed complete reorganization in March 1945.

The basic unit of the army was a group of six persons, typically young men living in a town or a market town. The first groups were mostly recruited either from members of the Communist party or from supporters of Danish Unity. Indeed, well before the launch of the SOE drive both the Communists and Danish Unity had started setting up separate task forces, some of which now became units of the projected army. From the spring of 1944 the Ring played an important part in both the organizing and the manning of the army. Through its network of contacts across the country, it helped to broaden the party-political base of the organization. In some towns it created a counterweight to the Communist groups by setting up military groups of Social Democratic workers.

To some extent, the professional army, too, contributed to the broadening of the political and social base. The so-called 0-groups, military task forces made up of professional soldiers or members of associations and clubs linked to the army which since the beginning of 1944 had been attached to the small general staff, were formally placed under the command of the freedom council. However, while in the provincial regions most such groups in July 1944 became integrated with the civilian military groups, in the Copenhagen region they remained a separate force directly under the control of the small general staff. Moreover, they secured their own supply of weapons, smuggled in from Sweden, which gave them an advantage over the civilian groups. Thus, rather than helping to unify the anti-German forces in the country, this arrangement in the capital served to accentuate the tension between the freedom council and the leadership of the professional army and its political masters.

The line of command within the resistance army, and in the movement as a whole, was not only a subject of conflict among the parties directly involved but also an issue between Denmark and the allies. Initially SOE and SHAEF (Supreme Headquarters Allied Expeditionary Forces) intended to give orders directly to each of the regions. The freedom council, however, insisted that all orders from SHAEF to the Danish resistance should go through its military committee. To facilitate such a procedure, the council replaced that committee, in June 1944, with a high-powered command committee, which included two of the most prominent members of the council (Fog and Jakobsen), the resident SOE chief, two officers representing the army and the navy and, after the dissolution of the police force, a representative of the illegal police. The idea was that the command committee should handle all orders from the allied powers prior to an invasion of Denmark, at which point SHAEF would assume direct control of the resistance forces.

In practice, however, the command committee became a link merely between London and regions 6 and 5 (Copenhagen and the islands east of the Great Belt). Toldstrup in region 1 retained direct contact with London, as did Bennike, who till the end of the occupation controlled telegraphic communication between the rest of Jutland and England. Orders from London to region 4 (Funen), too, went directly. To some extent, this confusion of the British–Danish line of command reflected conflicts of allegiance and divisions of loyalty within sections of the anti-German forces of the country. The most divisive conflict was between professional officers of the regular army and civilian leaders of the resistance movement. Although general Gørtz, with the approval of the politicians, in December 1943 had agreed that the task forces of the army should be coordinated with the civilian military groups then under organization, and all be placed under the command of the freedom council, the majority of officers engaged in illegal activities, prominent among them Bennike in Jutland, still saw the small general staff as their superior authority. Recognizing it as a makeshift agent of the hibernating government, the ultimate legal authority of the country, they looked to that body for instructions and guidance, rather than to the freedom council of self-appointed resistance leaders.

Another line of command with potential for undermining the authority of the freedom council and its various committees was that of the Communist party. While the leaders and members of the party, very much pioneers of resistance in Denmark, had entered into cooperation with other illegal groups and organizations in accordance with their doctrine of popular front against fascism, they still looked to Moscow for ideological inspiration and moral support. Highly disciplined, they could not allow their engagement in the national struggle against Nazi Germany to eclipse their commitment to the Communist cause. Their dual loyalty found expression in the propaganda of the Communist illegal press as well as in the way in which their leaders and representatives in the resistance were appointed or replaced. All of them had to be approved by the leadership of the party. With the liberation of Denmark and the end of the war approaching came a growing concern in non-Communist circles about the nature of the post-war economic and political programme of the Communist party. Such anxieties were reflected in the planning and preparations of Danish political and military leaders in the later stages of the occupation, and also seem to have been at the heart of British policy and initiatives towards Denmark, both before and after the allied invasion of France.

Despite the various disagreements and difficulties, the organization and arming of the resistance army went on at a rapidly increasing pace. The total number enlisted in May 1945 has been estimated at about 49,000, nearly twice what it had been the previous December. Probably less than half of them were armed, largely with weapons received from Britain in the last months of the war. Yet numerically, the army at that stage was by far the most substantial section of the whole resistance movement.

The link to the allied forces was consolidated when SHAEF, in September 1944, set up a liaison mission to Denmark under the command of major general R.H. Dewing, and two months later accepted a Danish mission to SHAEF representing lieutenant general Ebbe Gørtz. On the initiative of SOE, and with the approval of the freedom council, Gørtz had been designated commander-in-chief of all Danish resistance forces, to assume command in case of allied military operations on Danish soil, when he would be acting under the orders of the supreme commander, general Dwight Eisenhower.

The diplomatic background to the SOE decision to seek the designation of general Gørtz was the failure of a British attempt earlier in the year to persuade its allies to accept Denmark as an ally. Formalizing the link between the Danish resistance and allied forces might be another way of boosting the morale of the resistance movement, securing SOE control of the entire organization, easing the transition from occupation to liberation and protecting British interests in post-war Denmark. Mainly in an attempt to secure and maintain its grip on the resistance organization, the Danish section of SOE arranged for a directive to be drawn up to define the limits of Gørtz's freedom of action. The drafters of the directive, particularly concerned about the risk of serious divisions arising within the movement as a result of shifts in the balance of power between a weakened freedom council and a usurping small general staff of the army, warned against centralizing tendencies in the lines of command and communication and stressed the need to keep the various parts of the whole organization separate.

The first paragraph of the directive stated briefly that Gørtz, when commander-in-chief of the resistance army, had to obey orders coming from general Eisenhower. The final paragraph dealt at some length with the status of the Danish Brigade stationed in Sweden and known as Danforce. This unit had been set up on the initiative of the small general staff and in accordance with an agreement reached between Social Democratic leaders and the Swedish government. Intended by its founders and sponsors as a police force ready to deal with any chaotic situation which might arise as a result of the collapse of German rule in Denmark, it had been put under command of officers loyal to the dethroned politicians and kept at the disposal of the latter. To dispel lingering uncertainty about the deployment of the unit, the directive now stated bluntly that Danforce was part of the resistance forces under Gørtz's command, and formed a tactical reserve with the primary role of assisting in the liberation of Copenhagen and/or Zealand. Thus the brigade, which by May 1945 counted about 5,000 well-trained and armed conscripts and volunteers, would be ultimately under the command of SHAEF, like the rest of the Danish resistance forces.

As part of its attempt to regain control of developments in the field, SOE decided to send a new chief organizer to Denmark. Muus's second period in this position had come to an end in December 1944 when he, personally run-down and hotly pursued by the Gestapo, had been ordered to return to London for consultation and rest. Earlier in the year he had played an important part in the reorganization of the resistance movement and the establishment of the resistance army. However, in the course of this work he had distanced himself from the freedom council and moved closer to members of the small general staff, especially Schjødt-Eriksen, and to friends of leading politicians, in particular the influential Herman Dedichen. Rumours of financial irregularities and aspects of his lifestyle had further affected his standing among the leaders of the resistance movement, as well as his relations with some of his SOE masters.

The man who had been trained to take Muus's place, should the need arise, was Ole Lippmann. A young businessman with an international education and strong anti-totalitarian views, he had been one of Svend Truelsen's closest collaborators in the running of the illegal intelligence service after the evacuation of the army officers. Handpicked by Juncker and Truelsen, rather than by lieutenant commander Hollingworth who preferred to send Muus back to the field, Lippmann was more on the side of the civilian than of the military section of the resistance movement in the rivalry that was intensifying with the prospect of a German collapse. Well-briefed by his British superiors, he arrived in Denmark early in February 1945 and brought with him the directive drawn up for general Gørtz.

A fourth category, that of individuals enrolling in the armed forces of an allied power and joining the fight against Nazi Germany and its allies, completes the range of militant reactions to German occupation presented here. The most obvious cases were those of men trained by SOE and sent to Denmark as organizers and leaders of the resistance, as experts and instructors in sabotage or as radio telegraphists responsible for establishing and maintaining contact between British headquarters and the field. Like other Danes in British service, they had enrolled in the Buffs, the East Kent Regiment, in which the Danish king was an honorary colonel. Thus, they were under British orders when serving in Denmark. In the course of the war a total of 53 SOE agents were dispatched to Denmark, most of them dropped by parachute and some transferred by sea. More than half were evacuated, imprisoned or killed, leaving 23 active in the field in April 1945.

The first SOE leader, dropped over Denmark on 28 December 1941, was the ill-fated captain C.J. Bruhn, whose parachute failed to open. Captain C.M. Rottbøll followed in April 1942, but was killed in a scuffle and exchange of fire with Danish police in September the same year. Six months later his place was taken by captain, later major, Flemming B. Muus, who in October 1943 was called back to London for consultation. Two months later he was in Denmark again, where he stayed till his evacuation in December 1944. The last SOE leader, major Ole Lippmann, remained in Denmark till the end of the occupation.

Periodically, two other agents took over the leadership of SOE activities in Denmark. One was Mogens Hammer, who belonged to the first batch of Danish volunteers reporting for SOE training in January 1941. Parachuted into Denmark together with Bruhn, he found himself in the role of the only SOE agent in the country after the death of his superior. When eventually he, hotly pursued, returned to London in September 1942, he was asked to go back to Denmark immediately and assume provisional leadership after the death of Rottbøll. This position he held till the arrival of Muus in March 1943. Returning to England the following month, he spent the rest of the war serving in the British army. The other acting leader was captain Ole Geisler. Like Hammer an engineer by profession, he was parachuted into Denmark in February 1943 as leader of a team of four men. After a long period in Jutland, he moved to Copenhagen, where he became a member of the freedom council's military committee and later of its sabotage committee. Occasionally standing in for Muus as SOE's representative and later keeping in close touch with Lippmann, he acted as SOE's second in command.

Of the remaining agents serving in Denmark, only a few failed to live up to expectations, their main shortcoming being lax security. Especially in the first years of the occupation the Danish section of SOE had problems with the number and quality of its recruits. With no Danish exile government in London to attract suitable volunteers, the organization had to draw mainly on stranded sailors and Danes living abroad. Later, when refugees from Denmark began to arrive in England, mainly via Sweden, the recruitment situation improved somewhat. Another problem, however, was that a few of the most suitable of the men who had been trained at SOE schools preferred to serve with British forces elsewhere, rather than hang about, often for months, waiting for an opportunity to enter active service in Denmark.

Other Danes served SOE in an administrative capacity. The first was W. Michael Iversen, who, after 20 years managing a plantation in Malaya, happened to be in London in April 1940. His reaction to the German occupation and Danish policy was to rally Danes in Britain and encourage them to make an active contribution to the war. In touch with some of the people engaged in setting up SOE, he became the manager of the Danish section's recruitment office. After retiring in 1943, he spent the rest of the war serving in the British army, with the rank of captain. E. Borch Johansen came to SOE with a different background. Having been very active in transmitting intelligence and organizing resistance, he had been arrested by Danish police for his part in arranging the illegal departure for Britain of the Conservative leader Christmas Møller in April 1942, but had been allowed to escape. Together with Hammer, he canoed to Sweden, and made his way to London, where the Danish section wanted him to help with planning the drops of men and material over Denmark. He left SOE in 1943 and spent the rest of the war in the British army, with the rank of major.

The work within the Danish section of Flemming Juncker, from May 1944 in charge of organizing parachute drops, and of major Svend

Truelsen, from about the same time attached to SOE's head office in charge of intelligence work and later on the staff of the Danish section with responsibility for systematizing, processing and transmitting Danish intelligence, has already been mentioned. Together they became a formative influence on the policy towards Denmark of SOE (or Special Forces, as the organization became known after the fusion with the American OSS in May 1944) in the last year of the war.

Other Danes, acting independently of SOE, took great personal risks in attempting to escape to England to enrol in the British forces. Four outstanding cases may be mentioned. After 9 April 1940 lieutenant colonel T.P.A. Ørum took leave of absence without pay. Later in the year he decided to make for England and volunteer for active service in the Royal Air Force, having already encouraged others to take the same course. In December, however, he was arrested in Berlin and charged with espionage for Britain and treason, Denmark being deemed part of the German operational area. By a concession on the part of the German authorities, he and his accomplices were tried by a Danish court. In January 1941 he was dismissed from the Danish forces and sentenced to prison for life.

Flying officer Kaj Birksted was more successful. Only a few days after 9 April he managed to escape to Sweden and make his way to northern Norway, where he fought on the Norwegian side till the allied forces were evacuated, and he was transported to England. Eventually he was able to reach a Norwegian training camp in Canada known as 'Little Norway', where he trained as a fighter pilot. Having joined the Norwegian section of the Royal Air Force, he took part in several hundred missions over enemy territory and fought countless battles in the air, reaching the rank of wing commander and ending up as chief of the Norwegian section. In 1943 he joined the general staff of the RAF, and the following year took over as chief of its operational section.

A particularly daring escape from Denmark was that of lieutenant Thomas Sneum, who, together with a fellow officer, assembled a tiny sports plane near Odense and, in June 1941, managed to fly it to England. Here his aim was to join the armed forces. However, already well known to British intelligence authorities for important material he had gathered in Denmark and passed on to them – in particular information relating to a novel type of radar installation set up by the Germans on the island of Fanø on the Danish west coast – he was asked by SIS to return to Denmark and continue his intelligence work. Dropped by parachute in September 1941, he established contact with the cautious Danish intelligence officers, who soon found him too daring to work with. A situation developed in which Sneum, hotly pursued by the Danish police, again had to abandon his work on Danish soil. In March 1942 he made his way across the frozen-over Sound to Sweden and returned to England. Like Birksted, he spent the rest of the war serving with the Norwegian forces in the RAF.

The Dane who attained the highest distinction in British service was a seaman who joined a commando unit. Already in April 1940 Anders Lassen, ordinary seaman on one of A.P. Møller's tankers then in foreign waters, decided to volunteer for the British forces. Through Michael Iversen he secured a place among the first Danes to be trained as SOE parachutist agents. However, dissatisfied and impatient, he welcomed a transfer to special training for an amphibious commando unit. Ending up in a special training boat squadron, he took part in or led raids and campaigns in the Mediterranean region, especially Greece. He was awarded the Military Cross and two Bars to the Military Cross, and reached the rank of major. Fighting in the allied offensive in northern Italy, he lost his life a month before the end of the war in Europe. Posthumously he was awarded the Victoria Cross.

In addition to heroes still remembered, an unknown number of Danes, estimated to be in the region of 1,000 to 2,000 with 10 per cent of them women, joined the armed forces of the Commonwealth Countries or the United States and engaged in operations in various theatres of war. Without an exile government in London to attract and organize them, they fought alongside soldiers of other nationalities and played their part in allied efforts to defeat the enemies in Europe and the Far East.

The continuum of Danish reactions to German occupation presented above, ranging from wholehearted support for the occupying power at one extreme to armed resistance at the other, roughly corresponds to the historical development of such reactions over the five-year period. Wholehearted support of the Germans, always minimal, became negligible after the elections in March 1943. Willing cooperation, not motivated by ideological sympathy but by necessity and prudence, reached its highest point after Scavenius took over the foreign ministry is July 1940, and became much more discreet after the retreat of the government in August 1943. While opposition to the German authorities was largely passive in the first period of the occupation, later it frequently took decidedly active forms. With the rise and organization of the resistance movement, and the establishment of the freedom council in September 1943, various kinds of militant or armed resistance came to the fore. While the policy of limited cooperation with the Germans in the first years had been largely accepted and supported by the population, it subsequently became less popular. In the last few years, especially the final six months of the war, active resistance, armed as well as unarmed, rapidly gained considerable public support.

However, this tentative correspondence between the logical arrangement and the historical trend of Danish reactions is somewhat marred by the important development taking place during the last period of the war. With the liberation of Denmark approaching, leaders of the old political parties, all men associated with the policy of cooperation, moved closer to the leaders of the resistance. From one point of view, this development may be seen as part of the broad trend from cooperation to resistance. In its effects, however, it can also be recognized as counteractive in relation to that trend, in the sense that it led to compromise and some cooperation between the politicians and the resistance movement, and thus brought about a relationship in which the politicians, with their parties and organizations, eventually gained the upper hand.

The underlying concern of the political leaders at that stage of the war was to keep their political organizations intact, ready to assume their traditional roles in Danish politics as soon as the country had been liberated and the democratic system re-established. For that purpose the party leaders needed to recover their authority in the country and restore some of the credibility they had lost among the allies during the years of governmental cooperation with the enemy. It was after the general strike in Copenhagen in the summer of 1944, in the management of which the freedom council had demonstrated its authority and influence among the public, that the politicians took the more decisive steps to establish relations with the resistance movement. Having declined earlier invitations to secure representation of their parties in the freedom council, they now decided to have two of their men join a contact committee set up by the council in August 1944. They were H.C. Hansen from the Social Democrats and Aksel Møller from the Conservatives, both younger leaders who already had been involved in various forms of illegal activities. In the initial period of the work of the new committee, Aage Schoch and Børge Houmann represented the freedom council.

Within Denmark, the driving forces behind this whole development were Herman Dedichen and Flemming Muus. While Dedichen, in close touch with both the politicians and the officers and enjoying the confidence of the British, for long had worked for some reconciliation between the political and military establishment and the resistance, Muus, largely sharing the views of his close collaborator Dedichen, had moved closer to the politicians at the expense of his relations with the freedom council.

Abroad, the idea of contact and coordination between the two camps in Danish relations with the German authorities at this stage of the war had the support of the Western allies, especially Britain. The Foreign Office, mindful of its post-war interests in Denmark and the region and uncertain about Soviet policy and intentions for that country, wanted to end the occupation with a minimum of internal tension. Hence Britain tried to steer a middle course between the political and military establishment and the resistance movement, which in practice meant seeking to rehabilitate the former while occasionally checking the latter. This was the policy that first Muus and later Lippmann, both under British orders, pursued in the field, the former leaning towards the old establishment and the latter identifying more with the freedom council.

For all the parties most concerned, the old politicians and the freedom council as well as Britain, the two most important matters to be resolved were the status of Denmark in relation to the allied powers and the composition and programme of its government immediately after liberation. The problem of status was complicated by the conflict between the peacefully-occupied role of the state and the militant activities of the resistance movement and by the absence of the government and the non-existence of an exile government. Already in the earlier months of 1944 Britain and the United States had negotiated a joint declaration which practically recognized Denmark as an ally. However, they had failed to secure the assent of the Soviet Union, which had not forgotten that the Danish government had broken off diplomatic relations with Moscow immediately after the German attack in 1941. In the autumn of 1944, a few months after Thomas Døssing had been accepted in Moscow as representative of 'the fighting Denmark', the king and the leading politicians, without consulting the freedom council, had sent a message to the Soviet government in which they apologized for, and tried to explain, the diplomatic rupture in 1941 and the subsequent signing of the Anti-Comintern Pact.

When this approach, presumably mediated by Døssing, drew no response whatever from Moscow it finally became clear to the politicians that in matters of diplomacy they had to cooperate with the freedom council and, in relations with the Soviet Union, show their united support for the resistance movement. After considerable debate about the basis for their cooperation, the politicians and the freedom council prepared a joint appeal for allied status, which early in January 1945 went off to the Danish representatives in London, Washington and Moscow. A lengthy negotiation, involving many parties followed. For long, the greatest obstacle was Døssing, who found it difficult to accept the recent reconciliation between the politicians responsible for the policy of cooperation and the resistance movement he represented. Refusing to present and recommend the appeal to the Soviet authorities, he at one stage tried to impose new conditions for accepting the discredited politicians as partners of the freedom council. Here he could point out that his demands were in line with the attitude of the Soviet government. When the Germans capitulated and the occupation came to an end the matter of Denmark's formal status was still pending. Later in May, however, its government received an invitation to take part in the San Francisco conference, where allied powers would meet to set up the United Nations.

Since the joint appeal to the three great powers was intended as a diplomatic demonstration of national unity behind Danish resistance, it presupposed a degree of political agreement between the parties. To achieve this at that stage proved very difficult. When the politicians initially insisted on first agreeing on the text of the diplomatic document and only later discussing the political issues, a vehement debate ensued. The basis for the discussions became a memorandum prepared by Frode Jakobsen and Børge Houmann on behalf of the freedom council. It dealt with two crucial issues in particular, namely the composition of the liberation government and its programme for the post-war period, and also presented certain demands.

As to the composition of the future government, it was too soon to reach a detailed agreement, even on the relative strength of representation of the two sides. The previous winter the political parties had prepared a list of future ministers which was made up entirely of politicians from the parties of the former coalition government, and included some names that were unacceptable to the resistance movement. In the meantime, the idea of such a government had become quite unrealistic. The memorandum presented by the freedom council demanded representation for the four major resistance organizations, *Frit Danmark*, the Communists, Danish Unity and the Ring, as well as for the 'free Danes' abroad, and pointed towards an equal representation of the two sides. All that could be agreed now, however, was that a government would have to be formed in unison, and with participation of both sides.

As for the political programme of the post-war government, the memorandum presented three major demands: punishment of all persons who during the occupation had committed treason or other crimes which it had been impossible to deal with at the time; compensation for all who had suffered loss as a result of German persecution; and the end of Denmark's traditional and isolated neutrality and its full and binding entry into the projected United Nations. Those conditions the politicians found largely acceptable. Thus, for the purpose of drafting the joint appeal to the allied powers, the parties were able to agree on a formula which stated that they were united 'in seeking to maintain the solidarity of the Danish people also after the war, by forming the first free government of the country and determining its basic programme in unison'. At that stage, it was mainly the freedom council that laid down the terms for cooperation between the resistance movement and the old political parties. Four or five months later, a liberation government led by Vilhelm Buhl and composed half of politicians and half of representatives of the 'free Danes' abroad and the leading resistance organizations took charge. Before long the professional politicians managed to re-establish their control of the political process.

Diplomatically, Denmark's efforts during the last winter of the war were less than successful, its joint appeal for allied status getting stuck somewhere in Moscow. Yet, it did enjoy the diplomatic support and receive the implicit recognition of the two great Western allies.

Politically, Denmark managed to reach an understanding and develop a form of partnership between the old political establishment and the leadership of the resistance movement. This achievement, though perhaps less than convincing to the Russians, was acceptable to the Americans and more than welcome to the British. Indeed, the Foreign Office and SOE, now working together, had for long sought a reconciliation between the forces of tradition and continuity and the revisionist tendencies and ambitions in Danish politics, with a view to reaching a political equilibrium of national unity which would be stable enough to protect the country against divisive influences and interventionist initiatives from the Soviet Union, and durable enough to prepare it for a pro-British role in post-war Europe.

Militarily, the resistance army, organized on SOE initiative, was coordinated with the allied forces. Through the designation of general Gørtz and a series of declarations, directives and missions following the allied invasion of north-western Europe, both the civilian and the professional forces of the country were potentially integrated in the forces at the disposal of SHAEF. Thus Denmark, despite its passive conduct in the early years of the occupation, ended up firmly within the camp of the Western allies. While encouraged, guided and supported by Britain and other allies, it did so essentially through its own efforts.

3
Since 1945: From resistance to collaboration

While the history of Danish reactions to German occupation presented a broad development from cooperation to resistance, the huge historiography that since 1945 has been devoted to the subject has gone through a thematic movement more in the opposite direction. As regards focus as well as commitment, scholarly work on the occupation years has passed through three stages.

The historians writing in the first post-war decades concentrated on the Danish–German conflict and took less interest in divisions on the Danish side. Imbued with the anti-German feelings which had affected the overwhelming majority of the Danish people since the invasion in 1940 and impressed with the national solidarity that had emerged in the year of liberation, they were inclined to belittle the tensions and conflicts which had developed between official Denmark and those who were against the policy and practice of negotiating and cooperating with the German authorities. Acknowledging the historical coexistence of cooperation and resistance, such writers looked for some concord between the two kinds of reaction to German occupation. While some found an implicit compromise, others detected an underlying continuity between the earlier policy of cooperation and the later commitment to resistance. As presented, each notion implied a degree of complementarity between opposite reactions. The concept of complementarity helped historians and other writers to sustain the image of a nation united in opposition to the German enemy.

Later historians, writing in the 1970s and 1980s, were less impressed with the national concord of anti-German opposition and more aware of the divisions within the occupied nation. Shifting the focus from Danish–German conflict to Danish disagreements, they questioned some basic assumptions behind the earlier presentation of the history of reactions to occupation. Dealing with resistance and cooperation separately, they examined the former more critically and assessed the latter on its own merits. Thus they revived the conflict that had divided the nation in the middle years of the occupation.

The 1990s brought a second revisionist wave, which took the scholarly debate beyond the conflict between resistance and cooperation. Addressing the conduct of relatively minor groups of people who during the war, in some way or other, had collaborated with the Germans, and who had been largely ignored by earlier writers, a new generation of historians highlighted the moral dimension of Danish conduct during the war. On the one hand, they distanced themselves from the standpoint of the resistance movement by condemning some of its practices, especially liquidation of informers and others. On the other hand, they went well beyond accepting the policy of cooperation when they dealt sympathetically with the parts played by marginal groups hitherto not only excluded from scholarly consideration but also broadly condemned by the public. Thus the younger historians introduced a new note of discord both in scholarly and public debate about Danish behaviour during the German occupation. At both levels, that debate continued till well into the twenty-first century.

3.1. Concord

The historians who were inclined to present cooperation and resistance as alternate and ultimately complementary ways of opposing the German authorities included some who viewed the relationship between the two ways primarily from the angle of active resistance and some who saw it more from the perspective of limited cooperation. For the former, typically identifying with the resistance movement, it was bound to be difficult to accept the policy of cooperation in its entirety. For the latter, sometimes personally committed to that policy, it could be hard to endorse all of the practices of the resistance movement. Yet all such writers shared, at least to some extent, the idea of essential complementarity between reluctant cooperation and active opposition to the occupying power.

A clear case of presenting and assessing reactions to German occupation from a resistance perspective was that of Jørgen Hæstrup, who became the foremost historian of Danish opposition. A charismatic and enterprising history master in one of Odense's upper secondary schools, he had himself been active in the resistance. Like many others with a similar background, he became concerned about the emergence in the first post-war years of a so-called counter-movement, opposed to the resistance movement. Its supporters, many of them people with a less than heroic wartime record and some with an axe to grind, were critical, in particular, of the severe, and sometimes arbitrary, treatment meted out to collaborators by the Danish judicial system after the liberation. More generally, they seemed set to undermine the immense popularity, and considerable political influence, enjoyed by the resistance movement after the war.

However, any serious attempt to counter such efforts of denigration seemed bound to be thwarted by the obvious lack of factual knowledge about the structure, organization and activities of the resistance movement. To secure its rightful recognition in the long run, it became clear to Hæstrup in the spring of 1947, some historical research would be required. From his contacts with the SOE agent on Funen in 1943–44 he knew that the men trained in England and sent to Denmark to assist the resistance movement had maintained telegraphic contact with London, sending reports to headquarters and receiving instructions. Such written material, presumably filed in England, could be important sources. If it was not available, personal reports by the agents and others involved, whether they were written by themselves or were obtained by way of interview and gathered while the events were still relatively fresh in their memories, might help fill the gap in information about that period of Danish history.

Having received the consent of an initially rather sceptical keeper of the Danish public records and having secured the support of Aage Friis, then nestor of historical research, Hæstrup arranged to take a couple of months leave from his teaching duties towards the end of 1947. Confident that the wartime relationship with British military authorities offered the best entry to a study of the organization and activities of the Danish resistance movement, he decided first to visit London. After an instructive weekend with Flemming Juncker in Jutland and a useful meeting in Odense with Sir Bruce Lockhart, who had been in charge of British propaganda in the war, he left for England, armed with a suitable letter of introduction to Sir Colin Gubbins from Per Federspiel, SOE's paymaster in Denmark and now a member of the government.

In two weeks in London, Hæstrup met not only people who had held top positions within SOE, namely, in addition to major general Gubbins, Lord Selborne and Sir Charles Hambro, but also some of those who had run the Danish section of the secret organization, including lieutenant commander Ralph Hollingworth, Reginald Spink, commander Frank Noel Stagg and major Lawrence Lassen. The arguments he advanced for securing the SOE archives relating to Danish resistance were that they constituted a vital chapter of his country's history and ought to be in the custody of a Danish institution, and that it was not in British interests to withhold information about the activities of SOE in the occupied countries. If the efforts and achievements of SOE in such countries remained unknown or were forgotten the goodwill still enjoyed by Britain in Europe would evaporate. Here he went as far as suggesting a scholarly country-by-country presentation of the organization's achievements.

Of course, Hæstrup did not manage to have the SOE files, or a copy thereof, transferred to Danish custody, or even to secure access to this material. It was a time when the papers of that organization were still marked 'top secret' and, indeed, its very existence was being kept secret.[1] However, major N.G. Mott, responsible for watching over those archives, did help him in his work, by writing to the officers of the Danish section and authorizing them to speak freely to him, irrespective of their pledge of secrecy. Moreover, Mott referred him to professor W. J. M. McKenzie at Oxford, who had been charged with preparing a full account of the work of the Danish section. McKenzie, no stickler for War Office secretiveness, allowed him to read his 300-page report, and later sent him a copy confidentially. Thus, Hæstrup could return to Denmark confident that he had secured British approval for his research project. However, nearly all his contacts had been with SOE people. Only later did he become aware of the rivalries between that organization and other British bodies, which sometimes had different ideas about the conduct of the war in northern Europe.

Back in Odense and ready to start collecting reports from SOE agents and resistance leaders, Hæstrup soon discovered that there were rather more important sources of Danish occupation history to be located. Despite the need for secrecy and the rules of security, many important members of the resistance movement had stored away written material about their activities. For some, especially those running large organizations, it had been necessary for the efficient continuation of their work to retain records of various kinds. For others, in particular those stationed in neutral Sweden, it had been relatively safe to do so. Now such contemporary material, he found, was often stored in unsuitable places by people not fully aware of its significance. To secure it and make it available for future historians became his most urgent task. The next few years he came across, and secured for the public record office, 27 such collections of material and, in each case, sorted the papers, decoded messages and listed the contents, thus turning the collection into a proper archive. Twenty-five years later the total number of archives prepared and deposited had grown to 80.

In his account of this part of the research, Hæstrup drew attention to four archives in particular, namely those of Lorens Arne Duus Hansen, Erik Seidenfaden, Herman Dedichen and Ole Lippmann. Each of those men had not only been deeply involved in resistance activities but had also played a significant part in establishing or maintaining contact with sections of official Denmark. Duus Hansen, organizer and leader of radio communication with London and the free world, had been in close touch with the intelligence officers and sections of the police force. Seidenfaden, one of SOE's earliest contacts in Denmark and from 1943 leader of the Danish Press Service in Stockholm, had drawn on excellent connections with influential politicians in Copenhagen. Dedichen, a businessman with long-standing contacts to SOE and its agents, had offered his good offices and become a principal mediator between the resistance movement and the leaders of the major political parties. And Lippmann, as the last SOE chief in Denmark, had been under orders to smooth relations between army officers and civilian leaders of the resistance movement and to facilitate cooperation between the politicians and the freedom council.[2]

Among the many collections of documents that turned up at later stages of his research, Hæstrup singled out Ebbe Munck's, describing it as both the largest and the most important of all the archives that had been deposited in the public record office. Since 1940 Munck had been stationed in Stockholm, where he had served as unofficial link between both official bodies and illegal organizations in Denmark and various authorities in London and other capitals of the free world. Thus, in the earlier years he had represented the general staff of the army in dealings with the British legation in Stockholm, and in the later years the freedom council in its relations with the SOE office in the Swedish capital. Involved in some way or other in most of the more important secret negotiations and transactions with neutral Sweden and the allied powers, he had become a corner stone of Danish opposition to German occupation. Describing him as having been motivated from the very beginning of the occupation by a determination to transform Denmark from a country of capitulation to a country of resistance, Hæstrup went as far as claiming that Munck's efforts amounted to one of the most significant and decisive contributions to Danish foreign policy in the twentieth century. Like Seidenfaden in the last years of the war, he had worked from an office which was out of the reach of the Germans, and had been able to keep his files intact.[3]

Collecting reports from individuals who had been engaged in resistance turned out to be a task much more demanding, in terms of both time and effort, than expected. Since he had decided to concentrate on what he regarded as the main organs of the movement and their leaders, Hæstrup sought out people who had been associated with the Danish section of SOE. Thus, roughly four out of five of the 78 reports he managed to secure between the autumn of 1947 and the spring of 1949 were by SOE officers and their contacts. Even when he interviewed Communist resistance leaders, such as Mogens Fog, who represented the popular-front *Frit Danmark* in the freedom council, and Børge Houmann, who represented the Communist party and the sabotage organization BOPA, his point of departure was their relationship with SOE.[4] As the work progressed, he came to see the reports as supplementary to the archives, often using them to fill gaps in the documentary material available.

Only a small minority of the 78 informants wrote their reports entirely on their own, and even so only after an exchange of letters with Hæstrup. Several dictated their accounts to a secretary, or to a stenographer sent to them by Hæstrup. In most cases, however, he had to fall back on the interview method, meeting the informants in their offices or homes, or in his own home in Odense, and usually taking close notes in longhand but sometimes using the services of his stenographer. It was a method which allowed him occasionally to guide an informant and help him to focus on what was deemed significant. After the interview, the report was typed out and sent to the informant for corrections, and finally for signature. The first phase of Hæstrup's research came to an end in April 1949, when he deposited all archives and reports so far gathered in the public record office. The material was in principle kept secret for 25 years, but in practice soon made available selectively for historical research.

Having finished the pioneer work of discovering and procuring source material for a history of the resistance movement, Hæstrup returned to full-time teaching at Sct. Knuds Gymnasium. It was not till about two years later that he, after overcoming personal hesitations and professional considerations, decided to accept the challenge of writing the first part of the history himself. His major motivation was still, he explained later, to counter the growing disparagement of the resistance movement.[5] For any work to have the proper impact on the public debate, it would need to be of a strictly scholarly nature. He started research and writing in the summer of 1951. Though uncertain about the attitude to contemporary history of the academic authorities, he eventually decided to present the result of his work to Aarhus University in the form of a doctoral dissertation. In 1954 it was submitted and formally accepted, and in accordance with Danish practice, subsequently printed and published. Its title was *Kontakt med England 1940–43.*

The book immediately became a best-seller. Drawing on sources hitherto unknown and revealing a central relationship between Danish resistance and allied military and political efforts, it was a decisive contribution to knowledge of contemporary history and became a point of departure for further research. Very well written, with a wider readership in mind, it told a dramatic story about recent events, which acknowledged the patriotism of ordinary people and highlighted the heroism of outstanding individuals. The public defence of the dissertation attracted close to one thousand people, many of them prominent members of the resistance movement, and became a media event.

The two officially appointed opponents devoted some time to critical comments on the use of personal reports as historical sources. One of them, professor Sven Henningsen from Copenhagen University, also pointed out that the candidate had not consulted German sources. More important, Henningsen attacked him for obviously acting as spokesman for the views of the resistance movement and showing little understanding of the conduct of the politicians. In particular, he objected to the candidate's violent criticism of Erik Scavenius and his policy, and also pointed out that he had failed to give the politicians credit for their refusal to comply with German demands on 28 August 1943. The latter accusation led to a lengthy argument between Hæstrup and Henningsen, which was often interrupted by the applause of the largely pro-resistance audience.

However, reactions from the floor, while generally very supportive, also included some criticism and suggestions by prominent former members of the resistance movement. Flemming Juncker thought that the radio service had not been done full justice; Ebbe Munck stressed the need for viewing Danish resistance in a wider context; and Borch Johansen was sarcastic about the contributions of the intelligence officers. Børge Houmann, in a review of the book in the Communist paper *Land og Folk,* had already questioned the wisdom of choosing SOE activities as the starting-point for a treatise on Danish resistance.[6]

The following years Hæstrup continued his search for material about the resistance movement, now with the explicit support of the public record office. Again he secured a large number of individual reports, but soon gained the impression that the memories of the informants were not quite so reliable as those of the people he had approached half a dozen years earlier. Thus, the additional collections of contemporary papers, of which he now located, put in order and deposited as many as he had done in the late 1940s, gained in importance as sources. He was particularly pleased with the archives of Frode Jakobsen, the longest-serving member of the freedom council; of Thomas Døssing, the representative of 'the fighting Denmark' in Moscow; and of Svend Truelsen, in charge of intelligence work from 1943 to 1945, first in Denmark and later in the SOE headquarters in London.

While in his earlier search for material, as in the writing of *Kontakt med England*, he had focused on SOE activities, Hæstrup now turned his attention to the central organs of the resistance movement. He was particularly interested in documents and reports throwing light on the origins, development and role of the freedom council, the intelligence service, the foremost reception organizations and the centrally organized radio communication. More detailed studies, of for example the history of sabotage, the illegal press, the illegal boat service and the great strike movements, he left to later historians. Nor did he devote much time to exploring the relationship between leading politicians and the resistance movement, an omission he later regretted.[7]

However, while focusing on the structure and organization of the Danish movement, Hæstrup took the first steps towards a more comparative approach to the subject. Conversations with two young Norwegian historians engaged in similar research in their country had helped to broaden his conception of resistance. Soon he started to read up the rapidly growing literature about resistance in other European countries, including the Soviet Union, Greece, Yugoslavia, France, Holland, Poland and even Nazi Germany. The memoirs of British scholars and writers who had played heroic parts as liaison officers to resistance movements in the Balkans he found particularly absorbing. Soon he established contact with C.M. Woodhouse in London and F.W. Deakin in Oxford as well as with heads of institutes in Amsterdam and elsewhere devoted to research on anti-German resistance.

At this stage of his reading, Hæstrup was struck by the distinction between two levels of warfare in the Second World War. At the higher level, you had the regular war among states, fought with huge armies and other uniformed and organized forces and marked by decisive battles and important conferences. At a lower level, you had the struggle of peoples, in both Europe and Asia, resisting the forces of occupation and engaging in sabotage and other forms of underground activities, sometimes amounting to organized irregular warfare. While the former sort of warfare was highly visible and well known, the latter was largely covert and still fairly unknown. Yet, the struggle of subjugated peoples, he thought, was at least as important as the war among states.

Though thus well aware of the distinction between the arena of inter-state relations and the sphere of popular reaction, Hæstrup insisted on entitling his two-volume work on the Danish resistance organization in the 1943–45 period *Hemmelig alliance* (Secret Alliance). This had been the original title of his dissertation, but had been rejected by the committee set up by Aarhus University on the grounds that alliances existed only between states, not between a state and scattered illegal groups in another country. When he now revived the title for what he presented as a continuation of his dissertation he was stressing the central theme of all his work, namely the bond between Danish resistance and British efforts in the allied struggle with Nazi Germany. *Hemmelig alliance* appeared on 16 September 1959, the official birthday of the freedom council.[8] Like the dissertation, it attracted enormous attention, from scholars as well as the public. The first print run, of 5,000 copies, sold out the day of publication.

After completing a couple of briefer and more specialized treatises, Hæstrup started preparing his third major work on Danish reactions to German occupation, the first volume of which appeared in 1966 and the second in 1971. Entitled *...til landets bedste* (for the good of the country), it outlined the history of the quasi-governmental functions that the permanent heads of the central administration, in the absence of an acting government, carried out from August 1943 to May 1945.[9] This work represented a departure from the author's rather exclusive preoccupation with the resistance movement and showed a novel appreciation of the contribution of those who had been responsible for conducting Danish relations with the German authorities during the last 20 months of the occupation. In *Hemmelig alliance*, he later noted, he had devoted only 20 lines to that side of the story.[10] Now he found that the departmental heads, discreetly guided by their political masters, had played a part which had been not only essential for the country but, in a way, also advantageous for the resistance movement.

In retrospect, Hæstrup now saw the last period of Danish occupation history as split into two almost entirely separate worlds, of resistance managed by the freedom council and of Danish–German negotiations conducted by a council of permanent secretaries under political guidance. Acting without constitutional foundation and without prior agreement, those two organs of management had seen Denmark through a historic crisis by engaging in a largely involuntary interplay. Despite their contradictory tendencies, they had become complementary actors, each depending on the other. On the one hand, organized resistance had not only taken Denmark into the camp of the allied powers but had also mitigated the adverse political effects of the administration's limited cooperation with the enemy. On the other hand, such cooperation had not only protected the population against the worst possible effects of war and occupation but had also helped to create and sustain the conditions that allowed the resistance movement to continue its activities. While resistance had compensated for cooperation, cooperation had shielded resistance.[11] Thus Hæstrup, having become a historian of the occupation period rather than simply the historian of the resistance movement, perceived a concord between two opposite reactions to German occupation. Later historians labelled this notion the consensus perception of Danish conduct.

Yet, while he paid a handsome tribute to the devotion to duty shown by Nils Svenningsen, who as head of the ministry of foreign affairs intrepidly had conducted the negotiations with the German minister, and praised several other heads of departments, who discreetly had maintained contact with resistance leaders, Hæstrup's heart was still with the resistance movement. Resistance, he asserted, was essentially a home-grown product. Though it developed into a movement which received encouragement, instructions and arms from abroad, this reaction to German occupation had sprung from the national will. Disappointed by the government's capitulation on 9 April and increasingly frustrated by the presence and pressures of the occupying power, individuals across the country, usually acting independently, had found some way of expressing their opposition to the occupying power. Soon contacts had been established or developed among many like-minded people. Gradually, in step with the fortunes of the allied powers in the various theatres of war, resistance had taken more active and organized forms, eventually developing into something approaching a national underground movement. However, despite all the organization and reorganization taking place, the movement had remained by nature a 'gigantic improvisation'.[12]

As such, it was subject to continual re-creation. When a group was wiped out, whether through killing, arrest or escape, another set of people soon appeared to take its place. When a major crisis arose in Danish–German relations, as in August 1943 and in the summer of 1944, large sections of the population rose impulsively to manifest their opposition to the German authorities, mainly by joining street demonstrations and strikes. This view of the emergence, development and nature of Danish resistance became known among later historians as the spontaneity theory. Both that and the consensus interpretation of cooperation and resistance were criticized, and partly refuted, by the next generation of post-war historians.

These historians were in a position to examine Hæstrup's interpretations in historical perspective, and see them as, to some extent, conditioned, on the one hand, by the popular mood prevalent in Denmark in the immediate post-war years and, on the other hand, by the East–West tensions dominating European international politics in the first decades of the cold war. In their view, the consensus interpretation mirrored a nation-wide identification with anti-German resistance which gathered strength in the last stage of the occupation and reached its highest point immediately after the liberation. Likewise, the spontaneity theory rested on a profound faith in the democratic instincts and anti-authoritarian convictions which inspired the reactions of the Danish people, first, to the Nazi occupation during the war and later to the Communist challenge of the cold war.

In his identification with the patriotic spirit of the people, Hæstrup may have overestimated the moral and physical strength of the resistance movement as well as the solidarity of the public support it enjoyed. With his ideological orientation towards the Western allies, in the world war as well as in the cold war, he could be charged with having undervalued the role and influence of the Communists in Danish resistance, especially in its earlier years. Yet, despite the successive waves of revisionism that were directed against his story of occupation and resistance, Hæstrup's contribution to the history of the period remains monumental.

His writings became points of departure for many other historians. In the 1950s he gathered round him in Odense a small, informal group of colleagues, friends and former pupils who wanted to take up particular topics not fully explored in his work. In 1959 a high-powered association for the publication of source material and scholarly work relating to Denmark's most recent history (DNH) was set up in Copenhagen with him as founding member. The following year he was asked to prepare, together with Sven Henningsen and the archivist Johan Hvidtfeldt, a research programme for the study of the occupation period in Danish history. Once the problems of access to public records and funding of research projects had been solved he soon found himself, together with Hvidtfeldt, in the role of academic supervisor of the programme. As such, he became the principal source of inspiration and encouragement for younger colleagues, most of them educated after the war. He exercised his influence on fellow historians more through an infectious enthusiasm, seriousness and energy than through the kind of criticism that often goes with a more sceptical temperament. As a historian, he belonged to the more traditional school. Thus, he showed little interest in, or appreciation of, the type of historiography that draws on other disciplines too and, for example, combines a conventional historical approach and methodology with those of political or social studies.

Hæstrup did, however, venture into comparative studies. In the mid-1950s he discussed with Woodhouse in London and de Jong in Amsterdam, head of the Dutch institute for the study of occupation history, certain ideas which he had formed about joint or collective work on the history of the European resistance movements and their political importance. Part of his motivation was a conviction that popular resistance, armed rebellion and civil war, which had marked so many countries in Asia, Africa and Latin America in the post-war decades, would also be a dominant feature of world politics in the future.

In the later 1950s and the 1960s Hæstrup was an active participant in international conferences of resistance historians arranged in various Western European cities. In 1976 he consolidated his position as a historian of European resistance with a book about what had become known as the fourth arm. Entitled *Den 4. vaabenart*, it dealt with the main features of the histories of European resistance movements from 1939 to 1945. Two years later it appeared in an English translation under the Churchillian title *Europe Ablaze*.[13]

Despite his outstanding contribution to the study of modern Danish history, his lively and engaging style of writing and teaching and his growing international reputation, Hæstrup found it difficult to secure a suitable post in the Danish academic establishment. The faculty at Aarhus University, unwilling to offer him a professorship, apparently at one stage considered the possibility of finding him a position as amanuensis (roughly equal to assistant lecturer).[14] Half a dozen years later, in 1966 when he was 57 years old, he accepted an offer of a lectureship in history at a new university launched in Odense. There he remained till he retired.

Among those post-war historians, and other writers, who subscribed to the notion of cooperation and resistance complementing each other, but presented that relationship more from the perspective of the politicians responsible for formulating and conducting the policy of limited cooperation than from the angle of the resistance movement, the foremost case was that of the Social Democratic academic Hartvig Frisch. Having read history and classical philology at Copenhagen University, taught high school for several years and won a seat in parliament in 1926, he soon established himself as a leading intellectual of his party. As a prolific writer, on classical as well as contemporary topics, and a popular lecturer, he also became a major figure in Danish intellectual life of the inter-war period.

An important step towards his position of influential ideologist and political front figure in the major governing party was the publication in 1933 of *Pest over Europa: Bolshevisme – Fascisme – Nazisme*, which became Frisch's most famous book.[15] Dedicated to Thorvald Stauning, leader of the party and prime minister, on his sixtieth birthday, it was not merely a highly readable history of the emergence, rise and establishment of three ideological and political movements that were dominating much of Europe in the late 1930s. It was also a forceful attack on totalitarian ideas and governments and a spirited defence of democratic politics. As such, the book represented, in terms of the split between Communists and Social Democrats in Danish politics, a clear commitment to the processes of parliamentary democracy and a rejection of all ideas of a proletarian dictatorship. The book became highly influential, especially among the younger Social Democratic leaders. However, many of those reading its Nordic Preface may have been more impressed with the author's call for political cooperation among the working-class parties of the Nordic countries than with its tentative suggestions for a strengthening of the military means of protecting those democracies against pressures from neighbouring dictatorships, whether in the east or the south.

Six years later, after the outbreak of the Second World War, the four major political parties set up a committee of eight to facilitate parliamentary cooperation. The Social Democrats were represented by Hedtoft-Hansen, prominent among the younger leaders of the party, and Hartvig Frisch. The committee of nine, formed a few months after the German invasion to secure the continued cooperation of the five democratic parties, again had Frisch as a member. However, his reputation as the author of *Pest over Europa* and various articles directed against fascism and Nazism together with his performance in parliament made his position increasingly precarious. Shortly after a speech in parliament in November 1940, in which he berated the Danish Nazis, he decided, after consulting Stauning, to resign his posts as group chairman and spokesman of the party. In the summer of 1941 the Germans ordered him to stop his public lecturing activities. The following years he kept a very low profile in the political debate. While fully supporting the governmental policy of negotiating and cooperating with the occupying power, he devoted most of his energy to scholarly pursuits.

The official reason for Frisch's resignation from his party posts was that he wished to complete a doctoral dissertation that he had been working on for a couple of years. Only a few months later he was able to submit his work to the department of philosophy at Copenhagen University. At the subsequent public examination the dissertation, which dealt with the constitution of ancient Athens, received praise for being of interest to both classical philologists and historians. Almost immediately he was appointed to a vacant chair in classical philosophy at Copenhagen University. The rest of the war he spent most of his time on research, writing and teaching. Now and then, however, he was able to publish an article or deliver a lecture which, while formally dealing with some classical topic, had an obvious and pointed relevance to the contemporary situation of his country.

Despite his anti-Nazi writings, lectures and speeches in the 1930s and early 1940s, Frisch never engaged in active resistance to the occupying power. When Frode Jakobsen began to build up the resistance organization that became known as the Ring, one of the first people he approached for support was Frisch. In a brief conversation in the late summer of 1941 Frisch, initially under the impression that the plan merely was to start a new association of Social Democratic students and academics, immediately welcomed the initiative and promised his support. But when Jakobsen made it clear that the idea of the proposed organization was to go beyond stepping up intellectual and cultural opposition to the accommodating policy of the government and, eventually, engage in direct resistance to the Germans, he reacted strongly. According to Jakobsen's recollection, Frisch even seemed scared of such a prospect, and heatedly pointed out that it was neither governmental nor Social Democratic policy, and could hurt the country greatly. If that was what Jakobsen had in mind, Frisch added, he was not the man to get hold of. Instead he referred Jakobsen to men like Christmas Møller.[16]

When Frisch, both then and later, refused to engage in active resistance he seems unlikely to have taken his stand out of fear of what might happen to him and his family. Although, as an intellectual, he may have been a man of moral rather than of physical courage, his uncompromising anti-Nazi record shows him as being far from faint-hearted. His reasons for remaining passive seem to have been partly philosophical convictions and partly political considerations.

In several lectures about the political interaction of the city states of ancient Greece which he delivered in the early years of the occupation, Frisch focused on the phenomenon of power. Drawing on Thucydides, he rehearsed the argument that justice could be attained only between roughly equally strong states. As relations between powerful and imperialistic Athens and small and neutral Melos had shown, to oppose and resist a vastly superior power could lead a state to loss of independence and even extinction.[17]

To this realistic observation Frisch later added an essentially moral argument against active resistance. After the growth of sabotage, the abdication of the government and the establishment of the freedom council, he made a speech to first-year students at Copenhagen University in which he warned against resorting to the use of force. For a small nation in Denmark's present situation there were two ways ahead, he told the students. One was to stay within the law and strive to maintain and consolidate Danish democratic culture; another to adopt the policy of power, albeit in the inverted and distorted form forced upon the weaker party, and follow the law of vengeance, the law of the jungle. While recognizing that the latter course had the attraction of being active, violent, romantic and courageous, he firmly rejected it as 'secret anarchical terrorism'. Making it clear that he was referring to sabotage, he mentioned with loathing a recent such act which had cost three lives and endangered hundreds of Danes. As always, Frisch's appeal to his students to respect the law rested on faith in reason and humanism.[18]

The biographer of Frisch, while acknowledging the classical writings and analogies on which he based his philosophy of power and recognizing the rationalist ideology from which he derived his argumentation, found that there might be also a simpler reason for his rejection of illegal resistance to the occupying power. Frisch, he explained, was the Social Democrats' man. His political thought was conditioned by the legalism and the sense of responsibility which the party, in its pursuit of social welfare and its identification with the national interest, had developed in the 1930s – a process in which Frisch himself had played a significant part. Accordingly, he shared the party's commitment to keeping the national institutions intact, and accepted the Social Democratic view that this could be achieved only by accommodating the Germans, not through active resistance.[19]

A further party-political reason for Frisch's antagonism to the resistance movement and most of its activities may be found in his relationship with the Communists. In his youth, when he had been concerned about the split developing in the working class, he had maintained personal contact with some Communist circles. In the 1930s, however, a rupture had occurred in his relationship with DKP. Since then the Communists had treated him as their major tactical enemy, and he had built up a considerable resentment against them. When Communists, a few years into the occupation, took the lead in carrying out sabotage and organizing strikes, they became the foremost opponents of Frisch and other champions of the policy of cooperating with the Germans. Now he rarely missed an opportunity to assail them.[20]

After the rupture in Danish–German relations in 1943 Frisch maintained his line, still appealing to reason and common sense and calling for national solidarity, without resistance. At a conference of Social Democratic leaders and deputies shortly after the mass strikes in the summer of 1944, he discussed the role of the party after liberation. Presenting the resistance movement as the principal threat to the bright prospects of post-war Denmark, he referred to the 'epidemic of murder' that had raged in the country since the breakdown of law and order. In the same speech, he described the freedom council, despite the respect it had gained among the allies, as a stranger in Danish democracy.[21]

At the same time, he was taking steps to prepare the case that the party would present after the war in defence of its policy and conduct during the occupation. As early as the autumn of 1943 the Social Democratic leadership had started to plan a major historical publication about Denmark during the occupation. Frisch had been appointed editor-in-chief and principal contributor. Once the plan had been approved and the authors, all respectable Social Democrats, selected, he could begin to collect documentary material and think about the contents of the work. One of the biggest problems facing him was how to explain the collapse of the policy of cooperation in August 1943. Rejecting the idea that it was the resistance movement which had undermined popular support for the government and its conduct, he found the principal cause in developments in other European countries that summer. The fall of Mussolini in July had led to major strikes in Italy, which had spread to other countries, including Denmark, he explained in a speech to party members late in December.[22] About the same time he prepared a lecture on the Nordic countries and the war, which he gave in many parts of the country during the last 18 months of the occupation. Serving as a preliminary sketch for his contribution to the major work projected, it again presented developments in Denmark, and the other Nordic countries, in an international political context.

In May, only about a week after the liberation of Denmark, Frisch gave a talk in which he, in the words of his biographer, laid down the double strategy which would guide him through the political difficulties of the following period. While now fully acknowledging the efforts of the resistance movement, he warned against letting the glowing tribute to the members of that movement eclipse the very great contribution that had been made in the first years of the war by those responsible for establishing and maintaining national and democratic solidarity. As a result of their efforts, Danish Nazism 'had been ridden to death' and a Quisling form of government prevented.[23] Five days later he flew to America to help present the Danish case for membership of the United Nations. In addition to Frisch, who had been elected by the parliamentary parties, the Danish delegation to the San Francisco conference included professor Erik Husfeldt, selected by the freedom council, and Henrik Kauffmann, the wartime ambassador in Washington. During the following two years Frisch participated energetically in the work of the new institution as a delegate to its General Assembly.

While he managed to follow his double strategy on the international scene, in the domestic politics of post-war Denmark Frisch occasionally found himself in the role of outspoken critic of the resistance movement. Thus, he reacted negatively to popular efforts to 'purge' not only outright collaborators but also people responsible for the politics and administration of the country up to 29 August, and was particularly scathing about the vengeful passion with which some members of the resistance movement and, not least, many of its latter-day supporters pursued the drive. In a radio interview in August 1945 he drew an unfortunate parallel between events in the streets of Copenhagen after 5 May and what he had seen in Italy in the years before the fascists' march towards Rome in 1922.

Later in that interview he made some even more offensive remarks. He started by saying that he, in speeches both in the United States and after his return, had paid due respect to the resistance movement for its military resistance, but went on to argue that the movement in certain of its practices would one day have to submit to historical critique of its record. After all, the movement had for months been busy tearing to pieces the political parties for *their* policy, even though that, too, was a policy of resistance, only carried out under other conditions and by other means. The practice he singled out for condemnation was the liquidation of informers. Asserting that, if he had been a member of the freedom council, he would have been against this kind of action, on the grounds that it could have led to a German campaign of terror against the population, he described the executions of the infamous informers as pure and simple murder – in the form in which they had taken place, he added.[24]

As Frisch must have expected, the broadcasting of the interview led to an outcry in the press and sharp reactions from spokesmen of the resistance movement. The newspapers, which immediately after the liberation had joined in the general glorification of that movement, could not have been happy when he, in the course of the interview, reminded them that they practically all had been solidly in support of the cautious and protective line taken by the politicians during the occupation. Now they reacted by highlighting his most audacious comments and generally dissociating themselves from his censure of the resistance movement.

The papers also opened their correspondence columns to readers with something to say on the topics Frisch had raised so provocatively. Naturally, spokesmen of the resistance movement reacted strongly to what they recognized as an attempt to criminalize the liquidation of informers, maintaining that such acts could be both necessary and justified in what was essentially a situation of war. Mogens Fog, speaking at the 29 August commemoration of those killed by the Germans and their helpers during the occupation, took up a more general point made by Frisch in his recent interview. To say or imply that the active form of resistance grew out of a passive form, and thus present the reactions to occupation in terms of continuation and harmony, amounted to a falsification of history, Fog explained. Both before and after 29 August there were two quite different attitudes to the occupying power, each with its own view of what in the long run would benefit the soul of the people and the welfare of the country. Frisch, clinging to the policy of accommodation, had never understood, Fog asserted, the spirit that had carried the fight in Denmark through to a moral and real victory.[25]

Another weighty contribution to the debate was a long letter in the one-time illegal paper *Information* from Lis Jacobsen, an influential intellectual and close friend of Frisch. She acknowledged the consistency of his attitude and the coherence of his argumentation and paid tribute to his moral courage in openly and publicly giving his reasons, but rejected as deeply unjust the association he had made between the post-war activities of the resistance movement and the antics of early Italian fascism. She went on to defend the wartime activities of the resistance, including liquidation of informers which had been necessary. Finally, she told him very directly that his concern from beginning to end had been to behave as a faithful Social Democrat, which had led him to accept uncritically the party's conception of its role and duty during the war.[26]

Frisch got the last word in that particular debate. In a postscript to his *Tænkt og talt under Krigen* (Thought and said during the war), a book he published the following month, he clarified his position. Summing up his assessment of the political development during the occupation, he wrote,

> It is my deepest conviction that if the majority of responsible Danes had not stayed at their post to the end, and carried out their duty to serve the population, the illegal movement would not have been able to do its job to the extent it did. And, if the military achievements of the underground movement are to remain standing as a true memorial in the history of Denmark, it must be possible to direct criticism also at events which will never attract the united support of the public.[27]

However, Frisch's foremost contribution to the consensual interpretation of the period of Danish history was *Danmark besat og befriet* (Denmark occupied and liberated), the major work planned by the Social Democratic leaders soon after August 1943. Designed as a scholarly project with a broad popular appeal, it had a political purpose, namely to justify the line of cooperation pursued by official Denmark and, in particular, to defend the role played by the Social Democrats. The first volume, written by Frisch, appeared in the autumn of 1945 and took the story up to the eve of 29 August.

In presenting the case for the governmental policy of those years, Frisch dissociated himself from the line adopted by Scavenius when he became foreign minister in July 1940. Convinced that Germany would win the war and devoid of illusions about Danish neutrality, Scavenius had deemed it to be in the national interest to engage in active cooperation with the occupying power, and had declared his willingness to do so. Frisch labelled this policy 'collaboration', and found that Danish policy at that stage, when Germany was at the height of its power, had been motivated by opportunism. Here, however, he made a distinction between an opportunism enforced by perceived necessity and one motivated by desire and applied by choice. While Scavenius and his supporters in the government had been moved by an opportunism of the former kind, a number of individuals, mostly not in official positions and typically of anti-parliamentarian persuasions, had been guilty of the latter kind when they cultivated representatives of the occupying power.[28]

The policy of less deliberate and more limited cooperation favoured by the Social Democratic leaders and ministers was motivated more by prudence. Frisch presented it as a tactical measure, designed to prepare for a managed rupture of diplomatic and political relations with the occupying power. In support of his interpretation, he quoted a speech by Hedtoft-Hansen in February 1941, after the Germans had forced him and H.C. Hansen to resign their posts within their party. Addressing the party's executive committee and parliamentary group, Hedtoft-Hansen asked rhetorically how long the apparently unprincipled practice of humouring the Germans could go on. It was political tactics, he explained, partly aimed at an expected rupture of the relationship, preferably brought about jointly by all the democratic parties, and partly intended to prevent the formation of a Nazi government, which would force the country into partnership with the Axis powers. Those words, Frisch suggested, clearly expressed the special Danish complex of problems, which had not come to a head till 1943, when it reached a conclusion through the electoral victory in the spring and the final rupture in the autumn – after the Danish Nazis had been ridden to death. This connection between compromises with the Germans and fight against Nazism, he concluded, should always be kept in mind if one wanted to understand Danish democratic politics.[29]

Later historians have taken Frisch to task for quoting selectively from Hedtoft-Hansen's speech and creating the impression that he was looking for a rupture of relations with the Germans, whereas the speech read as whole shows that he did not want such an outcome. Like other Social Democratic leaders, and indeed Frisch himself, he preferred to continue the existing relationship with the Germans till the end of the occupation. Frisch has also been accused of exaggerating the danger of a Nazi take-over in his attempt to justify the policy of the government and the party. By such means, he managed to convey a degree of continuity between the policy of cooperation in the earlier period and the rise of resistance in the last years of the occupation, and to suggest some complementarity between the endeavours of the politicians and the activities of the resistance movement.

Frisch's identification with the policy of cooperation – or the policy of negotiation as he preferred to call it – and his adherence to the fiction of neutrality were revealed most clearly in his chapter about the sabotage that started in the summer and autumn of 1942. Discussing the reluctant reactions of the Danish population to Christmas Møller's call for sabotage broadcast by the BBC in September, he found that Christmas Møller had come to be seen as a man who, after starting his time in London as a Danish patriot, had developed into an English propagandist, who no longer considered the interest Denmark had in maintaining law and order. If Danish policy should be changed, which might well be a possibility, the decision should be taken, Frisch added, by king, government and parliament and not by irresponsible private individuals. He went on to discuss Vilhelm Buhl's radio appeal to the population, broadcast some days before Christmas Møller's BBC talk, in which the prime minister warned of the serious consequences a continuation of sabotage might have and urged members of the public to assist the authorities in the clearing up of such evil acts. Pointing out that Buhl's appeal should be seen in the context of its time, Frisch explained that it was all a matter of policy, and that a policy must rest on a morality. If Denmark should go on having a government, he concluded, it would have to be able to maintain the legal order of the country.[30]

The two further volumes of *Danmark besat og befriet* did not appear till three years later. The middle volume, written by 17 mostly prominent Social Democrats, dealt with economic and cultural aspects of the occupation. The third volume, again written by Frisch, presented the political history from 29 August 1943 to the liberation of Denmark 20 months later. Drawing on very many sources that had become available in the meantime, and which may have produced little evidence in support of his construct of a deliberate rupture by the party leaders of Danish–German relations, he did not elaborate, and seems totally to have abandoned this interpretation. He did, however, continue to present the politicians, and their discreet activities under the informal leadership of Buhl in the new situation, in a favourable light.

In Frisch's attitude to the resistance movement there was a marked change. While still highly critical of the injustice of liquidations, scathing about the provocative effects of what he called the policy of demonstration pursued by sections of the illegal press and reluctant to credit the freedom council with the management of the general strikes in 1944, he now found it easier to accept what he called active resistance. Noting the tacit approval by the political parties and the legal press of sabotage in the months after August 1943, he paid tribute to the courage of the young people engaged in that activity and to the efficiency of the men who issued the orders.[31] Later, dealing with the last months of the war, he described with some enthusiasm the wave of intense and effective sabotage of railways and factories in the months from New Year 1945 to the German capitulation, and deemed it the most brilliant military contribution of active Danish resistance.[32] Along the way, Frisch also found a way of correcting the impression left by his speech to first-year students at Copenhagen University in November 1943. His passionate denunciation of 'secret anarchical terrorism', he could now explain, had referred to reckless acts endangering innocent lives, not to strategic sabotage.[33]

While the first volume of the work had focused on the relationship between the Danish government and the German authorities, in this volume Frisch paid increasing attention to relations between official Denmark and the growing resistance movement, in particular between politicians of the dormant coalition government and members of the increasingly influential freedom council.

In tracing the emergence of that body, he quoted with emphatic approval Erling Foss, a founding member of the council, who in the summer of 1943 had warned of the dangers of getting at cross purposes with the political parties, who 'at heart work along the same lines'.[34] In discussing the later work of the freedom council, Frisch paid tribute to the influence of Herman Dedichen, who became an important contact and mediator between the council and the party leaders, especially Hedtoft-Hansen and Buhl, and departmental heads. Noting that earlier attempts by the freedom council to secure permanent representation of the principal political parties had been rejected because neither the Social Democrats nor the Conservatives wanted to compromise the legality of their parties, Frisch admitted that the general strikes in the summer of 1944 had demonstrated the need for a formal link between the two sides. Overcoming the animosity, suspicions and jealousy that had affected the party's relations with 'those anonymous men who so boldly acted as a Danish government', the Social Democratic leaders decided at a meeting in July to establish the necessary contact. They realized, he explained, that, unless such a connection was established, the collapse of Germany 'would present them with a dualism which could be extremely dangerous both for the country and for its democratic system of government'.[35] The Conservatives reached a similar decision. Thus, in August H.C. Hansen and Aksel Møller could join two members of the freedom council to form a contact committee of the council.

The theme of the concluding passages of the book was the connection between the policy carried on by the government and administration and the course chosen by the resistance movement. Surveying the immediate reactions of the leading Danish newspapers to the liberation in May 1945, Frisch quoted from what he described as a clear and well-balanced article in *Socialdemokraten* by Peder Tabor, one of the authors of the second volume of his work. Before 29 August there was no real cooperation between the legal political circles and the resistance movement, the author noted. Yet, in actual fact, there was a kind of division of labour between the two parties. Each acting in its own way and by its own means, they held different sections of the front in a struggle with a common goal. After 29 August, contact between the politicians and the freedom council was soon established, in response to external as well as internal needs of the country.[36] The doubleness at the heart of this view of the history of the five years of occupation characterized also the interpretation presented by Frisch, at this stage of his life.

Rather than opposing cooperation and resistance in his analysis, he distinguished between passive and active, or legal and illegal, opposition to the occupying power, and asserted that they had supplemented each other in a way which had served the country very well. In assessing the importance of the illegal struggle, he moved from the political and legal to the cultural and psychological level. The national rally and cultural solidarity of the early years, when the power of Hitlerism had been at its highest point, had been a mild and quiet power, a sign of high culture. However, though a wonderful experience, it had not been enough. The underground struggle for freedom had brought its completion, namely virility. The problem, as always, had been to balance the virtues of peaceful culture against the force of virile nature.

As so often when dealing with a basic issue of politics and morality, Frisch turned to classical writers, and once again drew on the wisdom of Socrates. Quoting from Plato's *Politicos*, he presented a debate between the young Socrates and an unnamed stranger which turned on the contrast between sober-mindedness and bravery. This contrast, Plato said, could divide a people and lead to deep enmity. Each quality, if unchecked and carried to the extreme, could lead to loss of freedom for the state. As Frisch now saw it, that issue had been at the heart of Denmark's difficulties both before, during and after the occupation. By its spirit and action, the resistance movement struggling for freedom had helped save the country from the dangers of annihilation inherent in the pursuit of internal and external peace and quiet at any price. On the other hand, there was the danger of bellicose inclinations and excessive heroism leading to enmity and hostilities with powerful neighbours. Drawing on the experience gained and writing at the outset of the cold war, Frisch concluded that the task for the present as well as the future of the country was to find the optimal combination of sober-mindedness and bravery – prudence and courage.[37]

By the time this volume appeared, the author was minister of education in a minority government formed late in 1947 by Hans Hedtoft (as he now called himself). Frisch remained in office till late in 1949, when he became seriously ill. He died a few months later, 57 years old.

In their contributions to the history of Denmark under occupation, Jørgen Hæstrup and Hartvig Frisch set out from opposite positions but moved closer to each other. Hæstrup started as a committed historian of the resistance movement but eventually embraced also the administrative relations with the German authorities after 29 August, in that way ending up more as a historian of the occupation years. Frisch began as an intellectual and politician devoted to the cause of the Social Democratic party and the policy of the coalition government but gradually acknowledged the role of the resistance movement, eventually focusing his attention on the relationship between different reactions to occupation.

Both writers found a synthesis of the conduct of the government and the activities of the resistance. For Hæstrup, well aware of the conflict between accommodation and resistance, it took the form of a compromise, between the line favoured by the politicians and the course pursued by the leaders of the resistance. For Frisch, eager to reconcile the position taken by his party, the government and the rest of official Denmark in the earlier years with the attitude adopted by the people towards the end of the war, the synthesis found expression in the notion of continuity, between legal and passive opposition and illegal and active resistance.[38] They broadly shared the notion of a complementarity of limited cooperation and active resistance and the image of a nation united in the pursuit of freedom. Thus, Hæstrup and Frisch may be seen as fathers of the consensus interpretation of occupation history.

Their interpretations of recent history reflected the general mood of the Danish population in the period of liberation. After years of suppressing deeply rooted anti-German feelings and hiding growing pro-allied sympathies, and with the ignominious memory of 9 April 1940 still in mind, most Danes were able to enjoy the ecstasy of May 1945, and perhaps even share the triumph of victory sweeping through Western Europe when the Germans finally capitulated. Other Danes, by now aware of having been clinging too long to governmental policy and having been less than forthcoming in their support for the resistance movement or perhaps, in some cases, even having something to hide about their past conduct, had their own reasons for joining in the general jubilation. Whether moved by relief and triumph or more by regret and even shame, the bulk of the population experienced a rush of patriotic emotions, which turned into a wave of national solidarity broad enough to submerge, for a while, most recent divisions of policy and attitude.

The consensus interpretation was also conditioned by the interests and concerns of the principal actors on the political and social scene of post-war Denmark. For the major parties and their leaders, eager to reassert their authority in the country, the notions of complementarity of cooperation and resistance, and of continuity between passive and active opposition, were welcome representations. So they were for much of the rest of official Denmark, including the royal family, the central and local administration, the armed forces, the remains of the police force and the major economic organizations, many of whose representatives felt that the difficulties they had faced during the occupation often had not been fully appreciated by the public they represented. Even for the resistance movement and its leaders there were advantages of a historical interpretation which stressed the quality of concord between different reactions to the occupation. It not only served to legitimize the existence and wartime activities of that movement but also presented it as the spearhead of opposition to the Germans, thus reducing the government and politicians to a preparatory function and secondary position in the struggle.

In the post-war months the foremost manifestation of compromise and consensus between the two sides was the composition of the liberation government, half politicians and half resistance leaders. Even in subsequent years there was some correspondence between the historical interpretation and the political situation of the country. From the later 1940s, Danish politics were conditioned externally by global tension between the superpowers and their allies, East–West division of Germany and Europe, and Danish membership of the US-led military alliance NATO. In such circumstances, the consensus theory of recent history had certain advantages, both as a means of coming to terms with the immediate past and as a guide in dealing with the current situation of the country. First, it rested, implicitly or explicitly, on a firm commitment to the democratic form of government, as developed in Denmark and other Nordic countries since the nineteenth century. Second, it was directed against Nazi Germany and its supporters and sympathizers in Denmark. Both Hæstrup and Frisch excluded collaborators from their analysis and interpretation of occupation history. Even Scavenius, with his policy of willing and active cooperation with the Germans, was considered beyond the pale. Third, the consensus construction gave less than full credit to the crucial work of the Communists in the resistance. Frisch's account was coloured by a degree of animosity towards the Communist party, the long-standing rival of the Social Democrats in the competition for working-class support. Hæstrup's focus on the link between SOE and Danish resistance gave his treatment of the period a marked list towards the Western allies.

Thus, in relation to both domestic and international politics, the consensus interpretation of Denmark's occupation history was not out of tune with the circumstances prevailing in the post-war years and the first decades of the cold war. For a long time, it remained the standard interpretation. It characterized various other scholarly works about that period, whether written by historians, journalists or politicians, and influenced many personal memoirs as well as numerous works of post-war fiction. Thus, it played a decisive part in the shaping of the nation's collective memory of its most traumatic experience in the twentieth century. It was not till the 1970s that a younger set of professional historians first challenged the consensus construction.

3.2. Conflict

Jørgen Hæstrup and Hartvig Frisch, and other writers of the post-war decades who had lived through the occupation, had experienced the conflicts that had divided the nation during much of the war and had also followed the developments that had shaped public opinion after the liberation. Their writings, whether motivated by a duty to honour the resistance movement or a concern to justify the political leaders, may be seen as attempts to come to terms with political and moral issues which had been raised by years of Nazi occupation, and which still were troubling the nation. In their search for a synthesis of cooperation and resistance, they tended to pass lightly over the political passivity and national introspection which had characterized most of the dismal first years after the invasion. Sometimes they were also inclined to gloss over the deepening divisions that had marked politics and society in the dramatic year leading up to the turning-point in Danish–German relations. They preferred to highlight the patriotic spirit and national solidarity that had come to the fore in the invigorating last period of the occupation, and had carried Denmark through the liberation and into the post-war period.

Most of the next generation of historians had only childhood memories of the occupation, and knew its history mainly from the writings and teaching of their elders. Not so influenced by the *résistancialism*, which in Denmark, as in other occupied countries, had coloured most post-war thinking about recent history, they were freer than earlier writers to scrutinize critically the efforts of resistance and to examine dispassionately the policy of cooperation. Sceptical about the notion of a national concord of opposition, they were able to recognize the conflict between opposite reactions to German occupation. Highly professional in their approach, they questioned various assumptions made and challenged some findings reached by the first scholars in the field. Thus they helped to dispel certain myths which for some time had seemed set to become part of the national heritage.

The revisionist wave got off to a dramatic start with a doctoral dissertation submitted to Odense University in 1971 by Aage Trommer, a member of the private group of former pupils, colleagues and friends formed round Hæstrup, and inspired by him to explore various aspects of occupation history.[39] Since 1960 Trommer had been researching the history of resistance in south Jutland, the part of Denmark known as region 3 in SOE's division of the country. In the course of this work, he had developed a special interest in sabotage, particularly railway sabotage, and had decided to carry out a separate study of this form of resistance, not only in that region but in all of Jutland and other parts of the country.

His aim was to assess the military significance to the allied powers of the railway sabotage carried out in Denmark during the Second World War. The assumption had always been that the two most important Danish contributions to the allied cause were the supply of military and political intelligence throughout the war and the anti-German sabotage in the last period of the occupation. Earlier writers dealing with the subject, foremost among them Hæstrup, had asserted, or assumed, that sabotage of the railway system had been an activity of considerable tactical significance, primarily because it delayed the transport of German troops from Denmark, or from Norway through Denmark, to various theatres of war south of the country. Sabotage leaders, including Vagn Bennike and Anton Toldstrup in Jutland, had expressed similar views, reinforcing their convictions with quotations from statements or messages from allied sources. Thus, Bennike could quote 'a high-ranking British officer' who had told him that, while earlier it had been assumed that the Germans could take two divisions through Jutland in a month, after the sabotage had reached its peak that figure had been reduced to only half a division.[40] Such writers, whether historians or resistance leaders, could also argue that the reactions of the Germans had demonstrated just how important it was for the occupying power to prevent or suppress such acts of sabotage.

In an attempt to verify claims of this nature, Trommer carried out a statistical examination of the effects of railway sabotage in Denmark. His most important primary sources were the archives of the Danish State Railways (DSB), which included timetables, lists of traffic movements, surveys of completed movements and reports of acts of sabotage, whether expected or carried out. To help him identify the army units carried, he used German military archives (available in the Danish national archives). Supplementary sources included a number of illegal wartime archives, including Vagn Bennike's, as well as some post-war reports provided by former members of the resistance movement.

Linking the identity of the German units carried by rail with the delays and disturbance caused by sabotage, he found that the effect had usually been minimal and the tactical importance nearly always insignificant. In his analysis, he applied a distinction used by the British in the development of their tactics of serial bombardment, between attrition and interception. The principle of attrition, aimed at the gradual wearing down of the general capacity of the railway system through numerous local actions, had been behind a good deal of Danish sabotage. However, it had proved practically ineffectual. To hold up German traffic that way, Trommer explained, was like trying to shoot an elephant with the pellets of an airgun.

The way of interception, designed to stop or delay certain traffic at a particular place and time, had been potentially more promising. But it required reliable advance information about the nature and timing of individual German movements as well as careful planning and coordination of the action required. To meet those conditions had rarely been possible. Except for two acts of sabotage, one in early February and another in mid-April 1945, which had created delays of possible tactical importance, such sabotage, he concluded, seemed to have had little effect on German movements.

Some of the responsibility for the poor result, he pointed out, lay with SOE, whose officers might not fully have thought out the tactics of railway sabotage. While encouraging and supporting such activities in the occupied countries, they also seemed to have failed to set up the organizational framework for effective sabotage of the intercepting kind. It was even possible, he suggested, that SOE, known to have been engaged in rivalry with other military bodies in Britain, for reasons of its own might have been inclined to exaggerate the importance for the allied cause of anti-German sabotage in general.[41]

Trommer stressed that his investigation was confined to the military effects of railway sabotage, and admitted that a detailed examination of the political or of the moral and ideological results of such sabotage might lead to different conclusions. Yet, in a postscript, he did touch upon the political importance of sabotage. In regard to domestic politics, he discussed its possible effects in the crisis of August 1943. Rejecting the common view that it was sabotage, of various kinds, which had triggered off the strike movement of that month, he asserted that it was only one among several possible factors leading to the strikes.

The primary significance of sabotage in that particular political context, he suggested, was to help prepare minds, on both the Danish and the German side, for recognizing that the days of the policy of negotiation were fast running out.[42]

In the international political context, too, it was difficult to separate sabotage from other influences at work. In Danish relations with the Soviet Union this form of resistance, in the earlier period very much the work of Communists, might have played a part in securing representation for the 'fighting Denmark' in Moscow, but apparently was not important enough to gain Soviet recognition of the state as a *de facto* ally. In relations with the Western allies, he concluded tentatively, sabotage was no more important than supply of intelligence and formation of military groups, both of which occasionally seemed to enjoy priority in allied military control and planning. Another factor of possible significance, he noted, might have been the anti-German and pro-allied attitude of the Danish public.

The public defence of the dissertation, which attracted about 800 people and lasted five hours, caused a stir. The candidate not only had to deal with the normal academic scrutiny of sources, methods and findings. Born in 1930, he also had to face verbal attacks and sarcastic comments from former members of the resistance movement, who could not reconcile his judgements on their work with their own recollections and convictions. Tage Kaarsted, an officially appointed opponent, and others criticized him strongly for having based his work almost entirely on statistics and contemporary reports, when so many of the actors involved were still alive and available. Another professor wondered whether railway sabotage had not been of military significance by tying down German troops who could have been useful at the fronts. Trommer denied this, arguing that the soldiers patrolling and guarding tracks and stations had been useless convalescents, but admitted that he had not examined this matter closely. The more passionate reactions to the dissertation came from former freedom fighters and others who identified with the resistance movement. They aimed their criticism mainly at the candidate's lack of personal experience of resistance. 'Unfortunately, sir,' Jens Toldstrup said pointedly about his work, 'you have overlooked the fact that a war was going on.'[43]

Two years later came Trommer's *Modstandsarbejde i nærbillede* (resistance activities close-up), a detailed account of the emergence, development and organization of the resistance in region 3. The sections dealing with the growth of resistance there cast a new light on recruitment for illegal work. Indeed, the author explicitly contradicted the notion of spontaneous recruitment advanced by Hæstrup. Thus, by implication, he dealt a blow to the conception of a people united in active or potential struggle with the occupying power, which was inherent in the consensual interpretation of occupation history.

Trommer showed convincingly that the typical origins of the resistance movement were not spontaneous reactions of numerous lone individuals exasperated by foreign occupation, but willing engagement of a limited number of members of certain political parties. On the whole, such activists came from the towns, while people rooted in the countryside gained a reputation for being more passive and, for a long time, reluctant to become engaged. Yet, even in the towns, until well into 1943, it was only a small number who became actively involved. The political parties to which most of them were affiliated were on the extremes of the political spectrum, the Communists on the left and Danish Unity and an activist wing of the Conservative youth organization on the right. The two first parties had for long been opposed to the parliamentary system, often accusing it of being out of date and corrupt. The reputation of such people could be a handicap in recruitment from among people with less extremist political views, especially in the earlier period.[44]

The pioneers in the resistance were the Communists, who were forced into illegal existence in June 1941. The others came mostly later, after the involvement of SOE, and often through cross-country clubs, scout associations and other youth organizations. Though the recruitment broadened and the numbers grew after August 1943, the Communists and Danish Unity, both represented in the freedom council, often maintained their leading roles. The initiatives for illegal activities in the region nearly always came from outside and from above, ultimately from Copenhagen, rather than from the level of groups and individuals. The major part of the work of the local leaders was to organize and, especially, to reorganize in order to repair the structural damage caused, in one town after another, by arrests, made first by Danish police and later by the Gestapo. In a certain sense, Trommer found, illegal work in south Jutland never went beyond the organizational stage.[45]

Another doctoral dissertation with revisionist aims appeared in 1979. Hans Kirchhoff's three-volume work *Augustoprøret 1943 – Samarbejdspolitikkens fald* (The August revolt 1943 – The collapse of the policy of cooperation), based on 10 years of painstaking research, described the causation of the break with the policy of cooperation and analysed the political and ideological dimensions of the conflict between resistance and cooperation. The author started by making it clear that his exposition was revisionistic in relation to the consensual conception characteristic of earlier national historiography. Rejecting the claimed concord between the popular uprising in August and the governmental rejection of German demands, he questioned the spontaneity of the strike movement and disputed the determination of the politicians, and others in positions of authority, to breach relations with the occupying power.[46]

After grass-roots research in all of the towns affected by anti-German demonstrations and strikes in August 1943, Kirchhoff was able to answer the question whether the movement was spontaneous or organized. He started by pointing out that when historians resort to describing a complicated course of events, such as a mass strike, as spontaneous, it is usually because they have omitted to examine the matter more closely, and have failed to appreciate that such an occurrence simply cannot come about without at least a certain amount of organization. On the other hand, when journalists or politicians use the same descriptive term, it is more likely to be for political reasons. Thus, when Communists, some writing at the same time and some later, stressed the spontaneous nature of the strikes, he thought, it was because they wanted to make them fit into their political programme of popular front. It was for the same reason that they invented the term *folkestrejke* (popular strike), which eventually took the place of 'general strike' in common parlance as well as in much post-war writing.[47]

Kirchhoff found no evidence to support the view, common at the time, that the rebellion was set off and managed by some 'general staff' in London or Copenhagen. The British authorities, caught by surprise, found it hard to catch up with the explosive developments in Denmark. In Copenhagen, even the committee of the Communist party was practically isolated from the rebellion, which was largely confined to major and minor provincial towns, and left out nearly till the end of the strikes. In the towns affected, the Communist leadership tended in the beginning to be cautious and reluctant to become involved, only jumping on the bandwagon when the strikes had already started seriously. For the party as a whole, committed to the tactics of popular front, it was important not to put obstacles in the way of the projected united front of the working class by appearing too aggressive for the comfort of the Social Democrats. However, once the town strikes were established, and supported by some sections of the wider public, the party stepped in and assumed control where it could, pressing for continuation of local strikes and calling for a general strike.

The real initiators and organizers of the local strikes seem to have been at the lowest level of decision-making, the factory floor. Here a dedicated Communist or a Social Democratic activist, perhaps encouraged by articles in illegal papers or by members of a local sabotage group, could take the first steps towards organizing a strike. Whether, as in the mass strike in Copenhagen the following summer, the initiative came from a Communist shop steward acting independently or from another worker of radical convictions, he did not stand alone in the summer of 1943. In building up, and maintaining, support for a strike, he could draw on fellow workers by then motivated by a potent mixture of feelings and beliefs – dissatisfaction, frustration and animosity as well as hope and expectation. Here the two most favourable conditioning influences at work in generating support for the strikes seem to have been a shared hatred of the Germans and all they stood for and a growing expectation that they would lose the war and be out of the country before long. Thus, the origins of the strikes may be seen as a match of individual initiative and spontaneous response.

In relation to enmity towards the Germans as a conditioning factor in the causation of strikes, Kirchhoff revealed another myth about the occupation. In 1943 and later it was widely believed that the occupying forces were pursuing a policy of deliberate violence in the streets and gratuitous brutality towards the demonstrators, from which it followed that the Danish youths involved in demonstrations and caught in clashes were essentially reacting to the conduct of the German troops. However, he found that the aggressive side in the clashes was usually the youths, and that the German forces, at all levels of command, showed considerable restraint practically everywhere. The Danes interpreted the German reaction as a sign of weakness and pushed on with their demonstrations and strikes. Paradoxically, German caution thus became an incentive to Danish challenge and resistance.[48]

Having dealt with the notion of the August rebellion as a spontaneous manifestation of the national spirit, a gigantic public improvisation, Kirchhoff turned to the reactions of those whom he described collectively as the opposition to the protest movement. They included practically all the authorities of official Denmark, government, parliament, central administration and local government as well as trade unions and other major economic organizations. Contrary to some later representation, they were all largely against the escalating street violence and spreading strikes which they recognized as a challenge to the government and an attack on the conduct of its relations with the German authorities. However, many civilian individuals, especially at local levels of administration, were caught in a conflict between their official duties and their private sympathies. So were many members and units of the police forces across the country. While in some towns the police made themselves very unpopular by reacting violently to revolts in the streets, elsewhere many officers rather took the side of the rebels, which angered politicians and many leaders of organizations – and did not escape the attention of the Germans either.

Throughout, the overriding concern of the trade union leaders was to put an end to the crisis. While claiming to be moved by responsibility for the welfare of the population, they also had narrower considerations in mind, namely to protect their organizations and influence against both external and internal enemies. They were afraid of a German take-over and much disturbed by the growing influence of the Communists. While the German threat turned out to be unjustified, the danger of the Communists remained. For the Social Democratic leaders, in the trade unions as in the party, the Communist tactic of united front was a challenge to their organizations, their power and their policies. Hence they were against sabotage, street demonstrations and illegal strikes, all of which appeared to them as exercises in united-front tactics initiated and managed by Communists. The hostile reaction to the rebellion found clear expression in the Social Democratic press across the country. One of the many papers quoted by Kirchhoff was *Sydsjællands Socialdemokrat*, which stated that 'we, as Danes, have no interest in helping the warring parties in this terrible war, we have only our country, ourselves and our families to consider, and there must be no other consideration when we act'.[49] The Radical Liberal press took the same line, though the tone was more moderate.

The trade unions were not the only organizations hostile to the rebellion. Most of the employers' associations and the chambers of commerce wanted to maintain the political and diplomatic status quo of the country. This view was reflected in the Liberal and the Conservative press, though their support for the governmental policy of cooperation was qualified, especially in some articles in Conservative papers.

Though the strikes spread to shops, offices and other non-industrial places of work and attracted a good deal of middle-class support, the rebellion never became a case of a united people taking up resistance against an occupying power, as it was later represented. Most people were passive, Kirchhoff concluded from his analysis, many were hesitant and uncertain and, most important, large groups of people with position and power actively opposed the rebellion. Thus, the crisis became a profoundly divisive experience for the nation. The aim of the August movement was to put an end to the policy of cooperation.

The concern of the establishment was to maintain the existing relationship with the German authorities. The basic issue was between two different reactions to occupation, defiance and resistance or negotiation and cooperation.

In his later writings, Kirchhoff made his findings available to a wider public. His main theme was not, as in most earlier writings about the occupation, the struggle between Danes and the occupying power. As indicated in the title and subtitle of a book published in 1987, *Kamp eller tilpasning. Politikerne og modstanden 1940–45* (Struggle or adaptation. The politicians and the resistance 1940–45), his concern remained the division within the nation.[50] Such a conflict, he pointed out in the introduction, could not be solved by a historian. It was essentially an issue of moral and existential nature. All a historian could do was to analyse the character and course of the conflict, reveal its forms of appearance and its motives, and try to outline its consequences. Even that, however, was not an easy task. It was a struggle against ignorance, prejudice and myths.[51]

One of the many myths he unmasked in this and later writings was that of the Social Democratic leaders all along wanting a rupture with the German authorities. Refuting Hartvig Frisch's tendentious presentation and interpretation of Hedtoft-Hansen's speech on 13 February 1941, he showed that the Social Democratic leadership, guided by the party's own survival strategy, was determined to postpone and avoid such a rupture and to continue the policy of cooperation with the occupying power.[52] When the government, under Buhl's leadership, decided to reject the German demands in August 1943 and accept the consequences, it did so primarily for reasons of domestic policy, namely fear of the growing influence of the Communists. In terms of the relationship with the Germans, the ministers always regretted the breach. Indeed, they managed discreetly to continue their practice of negotiating and cooperating, only operating through the central administration.

Both his earlier and his later works leave the impression that Kirchhoff's heart is not with the men responsible for the policy of cooperation. In a brief and personal passage in the introduction to his dissertation he went as far as offering the opinion that cooperation had outlived its day by 1943. Its *sacro egoismo* and its ever more explicit defence of certain political interests, and a certain political system, he explained, had led him to reject it.[53] A look at Trommer's major works from the early 1970s rather leaves the opposite impression of the personal attitudes of this author. Devoting many years to revealing the narrow recruitment for the early resistance and to questioning the military significance of a particular kind of sabotage – incidentally also casting doubt on its political importance – would scarcely be a likely research programme for a historian with an emotional commitment to the resistance.

However, there is no suggestion that political bias or personal motivations undermined the scholarship and compromised the findings of either of the two historians. Offensive or unwelcome to various interested parties though their conclusions might be, they could not be ignored. They played an important part in dispelling myths about the origins and achievements of active resistance as well as about the attitudes and conduct of the political parties and the major organizations before, during and after the rebellion of August 1943.

Once the practice of negotiating and cooperating with the occupying power no longer was seen, or at least presented, as complementary to active resistance, it became possible not only to explore the actual conflict between opposite reactions to occupation but also to examine the policy of cooperation by itself and assess it on its own merits. One result was a shift of focus in some revisionist writings towards the earlier years of the occupation. Several younger historians turned their attention to the period after the invasion, when there was no resistance movement and when negotiating and coming to terms with the German authorities to the great majority of people seemed the most reasonable, and perhaps the only possible way of dealing with the occupying power in the given national and international situation.

Here one of the earliest and most significant studies was Henrik S. Nissen's *1940. Studier i forhandlingspolitikken og samarbejdspolitikken* (1940. Studies in the negotiation policy and the cooperation policy), which appeared as a doctoral dissertation in 1973. It took the form of a number of more or less separate studies of relations among the five old political parties and of interaction between the government and the German authorities from April 1940 to January 1941. In the introduction to the book, the author indicated his revisionist intentions by stressing that he would not follow established historical practice and deal with Danish occupation politics from the point of view associated with the post-1945 judicial reckoning, which basically reflected the victory of the allied powers in the war. Rather than apportioning praise and blame according to moral and legal criteria developed in very different circumstances, he would view the policies of 1940 in terms of the conditions applying at the time when they were formulated.[54] At that stage of the war, the basic external influences conditioning Danish policy and conduct were the highly successful German military campaigns and the apparently very slim prospects of ultimate victory for Britain and its allies.

Another indication of Nissen's insistence on not passing judgement from hindsight was his tentative choice of terms for the two policies he studied. He avoided linking the word cooperation to Danish–German interaction in 1940, and thus departed from the terminology introduced by the illegal press in the later years of the war, and followed by post-war critics of wartime governmental policy as well as by many historians of his own generation. Instead he chose the more neutral term negotiation policy, which had been introduced by the officials of the foreign ministry and retrospectively used by Scavenius in his memoirs, and readily accepted by other politicians who had been involved in the post-invasion relationship with the Germans. Negotiation, and the accompanying words accommodation and concessions, seemed more suitable for a state of affairs in which neither the Danish nor the German party was quite clear about the form their interaction would take and the consequences it would have. It was only later, when the fortunes of the war had changed decisively, that the conduct and policy of the government in 1940 could be recognized as the beginning of an established relationship of cooperation between unequal parties, and thus be condemned as in several ways advantageous to the enemy.

The term cooperation Nissen reserved for the relationship among the five political parties, which soon after the invasion managed to overcome their differences and form a coalition government. Their policy of cooperation enjoyed wide popular support, and became the basis for the government's policy of negotiation with the occupation authorities.[55]

Nissen recognized that Danish negotiation policy was conditioned by international and national circumstances, ultimately by the course of the war among the great powers and more immediately by the situation of a small nation occupied by a great power. However, he also knew that policy is made by human beings deliberately acting and reacting within the limits of the situation in which they find themselves. Thus, he could analyse the disagreement between P. Munch, Radical Liberal foreign minister during the first few months of the occupation, and Christmas Møller, chairman of the Conservative party. Munch, adopting a pragmatic approach, pursued negotiations with the Germans as a way of settling matters that had to be dealt with. Christmas Møller, more concerned than most of his fellow ministers about the Danish image abroad and afraid that the country might be accused of collaborating with the enemy, warned of the dangers of being on a slippery slope of negotiating and giving way to the Germans.

Subsequently, in a long chapter about the negotiations in July and August about German plans for a future customs and monetary union and the Danish initiative in that respect, Nissen presented the confrontation between Scavenius and Christmas Møller about Danish policy. At a crucial stage of the negotiations Scavenius, moved by a cool small-state realism and guided by his principle of removing the nearest danger, insisted on accepting the German demands, while Christmas Møller, basing his case on German promises to respect Danish independence made on 9 April, refused to accept a voluntary renunciation of certain Danish rights involved in the projected post-war European order.

Such, and many other, debates about Danish policy in 1940 involved a range of politicians and sometimes also a few organizational leaders. Narrating the exchanges in some detail, Nissen made a point of presenting the position and arguments of each party sympathetically. He recognized that disagreements were essentially about the tactics to be employed in dealing with the Germans, and acknowledged that all participants were motivated by a determination to defend Danish interests. He accepted the policy of negotiation, which rested on the capitulation agreement of 9 April, and did not question the need to make concessions to accommodate the Germans in the country. Indeed, he saw no acceptable alternative. If the negotiations with the Germans broke down, the worst result, he believed, could be either direct rule by the occupying power or a collaborationist government based on the small Danish Nazi party, neither of which would be acceptable to the public, the great majority of which supported the negotiation policy. Moreover, the wave of a self-defensive national awakening sweeping the country in the summer and autumn of 1940 soon reinforced support for both the king and the coalition government as well as for its policy towards Germany.

Nissen did not see the negotiation policy as a step towards, or preparation for, active resistance to the occupation power. From the outset, its most important result was simply that negotiations did take place, and that the Danish authorities thus avoided becoming merely the administrative agents of Germany in an occupied country. The policy worked as long as it was possible to persuade the German authorities that they, too, had an interest in negotiating. The drawback was that it entailed concessions which tended to compromise what remained of the asserted Danish neutrality.[56] Thus, the policy became an exercise in maintaining the notion of sovereignty at the expense of the image of neutrality.

Nissen assumed that the policy of negotiation and the policy of cooperation were interdependent, and that both were dependent on the development of the world war and the state of public opinion in Denmark. The negotiating position of the Danes rested on the cohesion of the coalition government and on its parliamentary support. The cooperation of the political parties was based on shared recognition of a practical need to negotiate with the Germans and, in some respects, also on calculated advantages of doing so. As long as there was no prospect of an early German defeat in the war, he concluded his analysis, the political leadership and the Danish public were largely united in support of the policy of negotiation, provided concessions to Germany could appear as being necessary.

The two parties to the negotiations shared an interest in their continuation. The Danish negotiators, anxious to secure some acceptance of the sovereign rights of the state, defended or pursued diverse national interests in a changing situation. The Germans, preferring to secure control of the occupied country with a minimum of efforts, sought administrative, propagandist and, eventually, also economic advantages from the relationship. After various crises in the negotiations, in January 1941 an equilibrium was re-established, between German expectations and Danish willingness to make concessions. But it was an unstable equilibrium. Few people could then have told, Nissen observed, from which quarter it, in due course, would receive the decisive push.[57]

One step further in the historians' rehabilitation of the policy and practice of negotiating and cooperating with the Germans was taken the following decade, with a detailed study and thorough analysis of the events and context of 9 April. In 1987 Hans Branner, then best known for his work on neutral Denmark between the great powers at the outbreak of the First World War, published *Den 9. april – et politisk lærestykke?* (The 9th of April – a political lesson?). As indicated by the title, the book questioned the lesson often drawn from the traumatic experience of that day, according to which the German invasion and Danish capitulation had been largely results of the foreign and security policy adopted by Denmark in the pre-war period. Like his earlier work, the book was distinguished by the author's willingness and ability to combine the approach and methods of traditional historians with those of modern political scientists, in particular students of international relations.

The book, Branner explained in the preface, was an attempt, on the one hand, to bring together existing knowledge about the background for what happened on 9 April and, on the other hand, to present such knowledge in an overall setting, with a view to clarifying the basic conditions governing Danish foreign policy. At one level, he would give an account of concrete historical events and connections between them. At a higher level, he would deal with some matters of principle relating to the actual situation in April 1940, and would discuss the freedom of action of the Danish government, the major factors influencing its decision-making and the broad pattern of its foreign policy. At an even more abstract level, he would take up the same questions, but in a context more detached from the immediate historical situation, and would discuss them in the broad perspective of Danish foreign policy in the twentieth century. A major thesis of the book, he pointed out, was that the interpretation of the events of 9 April which had informed both public consciousness and political practice was far too unambiguous.[58]

In the theoretical part of the book, Branner dealt first with the government's freedom of action and decision-making on 9 April. He concluded that the decisions made in the morning of that day, namely to capitulate militarily, comply with the German demands and remain in office, were highly rational. Even with some machinery for crisis management in place, more reliable information available and greater awareness of possible alternatives, the government could not have reached other and better decisions, given its political objectives.[59] The decisive concern of the principal decision-makers was survival, of the population in the immediate situation and of the country as an independent state in post-war Europe. Divergent opinions, especially on the timing of the capitulation, as voiced by the army's representative general Prior and apparently motivated by military and political considerations as well as by moral feelings, did not affect the decisions.

The opposition parties did not take part in the discussions but – with the exception of Christmas Møller – did not oppose the decisions reached. However, their tacit consent rested on policies and judgements very different from those of the two governing parties. According to the Liberals and the Conservatives, the reasons why the government found itself in a situation of no choice in the morning of 9 April were its deficient defence policy in the 1930s and its irresponsible passivity in the days leading up to the invasion. In their view, 9 April marked the defeat of Social Democratic and Radical Liberal defence and foreign policy. That was the judgement which, towards the end of the occupation and after the war, found expression in the 'never more a 9th of April' slogan.

Though linked to only one particular interpretation of the experiences of 9 April, that motto was used in the post-war campaign to put an end to defenceless neutrality and start a rearmament programme. However, the political influence of this lesson of the recent past had been grossly exaggerated, Branner argued. When Denmark in 1949 took leave of its long-standing security and defence policy and joined the military alliance NATO the basic reason, he explained, was a radical change in the regional international situation, which now made it possible for the country to secure membership of such an alliance.[60]

The choices made and decisions taken by king and government on 9 April gained their real political importance by becoming the basis for Danish policy towards the occupying power for the following several years. Themselves representing a continuation of the course adopted by the Social Democratic and Radical Liberal coalition in the mid and late 1930s, they prepared the way for the broader coalition government's subsequent dealings with the representatives of Hitlerite Germany, in the more trying conditions of the period up to 1943. Thus, motivated by a determination to secure a degree of national independence by avoiding provoking the Germans, the Danish response to the invasion gave the policy of negotiation a good start.

The term Branner used to describe Danish foreign policy before and after 9 April was adaptation policy. He had taken it from the writings of James Rosenau, who saw all conduct of foreign policy as a matter of adapting to domestic and foreign demands and pressures and, for comparative purposes, distinguished various types of adaptation. In the concluding chapters of his book, Branner went on to examine the Danish policy in a comparative frame and present it in a historical perspective. Here he drew on, and contributed to, both the comparative analysis of foreign policy – admittedly one of the more problematic branches of the study of international politics – and the growing body of theoretical writings about the international conduct of small states.

During the occupation, when Denmark enjoyed only nominal independence and could maintain no more than a semblance of neutrality, its foreign policy could be seen as an extreme version of a particular type of adaptation. However, taken as a whole, Danish policy before and during the war was not unique, but in its essence comparable to that of a number of other European small states. In the later 1930s half a dozen such states, all affected by growing disillusionment with the League of Nations and rising tension among the great powers, took much the same course as Denmark and moved closer to a neutral position. However, their neutrality developed some novel characteristics. At the expense of the classical ideals of impartiality and equidistance, which had been associated with traditional neutrality, they allowed themselves to seek protection against the risk of being drawn into future hostilities by favouring the power that represented the greatest threat to peace. As in Denmark, their concern with security took precedence of their ideological sympathies with the democratic Western powers. Since Germany had become the strongest and most aggressive power in Europe, the partiality of those small neutrals also ran counter to traditional balance-of-power principles of foreign policy. The ultimate concern of the neutrals leaning towards Germany was about their survival as independent states after a major war.

In a closer comparison of Danish, Swedish and Norwegian policy and conduct towards Germany before and during the war, he again found parallels. Here, of course, there were some obvious differences between Denmark and its Scandinavian neighbours, in matters of both politics, diplomacy and defence. However, when viewed in the context of the three countries' location in relation to the great powers, those differences seemed less glaring. The underlying principle of adapting to the international environment by avoiding to provoke Germany and steering an anti balance-of power course operated in both the Swedish and the Danish case. The more general principle of adapting to the great-power constellation in the vicinity might again be seen at work in both the Danish and the Norwegian case in the days before and after 9 April 1940, even though Denmark was squarely within the German sphere of interest while Norway was of greater interest to the British. Whether compared with other neutrals in general or with its neighbours in particular, Branner concluded, Danish policy was not fundamentally different from that of comparable states. When, in conditions of crisis, it took different decisions and ended up in a different situation the basic reason was its greater dependence on Germany.

However, this defence of Danish policy towards Germany up to 1943 did lead the author to enquire how far adaptation could be taken without becoming meaningless. If its ultimate aim was to defend the independence of a country against not only military but also economic and cultural threats, such adaptation, if carried too far, could itself undermine national independence. From this point of view, he admitted, the more extreme form of adaptation policy adopted by Denmark in the 1930s and 1940s was of a character rather different from that of many other small states.

To broaden the basis of his analysis of small-state behaviour in crisis situations, Branner expanded the historical perspective and, in the concluding pages of the book, presented a brief overview of more than a hundred years of Danish security policy. Here he identified four different ways of reacting to threats to national security, three of which had come into play in the foreign policy of the Social Democratic and Radical Liberal coalition government of the 1930s. One, which had forerunners in the decades after 1864 and in the period before the First World War, had been described as pilot-fish policy, and involved steering close to the nearest great power. Another, also dating back to the nineteenth century, was known as lie-as-dead policy, calling for extreme passivity in international politics. The third, associated in particular with the inter-war period, and sometimes described as demonstration policy, had a more active character. Relying on joint action by small states, it was aimed at reforming international society by basing it on the rule of law instead of on the exercise of power. The three lines of policy coexisted till the end of the 1930s, when the pilot-fish course decidedly gained the upper hand in Danish foreign policy.

The fourth way of dealing with threats to Danish security, namely the policy of strength, had its roots in the earlier centuries of modern European history, when Denmark–Norway was still a major power in regional politics, but did not seriously come into play till 1949. By joining NATO, Denmark committed itself to a form of balance-of-power policy. Over the next several decades it participated politically and militarily in the activities of the American-led alliance, though with a number of significant reservations, which again were motivated mainly by a concern not to provoke the threatening great power and potential enemy. At the same time, it also continued to pursue, with other small states, the demonstration policy, mainly through active participation in numerous international organizations.

One of the most salient points made by Branner, in both his earlier and his later work, was that small states, even in situations of crisis, often have rather more freedom of action in foreign policy than their political leaders realize or acknowledge. Even those politicians who, typically in the name of small-state realism, invoke the doctrine of necessity have made a political and moral choice, he observed. Thus, though the forces of external compulsion were particularly strong on 9 April, the course taken by the Danish decision-makers was not the only possibility. However, the decisions they made he found the best possible in the circumstances. Nor does he seem to have any quarrel against the policy of defenceless and pro-German neutrality that led up to the Danish reactions to German invasion, or indeed against the policy of negotiation and concessions that flowed from the compliant decision-making that morning. The resistance movement, whose leaders and members, in later and, admittedly, far more favourable international situations, made different moral and political choices, is barely mentioned in the book. In his personal engagement, Branner, like Nissen, seems to be more with the government of negotiation and judicious accommodation than with the movement of defiance and armed resistance.

While Hæstrup and Frisch, both accomplished stylists with an educational mission, had aimed their writings at a wider public, the first generation of revisionist historians, self-consciously scholarly in their critical analysis, wrote more for each other, and of course for members of the public seriously interested in the debate about the occupation years of Danish history. Some of the works of the earlier writers are classics in the more literary tradition of Danish history-writing. The principal publications of those revisionist historians stand out as contributions to professional historiography.

3.3. Discord

The second wave of revisionist writings about the occupation period in Danish history developed in the 1990s, and was still running high well after the turn of the century. Largely the work of younger historians without personal recollections of the occupation and its aftermath, such writings left behind the major themes that had occupied the two previous generations, namely the shifting relationship between the Danish and German authorities and the resurgent conflict between official Denmark and the resistance movement. Untouched by wartime pressures and animosities and unmoved by post-war anti-German passions, the new generation of historians turned their attention to various groups of collaborators who had been largely ignored or given short shrift by earlier historians. Reacting to the harsh treatment some such people had suffered during the war and the severe sentences many of them had received soon after the liberation, those historians set out to examine the cases of groups of individuals who had been deemed guilty of unpatriotic conduct during the occupation.

Collaboration took many forms. A distinction has been made between economic and other ways of collaborating with the occupying power and its agents. While the former on the whole presented a grey area both morally and legally, the latter types appeared to be more clear-cut cases of unpatriotic behaviour. Economic collaboration covered companies and individuals gainfully supplying goods or services to German parties as well as workers providing labour for German employers whether in Germany or in Denmark. Both kinds were generally motivated by varying combinations of need, opportunity and official encouragement.

The last factor became a consideration of some importance in the judicial reckoning that, at the demand of the freedom council and on the basis of retroactive laws, took place in the post-war years. Many so-called *værnemagere*, especially some larger ones with long records of collaboration, could plead that they had traded with the Germans with the permission or encouragement, sometimes even at the explicit request, of the government or one of the established trade organizations, and thus had acted in the national interest as perceived at the time. For the workers it could be said that they, in a situation of high unemployment, not only had been driven by personal need but also strongly encouraged by their trade unions, and in some cases even pressed by ministerial authorities to accept work from the Germans.

Yet, a small number of *værnemagere* were punished for initiating what was called improper economic cooperation with the occupying power, while a larger number were sentenced to return profits deemed unlawful. A good many, especially larger companies, avoided being charged or escaped being convicted. Among the workers who had been in German employment, only those who had done uniformed guard duties in Germany were prosecuted. At the time, the judicial treatment of economic collaborators was a frustrating experience for supporters of the resistance movement, and for those actively engaged in the prosecutions. In retrospect, however, it can be seen that a more thorough retribution for economic collaboration had to be impeded by the fact that such private collaboration was an inevitable concomitant of a public policy committed to cooperating with the occupying power.[61]

At its worst, economic collaboration was driven by greed and opportunism. Nazi or pro-German sympathies were rarely, if ever, a motivation. In the non-economic forms of collaboration, however, such sympathies were often a defining characteristic. This applied not only to the political activities of the German minority population in south Jutland and of the Danish Nazi party (DNSAP) but also to the conduct of the four groups of collaborators to be considered here.

Most of the Danes who voluntarily enrolled in a German army unit and fought in the war or who joined a German police force operating in Denmark were ideologically motivated, though some were anti-Communist rather than pro-Nazi. The same may have been true of many of those individuals who acted as informers against the resistance movement. However, pro-German sympathies harboured by the women who associated with German soldiers seem more likely to have been of an emotional than of an ideological nature. Whatever the quality and degree of pro-German sympathies entertained by the last two groups of collaborators, their motivations may have been tempered with a measure of opportunism. Mixed though the motivations of the four groups of collaborators seem to have been, through their acts they all became identified with the German cause. Thus, they were roundly condemned by the public as traitors, and many of them prosecuted and severely punished after the liberation. Half a century after those deeds were done, historians could examine the conduct of such collaborators more dispassionately, if not downright sympathetically, than had been possible at an earlier stage.

In 1998 Claus Bundgaard Christensen, Niels Bo Poulsen and Peter Scharff Smith published a book which was based on the dissertation submitted for their finals at the Institute for History and Social Science of Roskilde University Centre. Entitled *Under hagekors og dannebrog. Danskere i Waffen SS* (Under the swastika and the Danish flag. Danes in the Waffen SS), it told the story of approximately 6,000 Danes who volunteered to fight in the German Nazi military organization, their background, training, roles in the war and fate after the German capitulation. Based on archival material in Denmark, Germany and a few other places and on letters, diaries and unpublished memoirs as well as interviews with some veterans, it became a contribution to both Danish wartime history and German military history.

The authors corrected the popular image of the Danish corps of the Waffen-SS as largely made up of antisocial and callous individuals. Mainly recruited through the German minority and DNSAP, the great majority were Nazis when they enrolled. As a result of intensive indoctrination during their training, a large number ended up as confirmed adherents of the Nazi ideology, confident of belonging to a superhuman elite of political soldiers inspired by high ideals. Some, however, were motivated more by anti-Bolshevism. This was characteristic especially of those who had fought for Finland in the 1939–40 war with the Soviet Union, and who after June 1941 decided to continue the crusade against Bolshevism by joining the German army units deployed on the Eastern front.

Some Danish officers and men joined the units of the Waffen-SS more out of antipathy to the defence policy of their government in the 1930s and frustration with the shameful capitulation on 9 April 1940. A smaller number joined up essentially to escape unemployment in Denmark, and others no doubt to exchange the boredom of the early years of occupation for a life of adventure on the battlefields abroad. Finally, the recruits included a group of social misfits in trouble with the local authorities in Denmark. Sociologically, the authors found, the members of those units on the whole represented a broad cross section of the Danish population. Contrary to what many people claimed in later years, they did not include a higher proportion of the criminal and the retarded than the rest of society did.

Nearly all the Danish volunteers in the Waffen-SS served in one or more of three units on the Eastern front, namely Division Wiking, Frikorps Danmark and Division Nordland. Frikorps Danmark, set up in connection with the attack on the Soviet Union, was formally non-political, which meant anti-Communist rather than Nazi-oriented. Also known as the Danish Legion, its flag and language of command were Danish. Its first commandant, C.P. Kryssing, was a Danish officer, not a member of DNSAP, who tried to steer a non-political course. When he resisted SS demands for indoctrination of the troops he was opposed by a group of Nazis within the corps, and eventually replaced by C.F. von Schalburg, former leader of DNSAP's youth section and a fanatical Nazi who hated Communists and Jews. When Schalburg was killed, in one of the earlier battles of the corps, his place was taken by K.B. Martinsen, also a convinced Nazi.

Danish volunteers took part in the attack on the Soviet Union, and experienced the *Blitzkrieg* with its rapid advances in the summer of 1941. In the following years, they were involved in a series of bloody defensive battles with the advancing Soviet army. In early May 1945 several hundred Danish SS volunteers participated in the German army's last stand in the streets of Berlin. Throughout the volunteers fought bravely, losing about 2,000 men, a third of the Danish force. In battle, their performance was marked by the brutality and ruthlessness that became characteristic of the war on the Eastern front. Thus, in an attack shortly after the killing of Schalburg they shot an unknown number of Russian prisoners of war.

Inevitably some Danish volunteers became involved also in the more political activities of the Waffen-SS, which were pursued in accordance with the ideological programme of Heinrich Himmler's broader SS organization. The authors of the book mention that about 100 Danes served in German concentration camps, that some Danish officers acted as observers when an SS extermination unit shot Jews and other civilians, that Division Wiking took an active part in the extermination of Jews in the western region of Ukraine, and that Frikorps Danmark at one stage was chosen to assist an SS brigade in atrocities against the civilian population of White Russia.[62] Earlier books about the exploits of the volunteers in the war, mostly written by SS veterans, had failed to mention this side of their activities, but had described in considerable detail the battles in which they fought, the heroics they displayed and the decorations they received.

Having read many of the volunteers' diaries and letters from the front and interviewed a number of veterans, the three authors were able to explain the conduct of the soldiers, in terms of their ideology and ideals as well as in relation to their experiences and situation. Like so many other things that had happened in the war with the Soviet Union, killing prisoners out of revenge was against the Geneva Conventions and clearly inhumane. For SS volunteers, however, Russian soldiers were Communist enemies who, according the Nazi ideology, belonged to a lower race. Exterminating Jews, and certain other categories of civilians, had become an essential part of the Nazi programme, and hence a primary task for sections of the SS organizations, including units of the Waffen-SS. Thus, those Danish volunteers unfortunate enough to have become involved in such actions might have been not only following orders but also acting in accordance with their political convictions.

That the Danish volunteers went on fighting long after the decisive defeats of the German forces and in the face of the relentless advance of the Soviet army, some persevering to the very end of the war, was not simply a result of their ideological convictions and political commitment. Among other reasons mentioned by the authors were the fighting spirit of their Danish officers, the bonds of solidarity uniting the soldiers of the corps and, perhaps not least, the lack of an alternative. Many were afraid of what might be in store for them if they returned to Denmark, where they knew they all were regarded as traitors.

After the liberation of Denmark and the end of the war more than 3,000 returning volunteers were sentenced by Danish courts, typically to two years' imprisonment, for having fought on the German side. The legal basis for the prosecution was the so-called penal code amendment of 1 June 1945, which retroactively made their participation in the war illegal. Thus the volunteers were punished for an act which had been lawful at the time when it was committed and, moreover, could be deemed consistent with Danish policy and diplomacy towards the occupying power. Giving in to German pressure, the government had signed the Anti-Comintern Pact, and thus at least ideologically lined Denmark up with Germany and its allies against the Soviet Union. Again in response to German pressure, it had allowed Danish officers to take leave of absence to join the Waffen-SS. The government had even agreed to let the Danish army be represented at various events for Frikorps Danmark on Danish soil. Indeed, the whole line taken by the government in relation to the recruitment for the Waffen-SS, the authors suggested, could be seen as an outstanding manifestation of the policy of cooperation.

The hostility the returning soldiers met from the population and the harsh and unjust treatment they received from the political and judicial system, on top of the suffering and losses they had endured during the later years of the war, further strengthened the solidarity of the former volunteers. Instead of regretting their choice and actions, some could see themselves as idealists who openly had fought for their ideological convictions and bravely lived up to their soldierly norms – only surrounded, now as then, by opportunistic politicians and a manipulable public. Such uniformly positive views of the volunteers' role in the Second World War found clear expression in the veterans' own historiography.[63]

Even more hated by the public than the Danes who had volunteered to fight abroad together with the Waffen-SS were the men who, in the last two years of the occupation, had decided to join the Schalburg Corps in Denmark. Set up in April 1943 on the instructions of Himmler and called after the heroic commandant of Frikorps Danmark, it was originally meant to recruit and train soldiers for the Waffen-SS as well as to Germanize Denmark in preparation for the Greater German *Reich* projected by Nazi ideologists. Divided into 10 main sections or departments, the corps covered a wide range of activities, including military, civilian and political undertakings, propaganda, intelligence and terrorism. Soon its principal function became to assist the German authorities in the fight against growing resistance in the country. Not least through its intelligence service (ET), the corps became deeply involved in terrorism and other acts of violence. Such activities, directed against both the public and the resistance movement, culminated with the general strike in the summer of 1944. As a result of difficulties with recruitment and disputes between the occupying power and its Danish leadership, the corps was dissolved on 1 February 1945.

The public, having noted that the Schalburg Corps went beyond fighting the resistance through acts of retaliation and deliberately worked to terrorize the population, was inclined to ascribe to the corps all destructive explosions and violent incidents for which the resistance could not take responsibility. The illegal press reinforced this tendency by constantly and indiscriminately accusing the corps of what became known as schalburgtage. The most provocative action of such a kind was the destruction of the concert hall and other parts of Tivoli, the historic and popular amusement park at the centre of Copenhagen, in late June 1944. It was clearly in revenge for the series of spectacular acts of sabotage preceding the demonstrations and general strike. The illegal press immediately accused the corps of being the perpetrator.

The hatred and scorn of the public was reflected in the severity of the punishments meted out to members of the corps in the first post-war years. Under a section of the retroactive legislation, dealing with uniformed service in the German police corps, about 700 Schalburg men received prison sentences ranging from two years to life, the typical sentence being four years simply for membership of the corps. Those guilty of torture, violence, robbery, murder, explosions, terror or treason received much longer sentences. Ten members, including the chief of the corps K.B. Martinsen, were executed. In 1948, however, the courts started to pardon those with shorter sentences. The last long-term prisoners were released in 1960.

The animosity and contempt for members of the Schalburg and similar Danish corps, which culminated in the period immediately after liberation when nearly everybody identified with the resistance movement, were shared by most post-war writers, including the first historians of the occupation years. While many simply ignored or dismissed its members as traitors, some writers went out of their way to condemn their character and question their motivation. Prominent among the latter was Vilhelm la Cour, who during the war had provoked both the Danish and the German authorities with a number of pamphlets written in the spirit of traditional anti-German nationalism. In a book about Denmark during the occupation, published in 1947, he fervently dealt with the terror committed by the Schalburg Corps and accused its members of being criminal and insane.[64] Fifty years later a young historian revised this assessment.

In 2000 Andreas Monrad Pedersen published *Schalburgkorpset*, a history of the corps and its members which was based on the dissertation submitted for his finals at Copenhagen University. He started by tackling the demonization of National Socialism and its henchmen immediately after the liberation and demonstrating its effects on Danish post-war society. This attitude, he acknowledged, was quite natural at that stage, after Germany had lost the war and the Nazi crimes against humanity had become public knowledge. To accept, let alone understand, people who had supported Hitler's regime was then impossible. To its contemporaries, the Schalburg Corps appeared as simply a servant of the occupying power and an instrument for arbitrary terror, and its members as generally criminal thugs and subnormal individuals, all engaged in treacherous activities.

This inclination to demonize and disparage, he pointed out, served an important social function in post-war Denmark. It helped to shift the responsibility for years of Danish cooperation with the occupying power on to a tiny minority of marginal Danes who, in a very obvious way, had collaborated with the Germans and fought the resistance. Drawing attention away from the economic, political and other forms of cooperation engaged in by much larger sections of the population, it played a part in maintaining the retrospective façade of a united nation steadfastly committed to opposing the occupying power. Thus, the tendency to demonize the collaborators, he noted, had a much needed healing effect on the Danish psyche. It allowed the nation to face the future with a clearer conscience.

Previous writings on the collaborators, the author pointed out, had been characterized not merely by demonization but also by a tendency towards sensationalism. The focus had generally been on the most spectacular events and the loudest statements. This approach had stood in the way of a strictly historical treatment of the Schalburg Corps. Now the time had come to see and present the corps in a new light, not in order to excuse and explain away the misdeeds of the Schalburg men, but to analyse the background, history and context of the activities of the corps and to examine the character, motivation and life of individual members.[65]

Pedersen's research into the organizational history of the corps showed a growing attachment to the occupying power in the period up to the general strike in September 1944. Schalburg men assisted German police in the raids and arrest of Jews in October 1943, and the intelligence service worked with German terror gangs in the earlier stage of the demonstrations and strikes in 1944. However, the majority of the killings and explosions that took place in the last years of the occupation were not the responsibility of the corps. They were mostly the work of terror groups organized by the Germans themselves, though sometimes carried out in accordance with information and advice about victims and locations supplied by ET. Thus, the explosions in Tivoli were not a case of schalburgtage but the work of the notorious Peter group, which later gained the reputation of having been the most violent and destructive terror gang operating in Denmark during the war. Though led by a former Schalburg man, it was part of the German security service.

In accordance with the defensive tactics employed by the German authorities at the height of the general strike, members of the corps were withdrawn from the streets of Copenhagen and barracked. In the later months of the occupation the corps, now under tighter German control, continued to take part in the activities of the German police, notably in connection with the action against the Danish police in September 1944. Its members also committed a variety of fairly minor and isolated acts of violence and thefts, especially in the final stage of the occupation. Thus the Schalburg Corps retained its function as the national scapegoat for practically all acts of violence and terror deemed to be pro-German or anti-resistance. As such, it served first the propaganda purposes of the illegal press and later, according to the author's interpretation, the psychological needs of the Danish population.[66]

Pedersen's sociological analysis of the membership of the corps showed that Schalburg men were not radically different from the rest of the population. While the officers came from the middle or upper-middle class, the men belonged to the lower social classes. Typically young and often poorly educated, they were normal both psychologically and intellectually. A high proportion (42 per cent) were unemployed when they joined, half had done civilian work for Germany and a quarter had a criminal record. The general picture was that of a marginalized group of young people in an insecure social situation who tried to improve their life by collaborating with the occupying power.

Though love of adventure and opportunism no doubt played a role in some cases, by far the most common motivation for joining the corps was ideological, typically pro-Nazi, anti-Communist and anti-Semitic. More than a third were members of DNSAP. Two thirds came from an environment which was marked by National Socialist ideas, whether a family, a political party, a German factory or Frikorps Danmark, and in which the Schalburg Corps was regarded as a respectable organization. The corps naturally produced its own *esprit de corps*, which reinforced the commitment of the members. In this connection it was worth noting that actual violence and terrorist activity was the responsibility of only a few departments of the corps and were carried out by a hard core of troops, and that service for the ordinary Schalburg man usually meant guard and patrol duties.

In discussing the sources of recruitment for the Schalburg Corps, Pedersen did not fail to draw attention to the parallel with the resistance movement. Both found most of their recruits in politically marginal groups of people who were dissatisfied with the existing system and state of affairs. While the corps drew heavily on the National Socialist milieu, the resistance movement, as Aage Trommer had shown, found its members in Communist circles and Danish Unity.[67]

The two revisionist historical works discussed here, on Frikorps Danmark and the Schalburg Corps, sought to redress the inadequate or savage treatment the two organizations and their members had received from earlier historians, who had been possessed by the ethos of resistance. Another book, also by a young historian and published about the same time, went one step further when it took up for reconsideration the sensitive subject of informers. It vehemently attacked politicians and writers who after the war had defended the practice of liquidating security risks. In doing so, it questioned the entire ethos of resistance.

In his *Stikkerdrab. Modstandsbevægelsernes likvidering af danskere under besættelsen* (Killing of informers. The resistance movements' liquidation of Danes during the occupation), which was based on the dissertation he had submitted for his finals in history at Aarhus University, Stefan Emkjær challenged the traditional conception of Danish resistance and questioned its political and moral context. In the title of the book he used the plural form of movements, he explained, because the singular stood for a construction which did not conform to the reality of resistance in Denmark. Even at the end of the occupation there was no unified and organized resistance movement.[68]

Nor could he accept the idea of an antithesis between resistance and cooperation which was supposed to present the population with a stark political and moral choice. Since the myth of peace occupation offered some protection for resistance activities, it allowed resistance and cooperation to coexist. Thus, the situation in Denmark was not so much an either-or as a both-and case. Even the international context of Danish resistance presented a degree of political and moral ambiguity. Since the primary cause of the Second World War, as Emkjær saw it, was the injustice of the Versailles treaty imposed on Germany, the war between the allied powers and the Axis was not so clear a case of good battling evil as generally assumed at the time.[69] Thus, those identifying with the resistance and defending its activities were not always entitled to claim the moral high ground.

Emkjær's position in respect to the post-war debate about the liquidation of informers and other security risks was clearly with the so-called anti-movement rather than with the resistance movement. His book was more than a historian's attempt to analyse and categorize all known cases of liquidation. It was also a dismissive critique of the freedom council, which had taken formal responsibility for all or most such killings, and a scathing attack on Frode Jakobsen, who after the liberation as resistance leader and minister had stood in the way of a proper examination of a large number of doubtful cases. Thus, the author managed to pass judgement, implicitly on those involved in the liquidations and more explicitly on those defending and protecting them.

Starting with the first known liquidation, which took place in May 1943, and drawing on archives available up to November 1947, Emkjær counted 409 cases. This list was not complete and excluded unsuccessful attempts, of which he had come across 96 cases. Of the 409 victims, 39 were women. About 70 per cent of all killings took place in the last six months of the occupation. His first concerns were to ascertain the organizational level at which the order to kill was given and the nature of the decision-making process preceding the order.

Contrary to what people had been led to believe in the post-war years, he found the orders usually came from a resistance group, typically from its leader but sometimes even from an individual member, and only rarely from a higher level of the organization. Though the group leader occasionally might have reported to his immediate superiors, the freedom council and the regional leaderships seemed unlikely to have been kept informed of individual liquidations, even though they carried the overall responsibility. Thus, the decision-making process would usually have been brief and informal.[70]

Having gone through the papers available, the author concluded that the vast majority of killings had been carried out on quite a summary basis. Only a small number of the victims (little more than 10 per cent) had been members of a terror corps or had acted as informers in a big way. As for the rest, the company a person kept could be a decisive consideration. Membership of a Nazi party, for example, could be deemed a legitimate ground for a liquidation. Though in some cases various forms of preliminary investigation, such as observation, searches, tests and interrogation had taken place, on the whole liquidation of security risks was done on the basis of suspicion rather than proof. In certain cases, revenge for the loss of fellow members of a group could not be ruled out as a motive.[71]

When Emkjær moved on to review the post-war debate about liquidations, he made it clear that he was on the side of those who, in response to claims made by relations of persons thought to have been killed unjustly, had pressed for presentation of documentary material about wartime executions. He criticized resistance leaders and politicians who, for reasons of their own, had refused to make such material available for a judicial case-by-case examination. In particular, he attacked Frode Jakobsen, who had supervised a cursory review of 125 cases and had produced only nine exonerations by the ministry.

The presentation of such a small number of public rehabilitations was motivated by political concerns, Emkjær argued, and might be taken to imply that the rest of killings had been justified and necessary. Now, having gone through the archives himself, he could state that this was far from the actual situation. Indeed, in many cases he found it difficult to see the difference between the killings that had been exonerated and those that had not. On the whole, the basis for the executions was flimsy.[72] That the ministry of justice later issued 20 'tarnished' declarations of rehabilitation, acquitting the victims of informing but asserting that they, through their conduct, had placed themselves in the danger zone, did not help much.

The reason Frode Jakobsen, and other members of the freedom council and the liberation government, had given for denying access to documents relating to liquidations was that the individuals who had carried out or ordered the killings needed protection. Emkjær did not accept this explanation. The real reason, he insisted, had been that it was considered essential for the authority of the freedom council and the image of the resistance movement that people should go on believing that the order to shoot informers and other security risks had come from a high level and that the decision had been reached only after careful examination of each case. For the same reason, the liquidators – some of them apparently professional assassins or others with links to the criminal underworld – had been instructed after the liberation to keep quiet about this side of their wartime activities. If the source of orders, the basis for decisions, the character of killers and the proportion of mistakes became generally known, the idea of a united and organized resistance movement managed and controlled by the freedom council would be unmasked as a fiction. The glory of one and the aura of the other would be gone.

Having already called Frode Jakobsen the spider at the centre of the web of culpable investigations set up after the liberation and described the liquidations as the dirty linen of the resistance movement, he wound up his argument with a few parting shots at the freedom council. With its academic discussions and public proclamations, it had existed in a political world of theory and dreams, not in the real world of men of action.[73]

In presenting a dark chapter of Danish resistance in a new light, Emkjær had the advantage over earlier historians of distance in time from the events and people he was judging. Not sharing the prejudices, convictions and commitments of the preceding generations of writers, he was free to cast doubt on the cause of the allied powers, to question the performance of the Danish resistance movement and to deny the conflict between resistance and cooperation, and could even allow himself to indulge in iconoclastic attacks on entities and individuals that acted in situations which were beyond his own experience.

But the distance in time was also a handicap. When he disqualified Danish resistance as a movement as well as when he condemned on moral, and would-be legal, grounds the practice of liquidation he tended to apply peacetime norms and rules to wartime conduct. Thus, he showed little understanding of the needs and norms of a resistance movement which, operating in a small, flat and densely populated country occupied by enemy military and police forces, depended on the loyalty of its members and the discretion of the public. In his censorious enquiry into summary liquidations of actual and potential security risks, Emkjær was inclined to allow later moral reactions to overshadow contemporary martial needs and political considerations.

An earlier neo-revisionist contribution to Danish occupation historiography, about another group of individuals who during and after the occupation had been punished or condemned for unpatriotic behaviour, also had a pronounced moral dimension. In *Tyskerpiger – under besættelse og retsopgør* (Pro-German girls – during occupation and judicial reckoning), Anette Warring examined the conduct, role and treatment of young Danish women who had engaged in intimate relations with soldiers of the occupation forces. A Ph.D. dissertation from the Institute for History and Social Science of Roskilde University Centre, it rested on police records and judicial sources as well as interviews with women involved. In approach and analysis, it drew on concepts from sociology, psychology and, not least, women's studies.

Instead of *tyskertøse* (pro-German tarts), or other offensive terms used during and after the war, Warring called the fraternizing women *tyskerpiger* (pro-German girls). She thought that there were perhaps at least 50,000 of them in the five years of the occupation – a figure roughly equal to the size of the resistance army at the time of the liberation. In a country in which the large majority of the population accepted that the correct behaviour towards members of the occupying forces was that of the cold shoulder, the public image of such women could not be flattering. They were generally taken to be stupid, ugly and of easy virtue, an image which remained long after the war and found expression in films and literature, even in some historiography. Warring, however, found that the fraternizing women formed a heterogeneous group. Coming from all social classes, they differed in most respects, including intelligence, appearance, age, marital status and political orientation. Yet most of them, she thought, were probably young women who did not live with their parents and who socially and educationally were below the average for the population.

She distinguished five types of pro-German girls, namely the prostitute, the woman who loved one soldier only, the woman who fraternized with one soldier after the other, the woman who openly engaged in general interaction with Germans, and the woman who was with

Germans out of pro-German attitudes and Nazi beliefs. Her analysis of their reasons for associating with German soldiers did not show any shared political or social motive, or point to any shared psychological characteristic. Yet, whatever the reasons, their decision to keep company with Germans in a situation of military occupation became an act vested with a degree of political significance. In particular, the behaviour of women who openly and publicly mixed with German soldiers appeared as a signal of sympathy for them and acceptance of their presence in the country. Through their conduct, the fraternizing women placed themselves on the side of the collaborators and in opposition to those who pursued the cold-shoulder line or engaged in active resistance.[74] However, only a tiny proportion of such women, about 300, seemed to have been guilty of informing for the Germans.

Much like Emkjær half a dozen years later, Warring was as interested in the motivation and role of those who passed judgement and carried out punishment as in the conduct of those who suffered the condemnation and retribution. As in other occupied countries, the typical punishment inflicted on a fraternizing woman was a cropping of her hair. Sometimes she was also stripped naked, and perhaps subjected to other forms of sexual humiliation. The first cropping recorded had already taken place in 1940; but it was in connection with the public disturbances in August 1943, and again in the days of the liberation, that the practice became more common. Sometimes such incidents led to street fights between German soldiers and Danish men, which left the Danish police in a difficult situation. The clashes also complicated relations between the Danish and the German authorities responsible for managing the fraternization.

The perpetrators of the punishments were mostly young men, typically workers, apprentices and errand boys. But they enjoyed the tacit understanding and acceptance of substantial sections of the public. In the months leading up to the August rebellions several Communist illegal papers helped to prepare the way for persecution of the pro-German women. When the punishments became more common occurrences the party refrained from intervening. Moreover, it was Communists who in several towns were behind a demand for the dismissal of female employees guilty of fraternization. Thus, Warring concluded, the Communist party and its members carried part of the responsibility for the harsh treatment of the women that summer.

During the following months the leadership of the Communist party warned its members against 'outright sadistic excesses in the treatment of the girls', which Warring saw as an indication that the party was well aware of the mixed nature of the motives behind the cropping actions, part patriotic and part gender-moral, sexual or private. Throughout the occupation, the harassment of pro-German women was a manifestation of the conflict between collaboration and resistance. However, it continued after the liberation, and became even more frequent and brutal. At this stage, the author thought, the motive was pure vengeance.[75]

Like other categories of collaborators, fraternizing women were rounded up and interned after the liberation, partly for their protection and partly for the purpose of possible prosecution. The public thirst for revenge for the most obvious form of collaboration was great. According to a Gallup poll carried out a month after the end of the occupation, as many as 75 per cent thought that pro-German women should be punished in some way. 1.3 per cent, more women than men, even wanted them executed. However, the retroactive laws passed by parliament did not include mere fraternization in the list of treasonable acts. So, unless charged with informing or some other criminal action, the interned women were set free, to live the rest of their lives with the shame and, in some cases, a guilty conscience.

The croppers, the men who in the days of liberation had attacked and punished pro-German women, were treated more mildly than under the occupation. Most cases were not reported to the police, and those that did go to court were dealt with in a rather arbitrary and inconsistent manner, and usually settled with a lenient sentence. The author noted that no organization, not even those representing women, protested against the treatment inflicted on such women, and concluded that this, together with the very mild sentences, showed that the Danish society largely accepted the croppings. Yet such acts even when carried out by members of the resistance movement exasperated at seeing various kinds of collaborators going unpunished, violated those democratic principles of law which Warring thought needed to be restored after five years of Nazi occupation.[76]

Fraternizing with German soldiers was not against the law during the occupation and was not deemed criminal in the post-war legislation. It was, however, regarded as in breach of the unwritten rules of the prevailing morality of the time. That morality, in Warring's analysis, had a national, a gender-related and a sexual component. The offending women had challenged each of those sets of norms. In a situation in which the acceptable political line was to cold-shoulder or to resist the occupying forces, they had acted unpatriotically by entering into intimate relations with German soldiers. Here they had made their choice and, whatever their personal motivations, had joined the ranks of collaborators.

In their breach of gender role and sexual morality, however, those women had been victims of a traditional mentality which linked women and their behaviour with the honour and fate of the nation. As mothers, educators and symbols, women were seen as having an important part to play in the processes which secured the nation's cohesion and identity as well as its independence and distinctness in international relations. By engaging emotionally and sexually with enemy soldiers, and thus implicitly rejecting Danish men, the women presented a threat to the established social and national order. The treatment of pro-German women after the liberation, Warring concluded her analysis, rested on 'the conception of women's sexuality as national property'.[77]

Focusing on their breaches of conventional morality, rather than on their admittedly unpatriotic conduct, allowed the author to introduce and apply concepts and criteria which had been developed decades after the women's fraternization and the croppers' lawless retaliation. Drawing on a modern gender ideology which focused on the role and rights of women, she could present the women of the 1940s as victims of an outmoded social mentality. Though she did not absolve the fraternizing women of their guilt of sexual collaboration, she directed her moral reprobation mainly at those who had punished and abused them.

Here a degree of similarity with Emkjær's work on informers and their killers might be noted. Inclined to apply his post-cold-war democratic legal and moral norms to a situation of wartime occupation half a century earlier, he denounced those guilty of approving or carrying out liquidations of suspected informers, and suggested that most of the men and women killed in this way had been more or less innocent. Both historians managed to place their group of collaborators in a better light by censuring their killers and tormentors. The result of their revisionist scholarship was a more nuanced picture of the collaborators, as well as of their castigators.

The four books presented in this section examined marginal groups of people who, in the heady times of the 1940s, had been deemed traitors, or at least considered beyond the pale of the professed national solidarity against the occupying power. Their authors were young historians who, lacking personal experience of the occupation, had no strong anti-German feelings. With at best early childhood memories of the post-war decades, they were not moved by the claimed national concord and not particularly interested in the manifest conflict between cooperation and resistance, the two themes that had marked earlier periods of historiography. Their contribution was to bring groups of former outcasts to the fore and reconsider their case. Revealing the identity and motives and examining the roles and treatment of such people, their works demolished a number of myths and contributed to the understanding of generally despised and overlooked groups.

That wave of revisionism marked the hitherto last stage in the long development in Danish historiography from more or less total commitment to resistance to some acceptance of collaboration. It was a process characterized by a gradual narrowing of focus and introversion of perspective, politically as well as morally. The first generation of historians, conscious of the importance of the country's relations with the allied powers in the later stages of the war, focused on the national struggle with the German occupier. The second generation, more aware of domestic political disagreements about the way to defend Danish interests, based most of their work on the opposition between cooperation and resistance as reactions to foreign occupation. The last generation, more interested in the fate of the outsiders in occupation history, devoted their attention to the character and role of groups of people who chose to collaborate with the Germans.

Morally, it was a regression from accepting patriotic duty in a time of European war with a Nazi enemy, through endorsing the safeguarding of internal Danish interests in a situation of foreign occupation, to upholding the democratic and human rights of deviant individuals acting in extreme political and social circumstances. If the theme of the first period of Danish historiography was national concord and, of the second, civil conflict, the theme of the last period, with its particularist focus and morally revisionist approach, became social discord.

3.4 Debate

The decade round the turn of the century, between the fiftieth and the sixtieth anniversary of the liberation of Denmark, produced many new and significant scholarly publications about the period of occupation. So did the following and the most recent years. It may be too soon to detect and identify one or more further stages of the historiography surveyed above. However, it is possible to classify, if rather roughly, the bulk of such material. The most obvious distinction is between writings examining the external dimension and writings focusing on the internal dimension of the country's situation in those five years. Two further categories of modern scholarly literature, namely that of general presentations of the history of the occupation of Denmark and that of its historiography of the subject, may complete the classification.

International

Within the category of scholarship devoted to the external dimension, a distinction may be made between a relatively small number of works which clarify and analyse the formal status of occupied Denmark in international society and a larger group which examine its actual relations with the major belligerents of the time. While the authors of the former set apply legal and moral criteria, those of the latter group deal with political, economic and military relations. While the former seek to clarify status and correct misconceptions, the latter add to existing knowledge of the country's interaction with the great powers of the region.

For some time, the formal status of occupied Denmark in relation to both the occupying power and other states, belligerent or not, was somewhat obscure. One difficulty, and source of confusion, was the duality of Danish thinking about neutrality that had developed in the inter-war years. One strand was that of traditional legal neutrality, the other that of so-called neo-neutrality.

Legal neutrality, as developed in European international relations of the nineteenth century and codified in the Hague Conventions from 1907, had its supporters mainly in the Conservative and Liberal opposition parties. Neo-neutrality, rooted in the pacifism of some Radical Liberals and the anti-militarism of many Social Democrats and developed in the optimistic internationalist spirit of the first decade of the League of Nations, had its champions in the two political parties that governed Denmark in the 1930s. Prescribing proactive diplomacy in pursuit of peace, it had a pronounced moral element.

The events of 9 April 1940 put an end to the legal neutrality of the Danish state. Though the Germans declared that they acted in order to defend its neutrality, the invasion and occupation naturally negated its territorial integrity and diplomatic impartiality. However, for those who believed that Danish neutrality was more than a legal concept and a formal status it was difficult to accept its sudden and total non-existence. Peter Munch, foreign minister since 1929 and Radical Liberal leader, recognized the end of neutrality as a legal attribute of the state but claimed that it had survived as a moral quality of the nation. For a long time, later Danish historians – perhaps misled by ambiguous statements made at the time by prominent individuals – concluded or assumed and accepted that the government, under reference to the notion of neo-neutrality, had claimed neutral status after the invasion.

In an article investigating Denmark's international legal status during the war, published in English in 2011, Karen Gram-Skjoldager reported that her research had revealed no evidence of Munch, or any other member of the government, having made such a claim.[78] The status which the government at that stage could accept was one of non-belligerence, a characterization which was in harmony with the internationalist ideology of the Radical Liberals. For Munch, of course, it was linked with the notion of moral neutrality. From the moment the king and the government on 9 April decided to give up resisting the invading forces the basic motivation behind Danish non-belligerence was, as it had been for its neutrality, to spare the country and its people the ravages of war.

Erik Scavenius, who at the request of the king replaced Munch as foreign minister in July 1940, was impressed with the German military victories and thought it wise for Denmark to adopt a more accommodating and even proactive attitude towards the occupying power. His years in office, first as foreign minister and, from November 1942 to August 1943, also as prime minister, became another phase in the history of the country's legal status. It was characterized by the concept of peaceful occupation. As developed by Erik Brüel, a lawyer and influential writer specializing in international law, that notion applied only to Denmark, not to countries which had been occupied belligerently. In principle, it protected the authority of the central political and legal institutions of the occupied state. Thus, the government could employ the notion when seeking to defend the execution of its internal sovereignty against intrusions by the occupying power. This became important in matters of jurisdiction, especially in cases involving illegal acts directed against the occupying authorities.

The fourth concept presented, analysed and discussed by Gram-Skjoldager, that of war, related to the phase in Danish–German relations that started with the events in the summer and autumn of 1943 and lasted until the liberation in May 1945. After the growth of sabotage, the public confrontations in August, the retreat of the government and the establishment of the freedom council the idea of Denmark being at war with Germany gradually gained ground. The claim, advanced by the freedom council and eventually supported by official Denmark, found some international support when Britain and the United States in June 1944 *de facto* acknowledged Denmark as an allied nation. A further indication of allied acceptance of the claim was the invitation to participate in the San Francisco Conference in June 1945.

However, the author found the matter of the possible role of Denmark as a belligerent party the most politicized of the legal questions pertaining to that country during the war, for the reason that it was closely tied to the basic political and moral dilemma between cooperation and resistance. Moreover, it was the most complex of the legal questions raised in the article, because it brought up the difficulties of defining 'war' and of determining the identity of 'Denmark' after the retreat of its government in 1943.

Having explored the informed debate that arose from those questions, she concluded the article with some general observations about the four concepts. Legal arguments advanced in support of neutrality, non-belligerence, peaceful occupation and war, she found, served as political instruments. As such they were closely linked with changing conceptions of Denmark's international position and national interests. Moreover, those legal concepts gradually took on a life of their own, and shaped Danish perceptions and political actions. The idea of peaceful occupation in particular affected not only politicians and officials but also later historians of that period in Danish history.

The utilitarian value to Danish politicians and officials of legal concepts of the formal status of occupied Denmark, with their accompanying argumentation, was a major theme also of a chapter which appeared two years later. Written by Niels Wium Olesen for a British publication, it was entitled 'The Obsession with Sovereignty: Cohabitation and Resistance in Denmark 1940-45'.[79] It presented the political advantages, reviewed the major disadvantages and discussed the moral difficulties of seeking to maintain more than a semblance of sovereignty in continual interaction with the occupying power.

From the beginning of the occupation Germany granted Denmark the status of a sovereign state, which the Danish authorities accepted and utilized to the utmost. However, Danish independence was severely curtailed in both external and internal relations. In the former dimension hardly anything was left of Danish sovereignty. In the latter, formal parity between occupier and occupied was largely an illusion because the German military presence consistently gave it the upper hand. Yet, the German authorities generally left it to the Danish government to exercise its internal sovereignty, as long as it did not conflict with German interests of a military nature. Matters at issue were dealt with through negotiation between representatives of the foreign ministries of the parties.

The foremost result for Denmark of such dynamics between the occupier and the occupied, the author noted, was the remarkable political and institutional continuity from the inter-war to the post-war years. Contrary to some other countries under German occupation, Denmark avoided a Nazi take-over of government and maintained its democratic system. Thus, it was able to have a parliamentary election in March 1943, and to keep support for DNSAP to a very low level. In some important matters, however, the government felt obliged to give in to German pressure, even when it meant violating basic democratic principles. Accepting censorship of the press, approving expulsion of certain members of parliament and organizing internment of Communists were cardinal cases of the system doing the dirty work for Nazi Germany.

In the political circumstances of the time, clinging to the notion of sovereignty and maintaining a semblance of independence at such costs could be seen by the decision-makers and their supporters as the politics of the lesser evil. But active members and supporters of the growing resistance movement would not accept that. Wium Olesen concluded with a brief presentation of the moral issue involved.

Bringing in Max Weber's distinction between the ethic of responsibility and the ethic of conviction, he distinguished between those guided by probable consequences and those guided by principles. Apparently tending to side with the former, he went on to add to the list of laudable results of the 'Danish line' with the Germans. Still, a problem remained.

Official Danish–German transactions had a touch of mutuality and voluntariness. Though largely fictional, they were not entirely without substance, since nobody really forced the Danes to negotiate. The tension was between the element of compulsion and the threat of a much worse alternative on one side and the element of voluntariness and mutuality along with a degree of complicity on the other side. That was the moral framework within which most discussion about the policy of negotiation and cooperation had taken place since 1940.

The occupation of Denmark suddenly put an end to practically all diplomatic, economic and social relations with Germany's enemies, but gradually broadened and deepened such relations with the occupying power. Since the turn of the century Danish–German interaction and cooperation in the economic sphere in particular have attracted the attention of many Danish historians and given rise to a number of scholarly debates. Again the underlying concern of the participants has often been with the moral dimension.

In 1998 Philip Giltner published a book entitled *In the Friendliest Manner*, which was based on his doctoral dissertation in History at the University of Toronto. Subtitled *German-Danish Economic Cooperation During the Nazi Occupation of 1940–1945*, it relied on both German and Danish sources.[80] He started by questioning Denmark's ethical position in the great struggle against Nazi dictatorship, noting that Danes usually had been less than eager to discuss this aspect of their past. That Denmark had survived German occupation better than any other occupied country in Europe was obvious. The reasons, however, were less than clear. Two conceivable causes often cited, namely the importance for the German war economy of Danish agricultural exports and the Aryan nature of the Danish population, he dismissed. The real reason was that Denmark, unlike all other occupied countries, from the outset chose to cooperate with the occupying power, and continued to do so even after the formal retreat of the Danish government in 1943.

This policy suited the Germans well. To the Nazi government, the basic importance of Denmark was strategic. Control of Danish territory provided access to Norway and barred entry to the Baltic. The overriding political concern had to be to maintain economic security and social stability in the country with a minimum of German effort. Negotiating with the Danish authorities in matters of importance and leaving most of the daily administration to them seemed the most efficient procedure. For the Danes, too, the so-called negotiation policy was advantageous. Based on the nonsensical notion of 'occupied neutrality', the arrangement generally left domestic matters in the hands of Danish authorities. Most important, it served as a protection against a more ruthless exploitation of the country. Through negotiation and management, the Danish government and administration made themselves indispensable to the German authorities. Thus Denmark defended its national interests, Giltner concluded, by cooperating with one of the most odious regimes of the modern era.

Half a dozen years later a book on much the same subject appeared in Denmark. Written by Ole Brandenborg Jensen, and also based on a Ph.D. thesis, it was entitled *Besættelsestidens Økonomiske og Erhvervmæssige Forhold*.[81] The subtitle too, *Studier i de Økonomiske Relationer mellem Danmark og Tyskland 1940–1945*, was rather more neutral than that of the earlier work. In the preface the author declared that the book should in no way be seen as a contribution to the current competition to expose various industrial groups and individuals that, in the bright light of hindsight, could be accused of collaboration and opportunism. On the contrary, he stated, the book was an attempt to describe and explain the actions of the parties in the context of their own times.

In general, he found, economic relations between the two countries were of relatively little importance, basically because the German authorities dealing with Denmark put political goals before economic concerns. Acknowledging the notion of Danish sovereignty in internal affairs, they usually left such matters to the Danes themselves. Subjects that did require German attention, and led to negotiation and cooperation between the parties, were most of the time to do with Danish export of goods to and imports from Germany, and employment of Danish workers in that country.

Danish export of fresh fish and agricultural products was not so important a part of the wartime nutrition of the German nation as earlier historians had assumed. Nor did it lead to significant shortages in Denmark. More important, it helped to pay for imports from Germany of goods traditionally supplied by Britain and essential for Danish production and the national economy, especially coal, fuel and steel. Such imports became tied up with the supply of Danish manpower for German factories. Probably well over 30,000 Danish workers were employed in Germany at any particular stage of the earlier years of the occupation. For a country at war and with major shortages of manpower, this was a not insignificant contribution. However, it was also a convenient solution for Denmark, whose government and trade unions at that time were still struggling with the problems of unemployment.

Much more problematic, the author admitted, was the Danish contribution, made in the last years of the occupation, to the construction of extensive defensive fortifications along the coast of Jutland. Forced through by decrees, instead of arrived at through negotiation and agreement with Danish authorities, it involved substantial participation in German military efforts. With eventually more than 100,000 Danes working on what became part of Germany's great Atlantic Wall, Danish involvement led to local shortages of labour, especially in agriculture. Consisting of about 8,000 concrete bunkers, the project also required large supplies of cement and timber from Danish sources. However, since the main objective of the Danish administration always had been to retain as much sovereignty in internal affairs as possible, the most serious aspect of the whole project was the way it had been imposed on the country.

Very few Danes actively engaged in various forms of official negotiation and cooperation with the occupying power were motivated by a desire to see Nazi Germany win the war. But nor were many of them driven by commitment to the allied cause. The overriding concern was simply to defend and pursue Danish political and economic interests in a situation of national emergency. When Brandenborg Jensen discussed the advantages and disadvantages for Denmark of such cooperation he implicitly accepted and endorsed that attitude. Regarding the people who carried the responsibility in those days as pragmatists, he thought that they should not be judged by post-war moral scruples. Giltner's work on the subject did not gain a mention in the book.

Several other economic historians contributing to the debate in the early years of the century were more critical of those who had engaged in economic cooperation with the occupying power. Their publications, again typically based on a Ph.D. dissertation, took up various kinds of such cooperation. Steen Andersen examined the history of some major companies of contractors from 1919 to 1947, but concentrated on the occupation period. His angle was their way of doing business in difficult political circumstances, and the order of priorities applied in decision-making.[82]

The record of Kampsax, one of the biggest companies, was politically ambiguous. It included major projects carried out by a subsidiary company for British authorities, such as road-building for transport of war materials to the Soviet Union before the battle of Stalingrad. However, the likely consequences for the course of the war were not a primary motive. It was more a case of the company taking on projects wherever it was profitable and possible.

The record of Christiani & Nielsen, another large company, was rather worse. It included seeking contracts in Norway for the building of submarine bases and plants for the production of aluminium for the German aircraft industry and, especially, undertaking extensive building by its German subsidiary of submarine bases and roads in France. All of it, the author emphasized, of obvious military importance. That company, he found, had gone well beyond the considerations dictated by the state of occupation. It could be deemed as showing 'improper initiative'.

In general, Andersen found, Danish contractors put profit before national loyalty in their relations with German authorities, which did not surprise him. More remarkable was their short-sightedness. They tended to continue their cooperation well after changes in the fortunes of war had led most of the Danish population to expect an allied victory.

In a book entitled *Hitlers spisekammer* (larder), made up of an abridged dissertation and various relevant articles, reports and papers and published in 2005, Joachim Lund examined and discussed Danish economic and commercial cooperation with Germany in occupied parts of Europe.[83] The German authorities, he found, had no wish to give Denmark a special role or to allocate it particular functions in the projected new order for Eastern Europe. German policy, it was clear, was conditioned by short-term considerations, and seriously affected by disagreement between governmental offices involved in the planning.

However, the Danish parties concerned, both the political and the commercial, were apparently quite willing to participate in the German project, whether in the Baltic states or in Russian and Ukrainian regions. Elsewhere in Europe too, the author found, there were German building projects and other planned activities which attracted Danish interest. If the concrete results of Danish efforts to engage in economic collaboration with the occupying power were rather limited it was mainly because of German reluctance and, simply, time running out. Lund concluded his critique by noting a significant parallel between political and economic collaboration in the early years of the occupation.

The same year Mogens R. Nissen's *Til fælles bedste – det danske landbrug under besættelsen* appeared.[84] Dealing with the history and role of Danish agriculture during the occupation, it focused on the importance of food exports to Germany. Challenging Brandenborg Jensen's conclusions on the matter, the author argued that such exports had a significant role, which grew with the duration of the war. Thus, his analysis of German statistics indicated that import of meat from Denmark rose from 4–5 per cent to 10–12 per cent of total consumption. The Danish contribution was relatively greatest in 1944–45, when Germany lost supplies from most of the countries it had previously conquered. However, the real importance of this form of economic cooperation, he stressed, was for the political relationship between the occupier and the occupied. The export helped to support the Danish policy of cooperation and to maintain the German policy of lenient occupation.

Nissen dealt also with the moral dimension of the wartime performance of the agricultural section of the Danish economy. Here he did not have an issue with Brandenborg Jensen. Neither of them saw that section as more given to voluntary collaboration with the Germans than its industrial and commercial counterpart was. Neither party was conspicuous for making economic sacrifices in the name of national solidarity.

Through their Ph.D. dissertations and other publications, Philip Giltner, Ole Brandenborg Jensen, Steen Andersen, Joachim Lund, Mogens R. Nissen and other young economic historians revealed, examined and discussed hitherto obscure aspects of the economic side of Danish–German relations. Whether reacting to prevarications or denials by interested parties or testing assumptions or assertions of earlier historians, they cast new light on the wartime policy and practice of cooperating with the dominant external power.

Danish relations with Germany's two foremost European enemies, Britain and the Soviet Union, developed later in the war and remained secret throughout the occupation. Initially of a largely military nature, they eventually acquired some tentative political and diplomatic qualities. The connection with Britain became the subject of Jørgen Hæstrup's first major work on Danish resistance. Provisionally entitled Secret Alliance, *Kontakt med England 1940–43* was written without access to SOE archives and published in 1954. Nearly half a century later relations between SOE and Danish resistance, and British policy towards occupied and liberated Denmark, were re-examined in Knud J. V. Jespersen's two-volume work *Med hjælp fra England. 1940–1945.*[85] It was based on British sources now available to historians. Its appearance led to another scholarly debate, this one about resistance instead of cooperation.

It started when a young historian Peter Edelberg made his mark with a challenging paper published in *Historisk Tidsskrift* under the title 'Arven fra Hæstrup' (the legacy from Hæstrup).[86] It was a critique of Hæstrup's conception of history and use of sources and a probe into his influence on later historians. The seminal doctoral dissertation *Kontakt med England* was intended and presented as objective history but was in fact, Edelberg pointed out, conditioned by political and ideological trends prevailing at the time of writing, the early stages of the cold war. It turned out to be a defence of the resistance movement, which to that author meant resistance supported and guided by Britain. Its focus was on SOE, and its heroes the agents parachuted into Denmark. That meant largely excluding the Communists and their engagement in the struggle.

He also criticized Hæstrup for idealizing the motivations and efforts of people involved in resistance, especially the SOE agents themselves. All from the outset inspired by patriotism, such people, it was implied, simply wanted to rid Denmark of Germans. Their less flattering activities, especially liquidation of informers, and various disagreements and conflicts dividing them were not dwelled upon. On the latter point Edelberg was well informed, having come across some 'personal files' in the SOE archives in London.

He went on to deal with the works of some of the foremost beneficiaries of the legacy from Hæstrup. While well aware of some of the shortcomings of Hæstrup's work, both Hans Kirchhoff and Aage Trommer implicitly subscribed to the master's view of historiography as a process of compilation, motivated by a quest for the truth and aimed at conveying a correct understanding. Though belonging to the second generation of occupation historians, they did not seem to appreciate that other scholars with different political interests and other ideological beliefs looking at the same material might discover a different truth and reach another understanding. Thus, like Hæstrup, they did not see a need for someone else to carry out a fresh examination of the material.

However, Edelberg's critique was directed mainly at the scholarship of Knud J.V. Jespersen. A specialist on the seventeenth century who already had written a book about the Danish brigade in Sweden, Jespersen had been asked by Hæstrup and Ole Lippmann, SOE's last leader in Denmark, to undertake the more crucial task. Thus Edelberg was able to deem his two-volume work another product of the influence of the old-boy network of SOE and resistance veterans.

Moreover, he found that Jespersen essentially belonged to the first generation of occupation historians, his first volume lying end-to-end with the master's writings, simply telling the story from the opposite angle. He was a 'back-to-front Hæstrup'. Basing his analysis only on the first volume, *Det lange tilløb 1940–1943* (The Long Run-up), published in 1998, he argued that Jespersen failed to take account of issues raised by second-generation historians relating to some of Hæstrup's theses, and also failed to explore the effect of political and ideological trends on earlier research into the occupation period.

Offered an opportunity to present a reply in the same issue of the journal, Jespersen rejected Edelberg's charges and argued that they were based on selective reading and overinterpretations. If Edelberg had taken the trouble to read also the second volume of his work he would have seen that the author's interpretations were not in keeping with the conservative and national tendencies Edelberg ascribed to him. Kirchhoff's and Trommer's answers followed in a later issue of the journal.[87] The former found the critique, when based on narrow, selective and disloyal reading, distorted in several respects. Defending Hæstrup he drew attention to the need for caution when writing about highly sensitive matters in the decades after the liberation of the country. Trommer agreed with Kirchhoff. Rejecting the charge of subscribing to the compilation approach to writing occupation history, he insisted that neither he nor Kirchhoff believed that one and only one adequate narrative of that period could be written. To conclude that they did was 'pure manipulation'. In an answer to the three respondents, printed in the same issue, Edelberg largely stuck to his guns, but paid tribute to their works as well as to Hæstrup's. With an acknowledgement of his own debt of gratitude to the latter for his achievement in collecting and analysing sources, Edelberg closed this brief inter-generational debate between historians.

As regards relations with the Soviet Union, it was again access to archival sources which led to fresh investigations and new findings. The most revealing material was the wartime communications between leaders of Denmark's Communist Party (DKP) and the Comintern. Reports, letters and other documents cast light on the difficult years of the non-aggression pact between the Soviet Union and Germany, on the challenging middle period of internment and growing resistance and on the crucial stages of liberation and transition to peacetime politics.

One important result of the research was a large volume of documents relating to the activities of DKP and the cross-party illegal paper and organization *Frit Danmark* between 1939 and 1943/44.[88] Edited by two foremost historians of the first revisionist generation, Kirchhoff and Trommer, it revealed, in its earlier part, the difficulties experienced by a political party which since 1935 had been committed to the strategy of popular front against fascism but which, from August 1939, had to justify the new Soviet policy towards Nazi Germany. The documents demonstrated how the party, while obviously far from being pro-German, always had to toe the line laid down by the Comintern. The later documents, supplemented by reports and letters from local branches in the country, showed how both the party and *Frit Danmark* struggled to establish and maintain the twin strategy of popular front and national front, which subsequently became the ordained line.

Documents pertaining to relations between DKP and Moscow towards the end of the occupation and in the post-war decades became sources for a book with a tell-tale title. In 1999 Bent Jensen, a leading sovietologist, published his *Bjørnen og haren* (the bear and the hare).[89] Having previously dealt with the gloomy role of Thomas Døssing as the representative in Moscow of Denmark's freedom council and having explained the mysterious Soviet occupation of the island of Bornholm after the German capitulation, he now analysed Denmark's relationship with the Soviet Union between 1945 and 1965.

Whatever the goals, policies and hopes of DKP leaders in the last months of the war, Jensen found no evidence of the Soviet leadership at that stage contemplating a military occupation of Denmark. Though very critical of the country's close cooperation with Germany during the occupation, the Soviet decision-makers accepted from the beginning of 1945 the formation of a broad coalition government in Copenhagen led by Vilhelm Buhl and with the freedom council as well as the political parties represented. The Soviet Union, he found, seemed to have come to accept Denmark as being within the British sphere of post-war influence. With little encouragement from Moscow and no alternative international backing in sight, any radical programme harboured and any revolutionary initiative contemplated by DKP's leaders in the transition from war to peace have their place more in the context of national politics.

National

Many scholarly historical writings, it seems, are inclined to present a sympathetic view of cooperation with the authorities of the occupying power, at least in its governmental and administrative forms. Criticism is usually directed more at corporate or personal instances of collaboration. On the other hand, such writings often seem to show a sceptical attitude to resistance, especially in its armed and organized appearance. Here a major concern is with the political programmes and post-war goals of the two political parties most closely associated with the resistance movement, namely DKP and Danish Unity (*Dansk Samling*).

From his study of Soviet sources, Bent Jensen concluded that the Russian masters were convinced that most of the Danish Communist leaders early in 1945 were intoxicated with wildly exaggerated ideas of their national popularity. Michael Kjeldsen, in an article analysing DKP's programme for the transition period and its concept of democracy, listed the reasons for the leaders' illusions.[90] At the national level, the strikes, protests and demonstrations of 1944 had strengthened the resistance movement and the freedom council, and thus enhanced the political influence of the party. Internationally, the example set by the Soviet Union in the war, the defects and risks associated with capitalism and the political achievements accomplished by Communist parties in other countries were also favourable influences. The post-war programme of the party presented in December 1944, 'The Will of the People – the Law of the Land', made it clear that the aim was 'to extend democracy' and bring socialism within reach. The assumption of political power was now clearly on the post-war agenda of the party.

Kjeldsen did not think that DKP was contemplating a military coup. On the other hand, it could hardly be said to be firmly committed to the doctrines and procedures of parliamentary democracy. Rather, its programme was to assume governmental power through extra-parliamentary efforts. By stirring propaganda and political action of many kinds, it would mobilize the masses and build up an overwhelming majority of people. For this purpose it was important to maintain the solidarity of the resistance movement.

Danish Unity, too, presented a political threat to the theory and practice of the parliamentary system. Based on a communitarian ideology with Christian and national roots, it rejected the sectarian rule by political parties that was bound up with parliamentary democracy, and championed instead elitist constitutional ideas. Though akin to the fascist movements emerging in inter-war Europe, it rejected German Nazism on both religious and national grounds. In the summer of 1940 its leaders were in touch with the Højgaard group of conservative nationalist businessmen, who planned to appeal to the king to appoint a government of distinguished and independent individuals. However, eventually the party decided to put its constitutional programme on hold. Early in 1941 its leader Arne Sørensen firmly declared Danish Unity loyal to the coalition government for the duration of the occupation.

The party appealed especially to self-employed people, white-collar workers, teachers, clergymen and students and attracted also a number of prominent intellectuals, notably the historian Vilhelm la Cour and the clergyman and author Kaj Munk. Many members and sympathizers joined local resistance groups, some establishing contact with SOE and reaching leading positions within the movement. When the freedom council was set up the party was offered a representative post, along with DKP and the principal resistance organizations. According to Henrik Lundbak's doctorial dissertation about the history of Danish Unity, published in 2001 under the title *Staten stærk og folket frit* (a strong state and a free people), Arne Sørensen preferred to appoint a deputy, and did not join the council till December 1943.[91] The reason for his hesitation was a fear that the freedom council was a front organization for the Communists.

Such fears were shared not only by members of other groups and parties right of centre on the political spectrum of the country. The Social Democrats, for whom the growing Communist movement was a potential rival, were also concerned. Others were disturbed by Danish Unity itself, with its fascist origins and extra-parliamentary programme. Yet others in the know may have been troubled by the fact that both of the political parties represented on the council had unconventional notions of the democratic form of constitution and government.

Most ordinary people too, not committed to either of the two parties represented or engaged in active resistance, were at first sceptical about the nature and role of the freedom council, which they first heard about in the illegal press in October 1943. However, its performance in the dramatic events of the following summer led to a marked change in the general attitude. Now accepted as the managing authority in situations of crisis, the freedom council had the backing of public opinion.

In recent years public attitudes and opinion have become a subject of serious study by Danish occupation historians. In 2000 Henning Poulsen published a humorous and ironic essay with the title 'Hvad mente danskerne?' (What did the Danes think).[92] Starting with German reports on the changing attitudes of individual Danes during the occupation, he went on to discuss critically the population's reactions to the two lines in Danish politics, cooperation and resistance. Speculating that the division between them might not have been so clear at the time, he suggested that the Danes in general supported both sides, though perhaps with changing emphasis. It was perfectly possible to regard resistance as desirable and political cooperation (or simply politics, as he sometimes prefers to call it) as comforting.

Seven years later a rather more substantial work on the subject appeared. Written by Palle Roslyng-Jensen and entitled *Danskerne og besættelsen* (The Danes and the occupation), it was based on about 70 diaries and other contemporary material from the six years of the war.[93] With diaries kept by individuals in positions with supreme responsibility, whether in the administration or in the resistance, excluded, the collection of diarists comprised a rich variety of ordinary Danes of that time. The analysis was presented chronologically in a dozen chapters, each structured round military and diplomatic developments in the war and political and social events in Denmark.

As a source of information about the attitudes, reactions and opinions of ordinary – though articulate – people, the book is a contribution to the comparative study of the formation and influence of public opinion in wartime Europe. However, with its many insights into the private lives of a broad range of diarists, it may also be seen as a composite and intimate account of everyday life in occupied Denmark. This social angle became a feature of some recent scholarly writings about that period of national history.

General

In 2005, the sixtieth anniversary of the liberation of Denmark, two books appeared to mark the occasion. They had three qualities in common. They provided an overview of all major aspects of the occupation, embraced all levels of Danish society and presented the five years in the context of the preceding as well as the following period of Danish history.

Historical continuity had already been the professed theme of the substantial Festschrift published two years earlier, under the title *Fra mellemkrigstid til efterkrigstid* (From inter-war time to post-war time). The continuity presented in the two later works may be described more precisely as the development, defence and restoration of the democratic tradition of the nation.

Nearly half of Bo Lidegaard's major work *Kampen om Danmark 1933–45* (The fight about Denmark) is about the years before and the time after the occupation.[94] The central part is broadly about a great national struggle of a coalition made up of successive governments, major institutions and the majority of the population against the forces supporting the totalitarian ideologies of Germany and the Soviet Union. Here all sections of the resistance movement are counted as part of the victorious democratic front. 1945, in this interpretation of Danish history, marks not only the victory of the democratic coalition but, significantly, also the return to normality.

The other major general work of that year also presents the country under occupation as a product of the Denmark of the 1930s, which was broadly shaped by coalition governments of Social Democrats and Radical Liberals. Here the historical continuity may be identified as largely Social Democratic. In dealing with the catastrophic impact of the invasion on 9 April, the authors stress the importance of the many social, economic and administrative institutions that survived and managed to continue their work under occupation, and beyond liberation. A revised edition of a work first appearing in 1995, and revised again in 2015, it is entitled *Danmark besat: Krig og hverdag 1940–45* (Denmark occupied: war and daily life).[95] About 800 pages long, it is the work of four historians with a wide range of scholarly specialities: Claus Bundgaard Christensen, Joachim Lund, Niels Wium Olesen and Jacob Sørensen. Regarded as the standard work on the occupation period, it is used at all universities in Denmark.

Not all recent general works plough the continuity furrow. Henning Poulsen's brief and readable *Besættelsesårene 1940–1945* (The occupation years) of 2002 starts with 9 April and ends with the restoration and the judicial reckoning in 1945 – and a one-line paragraph about life going on.[96]

The books discussed or mentioned in this sub-section are a small selection from a large number of recent historical publications on the subject. A critical review of scholarly occupation literature of the last decade of the twentieth and first half decade of the present centuries is available in the form of three articles which appeared, with five-year intervals, in *Historisk Tidsskrift*. Written by Palle Roslyng-Jensen, they examine significant contributions, discuss analytic distinctions, bring out major themes and, sometimes, point to promising fields for new research.

The theme of the first article, which appeared in 1995, is 'idealists and "materialists" in the occupation research'.[97] Devoted to the anniversary of the liberation and the latest literature in the field, it takes up the conceptual distinction between consensus and conflict, and notes a paradox. While the broader sections of the public, as revealed in celebrations throughout the country, have moved towards the consensus perspective on the occupation, the scholars have mainly accentuated a conflict perspective on the period. The latter tendency even makes the author wonder whether the distinction between the two concepts is becoming a stereotype.

The second article, published in 2001, is a continuation of the first and surveys the occupation literature since 1995.[98] It again characterizes and presents contributions according to analytic distinctions and themes. The general theme now is 'a national or an ideological historiography?' The author maintains that the experience of the occupation remains decisive for the formation of the national identity of the Danes. In the post-war years structured round the national state and expressed in novel foreign and defence policies, it has since become associated more with the Danish society, and expressed in social care at home and support for humanitarian causes abroad. The other main angle on the occupation research is more ideological. Its starting-points are the cold war between East and West and the conflict between right and left in Danish politics, each with its background in the occupation period. Many, though not all, of the scholarly writings of the last years of the twentieth century, the author finds, reflect one or both of those perspectives.

For the third article, published in 2006, it has become even more difficult to find a general theme.[99] Limiting his field to writings which present new tendencies in occupation research or contribute new knowledge, Roslyng-Jensen settles for 'post-modernistic variation and continuing boom'. It is no longer possible, as it still was in 2001, to characterize a substantial part of recent literature as, in some form or other, representing a revisionist approach. The relevant writings of the last five or six years, he finds, cover all degrees and combinations of consensus and conflict views. His overview starts with various general surveys of the occupation, and goes on to deal with publications about everyday life and consciousness history – all relatively new categories of occupation historiography.

On balance, the selected scholarly writings surveyed here appear to be oriented more towards consensus. After generations of revisionist scholarship featuring conflict and discord, the debate among modern historians may again be pointing towards some kind of concord in national reactions to foreign occupation. Signs of this may be seen in sympathetic views of governmental cooperation, typically deemed necessary or wise, and perhaps even in critical assessments of organized resistance, now often found heterogeneous and inferior, as well as in analysis of the interaction between the two.

Attempts to evade the basic dichotomy between cooperation and resistance, for example by postulating the development of a functional complementarity in which they, in effect, shield and exonerate each other, may be seen as pointing in the same direction. So may various creative efforts to find alternative dichotomies, some involving a renaming of cooperation (negotiation, politics, cohabitation). Such views and efforts may appear to be largely attempts to smooth over the adversity of the dichotomy.

Rather more significant may be the two novel tendencies in modern occupation historiography noted above, namely to broaden the social perspective and to extend the historical context. Examining the everyday life of ordinary people can bring out elements of the local situation and qualities of social interaction which may have remained largely unaffected by the occupation. Studying trends and qualities of Danish policy in the perspective of both the pre-war and the post-war period can reveal distinct continuities. From that angle the policy of cooperation, too, can be regarded as in some respects a continuation, in different circumstances, of the Danish policy of steering close to Germany at crucial stages of the history of the League of Nations. In that perspective the resistance movement may come close to appearing as an aberration.

Both the interest in everyday life and the search for continuity indicate a preoccupation with normality. This could conceivably be motivated by a lingering national need to overcome the historic trauma of invasion and occupation. Concentrating on shared habits and established traditions, instead of on the values and attitudes that divided people, might assist the process. So might some of the more recent enquiries into consciousness and searches for a Danish identity, complemented by a variety of less academic intellectual and cultural exercises in national introspection. Thus, modern occupation history might, conceivably, one day be recognized as essentially part of a national effort to negate the tragic quality of the five-year drama.

3.5. Discourse

For a long time, the professional debate presented in this part had only limited influence on contemporaneous public discourse about Danish reactions to German occupation. Yet, the starting-point of such discourse was much the same as that of professional historiography. Most of the personal memoirs, popular accounts and fictional works, as well as the films, plays and, not least, the press appearing in the first post-war decades presented a picture of a nation united in opposition to the occupying power. Such material often seemed to suggest that more or less everybody – apart from small groups of Nazis and other traitors – had been engaged in passive or active resistance.

Like the works of the first generation of historians and other scholars, public discourse at that stage claimed or assumed the existence of a degree of harmony which rested on some kind of compromise between those committed to political and administrative cooperation with the occupying power and those engaged in active resistance. This notion of national concord could be traced back to the last period of the occupation and the immediate post-war situation. Another characteristic of such discourse was a tendency to backdate by a few years the struggle against the Germans and to turn a blind eye to the combination of official cooperation and public passivity marking the first years of the occupation.

When the first wave of scholarly revisionism challenged the notion of national concord, whether by highlighting the conflict between cooperation and resistance or by dealing with the former separately and on its own merits, public discourse did not follow suit. In the 1960s, and even more so in the 1970s, the established inclination to play down any surviving notions of dissention between the politicians and the resistance and play up the image of wartime solidarity was rather reinforced in the public debate. The discourse of commemoration then gathering strength provided the best examples of such exercises in historical projection. The trend towards national self-flattery continued in the following decades, perhaps reaching its climax with the parliamentary debates in the spring of 1995 on the occasion of the fiftieth anniversary of liberation.

In an account of the occupation period as collective memory of the Danish people published in 1998, Claus Bryld and Anette Warring sought to show how, in the course of half a century, a history had been constructed and a memory transmitted of those momentous five years.[100] Drawing on German and other European scholarship, they introduced the concept of historical culture, and structured their book around its three dimensions, namely the political or volitional, the aesthetic or emotional and the cognitive. Exploring the political dimension, they explained how the post-war need for patriotic memories soon became tied up with the cold war and membership of NATO, which called for a demonstration of willingness to engage in military cooperation with democratic allies. In this setting, the image of resistance as the typical Danish reaction to occupation emerged.

On the aesthetic-emotional level, too, the nation needed a collective memory of its recent past which it could identify with and be proud of. This need, according to the authors, was met largely through the development of a commemorative culture. The erection of monuments, the celebration of anniversaries, other memorial ceremonies as well as various symbolic rituals helped to establish and maintain a shared tradition of remembrance. Such a construction, however, had little or nothing to do with the actual events of the period of occupation. As a result of the process, the discourse became imbued with mythical qualities.

In the cognitive dimension, the historical research carried out in the 1970s, together with various public debates taking place between 1970 and 1995, did help to present a more realistic picture of the occupation years. However, meaningful debate on the subject was often obstructed, the authors complained, by veteran circles of the resistance movement intervening to exclude particular lines of enquiry and seeking to monopolize the interpretation of history. Here they enjoyed the support of politicians who did not want to fall foul of the veteran organizations. Often the result was that the media simply dropped the subject and allowed the debate to peter out. Bryld and Warring's book can be seen as an attempt to redress the balance in the public discourse about Danish reactions to German occupation.

In the years following the publication of that book, the balance in both academic debate and public discourse swung against the resistance movement. The challenging programme and iconoclastic style of the second wave of historical revisionism, then gathering strength, caught the interest of a wider public and brought general discourse more into line with scholarly debate. At both levels, there was not only a greater willingness to accept and endorse the policy of cooperation, and even to understand and condone the actions of various groups of collaborators, but also a marked tendency to denigrate the efforts of the resistance movement and question the conduct of some of its leaders. The most obvious reasons for such attitudes were the passing away of veterans and other early spokesmen of the resistance movement and the emergence of a new generation of historians and other opinion formers with no personal experience of the occupation years. However, certain major changes in the international political situation and some novel issues of domestic politics may also have been at work, as conditioning influences.

The end of the cold war, the collapse of the Communist order in Eastern Europe and the break-up of the Soviet Union made the experience of patriotic resistance to an occupying great power seem less relevant than it had been during the East–West political and military division of Europe. Nor could the memory of such resistance, which had been mainly nationally inspired, have much bearing on the quasi-globalized concerns of the Western nations with democracy, free trade and human rights in the post-cold war world.

On the other hand, the US-led interventions and wars to combat fundamentalist terrorism and prevent proliferation of weapons of mass destruction did seem to be of some relevance to Danish debate about wartime cooperation and resistance. Raising political issues for the Danes too, they could influence that debate indirectly. Those who opposed Danish participation in the wars in Iraq and Afghanistan, broadly representing the left-of-centre tradition of neutrality and disengagement in power politics, were more likely to side with the wartime government in the debate about the occupation. Those who supported the case for taking part in the wars, in principle inclined towards engagement in international politics, were more disposed to see armed resistance to the Germans as an inspiring example. Thus the political conflict about the wars in Asia may have helped to harden the lines in the historical debate about the occupation.

Each of the anniversaries of the crisis in August 1943 and the liberation in May 1945 gave rise to a flare-up of the public debate about cooperation and resistance during the occupation. On 29 August 2003 Anders Fogh Rasmussen, Liberal leader and prime minister in a right-of-centre coalition government, made a speech at the naval college, which appeared in the national daily *Politiken* the same day. In what appeared to be something of a pep talk to the cadets and their officers, he started by saluting the decision of the government 60 years ago, at long last, to put an end to cooperation with the occupying power, and by praising the action of the naval officers who had deprived the Germans of the Danish fleet by scuttling the ships or taking them to neutral Sweden. Those events, he asserted, had helped to improve Denmark's reputation among the allied powers.

He went on to launch a scathing attack on the Danish establishment of the time, which for three years had pursued a policy of actively accommodating the occupying power in the hope of retaining a degree of sovereignty for the country. That policy he described as politically naïve and morally reprehensible. It was the growing dissatisfaction of the public with the policy of the government, he explained, together with the brave efforts of members of the resistance, that had put an end to such cooperation, and secured a place for Denmark on the right side in the struggle against the Nazis. Fogh Rasmussen finished his talk with a tribute to those who, as members of the resistance, had fought in defence of freedom and democracy.

Various other writers expressed similar views in articles and speeches marking the same anniversary. But soon a number of historians reacted to the political and moral charges directed at the wartime government and its policies. Perhaps the most robust retort to Fogh Rasmussen came from Hans Kirchhoff, otherwise better known for defending the resistance movement. In an article published in *Information* some weeks after the anniversary, he accused the prime minister and others of demonizing the policy and practice of cooperation with the Germans and misusing occupation history for their own political purposes.

They had failed, he pointed out, not only to mention the risk of a Nazi coup, which had been a major motive of the policy of cooperation in the first year or two, but also to acknowledge the fear of the Communists, who had been behind most of the sabotage and whose activities ultimately had threatened the proclaimed peaceful nature of the occupation. Is it really less moral, he asked, to want to protect democratic institutions against Nazification, or defend the economy against pillage and ruination or protect the population against hunger deportations? Resistance, he explained, could not be an alternative to cooperation in the first years of occupation, at least not for the politicians, civil servants and institutions saddled with the responsibility for the lives and welfare of millions of people. However, Kirchhoff finished his article with a warm tribute to the resistance movement for having broken with state egotism and sided with the anti-Nazi forces.[101]

About 18 months later the debate flared up again, in connection with preparations for the 4th of May celebrations. Once again the initiative came from the prime minister. In an introduction to some educational material presented on the website of the ministry of education, he recalled that many Danes under Nazi occupation had found themselves presented with the choice between resistance and cooperation, between doing the right thing, and thus exposing themselves to great personal risks, and going with the tide and putting their own wealth and safety first. That choice, he observed, could still bring feelings to boiling-point.

Subsequently Fogh Rasmussen, reacting to the hostile response of most historians to his views and judgements on occupation history, developed his arguments and answered his critics in a feature article in *Jyllands-Posten*, a leading right-of-centre daily. The sixtieth anniversary of liberation, as he saw it, had three messages. The Danish people owed a great debt of gratitude to the resistance fighters, who, through sabotage against the Germans and cooperation with the allies, had defied the politicians and secured the country a place on the right side in the anti-Nazi struggle. They had saved the honour of the nation. Second, the policy of actively accommodating the Germans, he reiterated, had constituted a political and moral failure. Denmark had got through the war cheaply by letting others do the work of fighting the Germans. Third, it was possible to learn from history, and avoid repeating the failures of the past. As for the critique by the historians, Fogh Rasmussen asserted his right to pass judgement on the policies and conduct of the occupation years, as people living at the time had been able to do, and stressed the need to acknowledge past mistakes.[102]

In the media debate the prime minister had the support of some politicians, many journalists and a few surviving members of the resistance movement. In the same issue of *Jyllands-Posten* Bertel Haarder, Liberal minister of education and ecclesiastic affairs, dealt critically with the revisionist writings of Radical Liberal historians and denounced their efforts to rehabilitate Erik Scavenius and reassess his policy. They presented Scavenius as a political realist. Yet, as a politician who, for much too long, had based his policy on a misjudgement of the Nazis' prospect of winning the war and who consistently had failed to take account of the attitude of the Danish public, he should not, in Haarder's view, be deemed a great statesman, let alone be held up as a true hero of the occupation.

The foremost spokesman of the veterans of the resistance was the 85-year-old Jørgen Kieler, a retired specialist in cancer research who, as active member of the sabotage organization Holger Danske, had been arrested, sentenced to death by the Germans and instead sent to a concentration camp in Germany. In interviews and articles in the months leading up to the anniversary in May 2005 he warmly endorsed Fogh Rasmussen's condemnation of the policy of cooperation. That policy, he insisted, had been mendacious from the very beginning and had led to a series of unnecessary and provocative initiatives in collaboration. Those who were angry about the prime minister's statements he labelled as adherents of the so-called anti-movement of the post-war years. Amply supported by many younger historians, they sought to disparage the resistance movement and to present collaboration as the most effective defence of democracy.[103]

The weightiest argument in support of the policies towards Germany pursued by the Danish governments in the later part of the 1930s and the first years of the occupation was Bo Lidegaard's *Kampen om Danmark 1933–1945*, published at the height of the public debate in 2005. His earlier works included a book about the role of Henrik Kauffmann in Danish diplomacy and a volume in a major series about the history of Danish foreign policy. The latter work, entitled *Overleveren 1914–1945* (The Survivor), was remarkable for its sympathetic treatment of Erik Scavenius and its positive assessment of his policies. It credited Danish policy and diplomacy in the world wars with having served the interests of the country and the future of its democratic system as well as had been possible in the circumstances. This finding served as a point of departure for the argument he presented in *Kampen om Danmark*.

There had been no reasonable alternative, Lidegaard argued, either to the appeasement policy of the 1930s or to the cooperative policy during the occupation. However, at both stages, the cautious and accommodating conduct of external relations had been compensated by a sharper line against Nazi and fascist tendencies within Danish society. Indeed, the overriding theme of the whole period he was dealing with had been the domestic defence of Danish democracy, against its rightist as well as its leftist critics and enemies within. Thus, the basic issue in the debate about the policy of cooperation was just how far a democracy can go in making concessions to an occupying power and compromising its legal principles without negating its essential idea and losing its legitimacy. That was the point reached in August 1943.[104]

Resistance, according to Lidegaard, had been primarily a political and moral, rather than a military, phenomenon. Sabotage had been a protest against the policy of cooperation more than an attack on German military power. As such it had been a demonstration of the will to resist the Germans. The fight for Denmark had been won through the interaction of cooperation and resistance. While cooperation, judged on its own terms, had been the right and sensible policy, it would have been a disaster if it had not been complemented by active resistance. Like Kirchhoff, Lidegaard could not defend the politicians and their policy and conduct in the earlier years of the occupation without acknowledging the decisive importance of the resistance movement in the later period.[105]

Seeking explanations for the recurrent attacks in more recent years on the policy of cooperation, typically followed by heated public debates between advocates of different interpretations of occupation history, Lidegaard went beyond current political needs and interests of the parties involved and considered also possible psychological motivations. Here he brought in the notion of a collective survivor's syndrome. Underlying the debate, he noted, was a self-accusation: where did we go wrong when we managed to get through the war so easily? The response he described as a new national epos about moral failure and shameful subservience in face of injustice; about a government, parliament and people failing to understand the innermost nature of Nazism. However, such views, he pointed out, ignored the development from cooperation in 1940 to resistance a few years later, and did not take the Communist dimension of resistance into account. Passing moral judgement on cooperation and resistance, Lidegaard concluded, was not so easy.[106]

Conclusion

During the period of occupation, taken as a whole, the basic political issue was between cooperation and resistance. After 1945 the relationship between those opposing reactions to German occupation became a major theme of both academic historiography and public discourse. However, cooperation as well as resistance are terms which cover a fairly broad range of policies and conduct.

A distinction has been made between willing and reluctant cooperation with the occupying power. The former was characterized by some miscalculated diplomatic initiatives and a measure of economic opportunism, the latter more by protracted negotiations and limited concessions. Yet, both forms were motivated by a concern to protect the population and institutions of the country, in particular its democratic system of politics. At no stage was official cooperation with the occupying authorities inspired by Nazi or even pro-German sympathies. The policy of cooperation enjoyed the support of the government, the major political parties, the parliament, the king, the administration, the major economic institutions and, at least up to August 1943, the vast majority of the population.

As regards resistance to the occupying power, a relevant distinction is between unarmed and the more militant kinds. The former comprised services to the allied cause by the merchant navy, organized intelligence gathering for Britain and its allies and propaganda against the Danish government and the German authorities by the illegal press. The militant kinds of resistance took the forms of sabotage and liquidations, demonstrations and strikes, organization of an army of resistance and active service by volunteers in the forces of an allied power. While most of the unarmed activities were maintained throughout the occupation, the militant efforts made their mark in the last two years before liberation. The general shift in public opinion was from broad support for reluctant cooperation with the occupying power in the earlier years to growing identification with armed resistance in the last stages of the war. While most pioneers of such resistance came from right-of-centre parties or the Communists, the resistance movement, emerging in the last years, drew its members from across the political spectrum of the country.

The wartime political issue between cooperation and resistance had a psychological as well as a moral side, both of which aspects characterized also later historical debate about the occupation. In February 1945, when representatives of the freedom council and political leaders were arguing about the composition of the liberation government, Frode Jakobsen wrote an article in which he drew attention to the psychological dimension of the conflict. Referring to the humiliating period of the Scavenius policy of deliberate cooperation, he called for a very different national will, as well as a different sense of reality, to guide the new government. The old political leaders had called themselves 'realpoliticians', he wrote, and considered the men of the resistance to be fantasts. But it was the fantasts, he observed, who had faced up to the hard reality and chosen the line that had prevailed. Whereas the realpoliticians, with their lack of imagination and parochial outlook, had proved themselves unable to look into the future, and into the world beyond Denmark.[1]

While spokesmen of the resistance stressed the virtues of patriotic emotions and courage, the politicians of the time, as well as later defenders of the wartime establishment, emphasized the need for reason and cool intelligence in the management of relations with the occupying power. Till a late stage, those identifying with the policy of cooperation were inclined to disparage their opponents as heroes and idealists. In broader psychological categories, the issue may be seen as a conflict between pessimism and optimism. While the pessimists ruled in the first three or four years of the war, the optimists gained support and influence in the last year or two, after the fortunes of war had turned against the German armies and the prospect of liberation had moved closer.

The moral dimension of the conflict between cooperation and resistance was related to the occupational roles of the participants. In a letter to Christmas Møller in London written in August 1944, soon after the general strike in Copenhagen, Mogens Fog touched upon the differences of morality between the politicians and the resistance leaders. What divided the two sides, he said, was not different ideas about tactics but basic views of life. 'The only word they know is "protect" – and at any price – while we are familiar with the notion of "to sacrifice", where it can bring about spiritual or material benefit'. A real fight for spiritual values was beyond most of the old politicians.[2] The true lesson of the occupation, he stated in a volume of memoirs written many years later, was that so many people voluntarily, in response to an inner personal call, had given up their secure everyday life because the external circumstances had violated those higher values on which their life rested.[3]

The old politicians to whom Fog was referring in his letter could have answered his charge by claiming that they, as ministers in the coalition government, carried the responsibility for safeguarding the lives and interests of the population and protecting the institutions and political traditions of the country. In a situation of great danger for the nation and of uncertain duration, they were acting in accordance with their professional duty when they negotiated with the Germans, proposed compromises and made concessions. As long as they could continue the exchange with the occupying power they were keeping the country running, and gaining time. While the representatives of the resistance movement, often intellectuals or members of a profession, typically were motivated by an ethics of conscience, high values and courage, the politicians supporting the policy of cooperation were guided more by an ethics of responsibility, duty and caution.

The choice between cooperating with and resisting the occupying authorities was not one which everybody had to make. For the individual Dane, the historians Henning Poulsen and Niels Wium Olesen have pointed out, it was quite possible to support the policy of cooperation, hate the Germans and sympathize with the resistance movement, all at the same time.[4] Thus, for many ordinary people it was more a both-and situation. For government employees, and those working for the major institutions of the country, there was, most of the time, only little choice. The first three years of the occupation, when resistance made little sense to men of responsibility, they could rarely see an alternative to following the lines laid down by the government and other national authorities. Yet, there were always exceptions, such as a civil servant who maintained secret contact to resistance circles, or a police officer who turned a blind eye or allowed a resister to escape.

However, when an alternative to cooperation did present itself, it was mostly individuals or groups not personally accountable to established authorities who responded by rejecting the governmental line and engaging in some form of active resistance. For them, it was a real choice between opposite courses, both before and after August 1943. For the Communists, who had been lying low since the signing of the Nazi–Soviet pact in August 1939 but had been making some preparations for illegal existence, the decision was facilitated by Danish legislation. By banning their party and interning many of its leaders soon after the German attack on the Soviet Union in June 1941, the Danish government in effect played a part in driving its members into illegality and militancy. In the last year of the occupation, especially in the last months, when many other people from most walks of life came out in support of the resistance movement, the choice was rather easier than it had been at earlier stages.

Whatever the response of sections of society and individuals to the dichotomy of cooperation and resistance, it was the tension between those opposite reactions that shaped the history of Denmark under occupation, and structured most of the historiographical debate and public discourse of later generations. Both cooperation with the occupying power and resistance to its presence and intrusions can be seen as wartime manifestations of long traditions of Danish conduct of relations with neighbouring great powers.

Governmental and administrative cooperation with the German authorities, conducted in the hope of maintaining a degree of sovereignty, was a continuation, in aggravated circumstances, of the Radical Liberal and Social Democratic policy towards Germany in the 1930s. This policy, derived from geopolitical determinism and faith in the superior virtue of Danish neo-neutrality, carried the marks of Radical Liberal pacifism and Social Democratic anti-militarism. It can be seen as a development from other policies of non-engagement in great-power politics pursued in still earlier periods of Danish history.

Cooperation with the occupying power served various socio-economic interests of the political parties of the coalition government. For the Social Democrats and Radical Liberals, whose pre-war governments had laid the foundations of a modern welfare state, it was essential to maintain the political structure and social legislation of the country, whatever the outcome of the war. Indeed, some of the more dedicated social reformers seemed inclined to view the occupation by foreign troops mainly as an interruption of their efforts to create a model society. For the Liberals, the economic benefits of the occupation could not be ignored. Many of the supporters of the party, the bulk of whom were farmers, found the rise in the prices of butter and bacon rather more interesting than the growing resistance in the towns. And most of those Conservatives who represented trades and industries were for long disturbed by the pro-resistance attitudes and activities of many members of sections of their party. On the whole, the material interests of the four parties in maintaining a degree of cooperation with the Germans weighed more heavily in the earlier years of the occupation, when the outcome of the war still seemed far from certain.

Active resistance, with or without arms, can be seen as a revival of a tradition of engagement in international politics much older than that of disengagement. Though it had fallen into abeyance since the traumatic defeat of the country in the war of 1864, traces of it may be detected in the critical reactions of Conservative and Liberal politicians to the capitulation on 9 April 1940 and their opposition to the foreign and defence policies of the 1930s as well as in the rejection by the upper house of parliament of successive proposals for disarmament tabled by the governments of the 1920s. Before that, the most striking manifestations of the survival of former preparedness to engage forcefully in European politics were the two patriotic wars with Prussia and the German Confederation over Schleswig-Holstein in the mid-nineteenth century and the less enthusiastic involvement in the later stages of the Napoleonic Wars. The origins of the tradition, however, are to be found in earlier centuries, when Denmark–Norway, together with Sweden, were still great or major powers, actively engaging in the power politics of the northern region of Europe in pursuit or defence of the interests of the state or its king.

While sabotage, and other militant measures employed by the resistance, politically might be aimed also at the Danish authorities engaged in cooperation, militarily such actions were directed at the occupying power. They were a local contribution to the European war against the forces and ideology of Nazi Germany and its allies. Though motivated by patriotic feelings and presented as a national effort, Danish resistance had to be coordinated with the plans and efforts of the allied powers. While the Communists looked to Moscow for direction and guidance, the non-Communist leaders of the resistance accepted instruction and support from London. The latter relationship proved by far the more important for the development and organization of resistance in Denmark.

The general directives issued by Moscow for the benefit of European Communist parties naturally applied to Denmark too. Thus, the Danish leadership adopted the tactical principle of popular front against the Nazi enemy, gave priority to national liberation and engaged in militant anti-German activities. However, as a result of limited Soviet interest in the political life of Denmark and a sceptical attitude to its efforts at resistance, Moscow's influence during the occupation became mainly ideological. Through a well-organized illegal press, the Communists spearheaded the Danish counter-offensive to the German propaganda apparatus.

Practically from the beginning of the occupation there were resistance-minded individuals in Denmark who managed to maintain or establish contact with England, whether through neutral Sweden or some other way. After the setting up of SOE, the way to the military and political authorities in London usually went through its Danish section. Thus, the reports that a group of Danish intelligence officers secretly started to prepare for Britain soon after the invasion of the country, and continued to supply till the Germans capitulated, went to that office, much of the time via Ebbe Munck and the SOE representative in Stockholm. When sabotage, strikes and street demonstrations in Denmark began seriously to affect the country's relations with the occupying power, it was through the same office that British authorities sought to manage and control Danish resistance, sometimes encouraging and sometimes restraining militant activities.[5]

For a long time, before Denmark had an organized movement to carry out sabotage, SOE, cautioned by the Foreign Office and warned by the Danish intelligence officers, refrained from encouraging such activities. It was not till the spring of 1943, well after the Communists had started their offensive, that SOE began to exercise real influence on this form of resistance. With a dynamic leader and a number of instructors and organizers, all Danes trained in England, now in place, it was in a position to strengthen existing and set up new groups in a number of major towns, supply them with necessary materials, especially plastic explosives, and provide guidance about targets and timing. After a marked intensification of industrial as well as railway sabotage in the summer and later part of 1943, SOE called for a pause in such activities in the earlier months of 1944. The retreat of the German armies after the invasion of Normandy and the approach of allied forces led to a greater need for more selective forms of sabotage. In accordance with orders issued by allied headquarters, the resistance now concentrated on mining German troop movements, particularly in Jutland.

During the last 18 months of the war, when the European branch of SOE was merged with its American counterpart OSS under the name of Special Forces, the primary task allocated to Denmark was to prepare its rapidly growing resistance movement for a local supporting role in the final stage of the war and the transition to peace. To secure direct allied control of the units of the movement, the country was divided into six regions, each with a separate structure and own leadership. Within this framework, an underground army, recruited across party-political divisions and officered by professional soldiers and resistance fighters, was set up. It was equipped, albeit sparsely, with British and some American arms and materials, dropped or shipped into the country. Much of the work of establishing this army was carried out by a military committee set up by the freedom council.

The Foreign Office, having come to regard Denmark as a significant part of a projected post-war British sphere of influence on the Continent, had a political interest in securing a smooth transition from occupation and resistance to liberation and restoration of constitutional government and political stability in the country. Thus, its relations with Denmark in the later stages of the war were largely directed towards managing the tension between the freedom council and the political leaders and loyal army officers, and towards avoiding hostilities between the Communists and other members of the resistance movement. That generally meant balancing between encouraging and supporting the efforts of resistance and cautioning and restraining some of the leaders and representatives of the movement. This conciliatory policy found expression in two significant diplomatic initiatives. One was British sponsorship for the Danish request for allied status, presented jointly by members of the freedom council and representatives of the major political parties. The other was British acceptance and support for a liberation government headed by the Social Democratic leader Vilhelm Buhl and with the old political parties and the major sections of the resistance movement represented equally.

The later stages of the occupation and earlier post-war years were a period marked by compromise in political decision-making and reconciliation in historical interpretation. Yet, the conflict between cooperation and resistance as reactions to German occupation remained. In the last analysis, it rested on an antithesis of mental attitudes, of introversion and a tendency towards national self-sufficiency against extroversion and a disposition to international solidarity. The former, rooted not only in the trauma of 1864 and earlier losses but also in the gains of neutrality in the First World War, was manifested in a willingness to accept the possibility of German victory in the war and a resolve to protect narrow Danish political and material interests. The latter attitude, drawing on the more heroic periods and incidents in Danish history, found expression in faith in the ultimate victory of the allied powers and in courage to join the anti-Nazi struggle through armed resistance.

International solidarity and courageous engagement marked both Communist and non-Communist resistance. The Communists, ideologically guided by the Soviet Union in a spirit of socialist internationalism, pursued their socialist goals within a framework of cross-party anti-Nazi resistance. The non-Communist resisters, motivated by patriotic emotions and supported by Britain, restored national honour through cooperation with Western allies.

Notes

Chapter 1

1 O. Feldbæk, *Danmarks historie,* iv: *Tiden 1730–1814* (Copenhagen: Gyldendal, 1982), 276.

2 Later writers, notably the diplomat Peter Vedel and the historians Edvard Holm and Aage Friis, quoted Bernstorff's comment on war and treated it as evidence of the moral superiority of a statesman pursuing a policy of peace. Writing in the late nineteenth and early twentieth centuries, they were inclined to vest the peculiar type of neutrality practised in the earlier century with legal and moral qualities which the policy of neutrality had begun to acquire only in the later part of the nineteenth century. For a brief survey of such historiography, see C. Holbraad, *Danish Neutrality: A Study in the Foreign Policy of a Small State* (Oxford: Clarendon Press, 1991), 3–7.

3 G. Nørregaard, *Danmark mellem øst og vest 1824–39* (Copenhagen: Gyldendal, 1969), 131.

4 One of the liberal leaders, D.C. Monrad, who had headed the government at a crucial stage of the war, said on 9 November 1864, 'I fear that it will be impossible for this small country that will be left to maintain its political independence' (E. Møller, *Helstatens Fald*, part 2, 1864 (Copenhagen: G.E.C. Gad, 1958), 191).

5 H. Nielsen, *Dansk udenrigspolitik 1875–1894 med særligt henblik paa beslutningsprocessen* (Odense: Odense Universitetsforlag, 1977), 58–9; the context was the crisis over the Eastern Question in the spring of 1878.

6 E. Scavenius, *Dansk udenrigspolitik under den første verdenskrig* (Copenhagen: Fremad, 1959), 16.

7 Scavenius, *Dansk udenrigspolitik*, 17–19.

8 The critic was the diplomat A.V.A. Dotezac (E. Halicz, *Danish Neutrality during the Crimean War (1853–1856): Denmark between the Hammer and the Anvil*, trans. J. Cave (Odense: Odense University Press, 1977), 128.

9 V. Sjøqvist, *Danmarks udenrigspolitik 1933–1940* (Copenhagen: Gyldendal, 1966), 29–30.

10 J. Hæstrup et al. (eds), *Kilder til modstandsbevægelsens historie* (Copenhagen: Gyldendal, 1972), 191–3. The reference was to the United Nations, which the allied powers were planning to set up after the war.

Chapter 2

1 E. Scavenius, *Dansk udenrigspolitik under den første verdenskrig,* 11.

2 E. Scavenius, *Forhandlingspolitiken under Besættelsen* (Copenhagen: Steen Hasselbalchs Forlag, 1948), 7–9.

3 V. Sjøqvist, *Erik Scavenius: Danmarks udenrigsminister under to verdenskrige. Statsminister 1942–1945* (Copenhagen: Gyldendal, 1973), vol. ii, 89–90.

4 Erling Bjøl reported that Erik Seidenfaden, editor of *Information*, told him that the man behind the circular of 2 September was Hans Hedtoft (E. Bjøl, *Set i bakspejlet* (Copenhagen: Politikens Forlag, 1993), 162–3.

5 The most famous story, about the king declaring his intention to wear the Star of David himself, was an invention. As the result of an interaction between the German minister, Cecil von Renthe-Fink, and the Danish authorities, no legislation discriminating between Jews and others was passed in Denmark. However, the story, which has been traced back to a cartoon in a Swedish newspaper in January 1942, did no harm to the reputation of the king abroad, especially in the United States. It also fitted in well with British propaganda aimed at building up the king.

Chapter 3

1 For Hæstrup's meetings with SOE officials in London and his arguments for getting hold of the wartime files of the organization, see the account he wrote of his 25 years of research into Danish history during the German occupation, *Dørene åbnes. En forsknings historie* (Odense: Odense Universitetsforlag, 1973), 34.
2 *Dørene åbnes*, 44–53.
3 *Dørene åbnes*, 56–8.
4 *Dørene åbnes*, 80–1.
5 *Dørene åbnes*, 89–91.
6 *Dørene åbnes*, 93–4.
7 *Dørene åbnes*, 114–5.
8 *Hemmelig alliance. Hovedtræk af den danske modstandsorganisations udvikling 1943–1945*, vols. i, ii (Copenhagen: Thanning og Appels Forlag, 1959). An English translation of *Kontakt med England 1940–43* and *Hemmelig alliance* appeared in 1976–7 in the form of a three-volume work entitled *Secret Alliance. A Study of the Danish Resistance Movement, 1940–45* (Odense: Odense Universitetsforlag).
9 *...til landets bedste –. Hovedtræk af departementschefsstyrets virke 1943–45*, vols i, ii (Copenhagen: Gyldendal).
10 *Dørene åbnes*, 197.
11 *...til landets bedste –*, vol. i, 11–12, and *Dørene åbnes*, 197–8.
12 *Kontakt med England*, 9–10 and 35, and *Hemmelig alliance*, vol i, 10–11.
13 *Europe Ablaze. An Analysis of the History of the European Resistance Movements 1939–45* (Odense: Odense Universitetsforlag, 1978).
14 *Dørene åbnes*, 135–6.
15 The book was blacklisted, and remaining copies confiscated, after the German invasion of Denmark. A second edition was published in 1950 by Fremad, Copenhagen.
16 F. Jakobsen, *I Danmarks frihedsråd* (Copenhagen: Gyldendal, 1975), vol i, 21–3.
17 N.F. Christiansen, *Hartvig Frisch. Mennesket og politikeren. En biografi* (Copenhagen: Christian Ejlers Forlag, 1993), 226–8.
18 Christiansen, *Hartvig Frisch*, 232–4. The oration was delivered on 13 November 1943.
19 Christiansen, *Hartvig Frisch*, 236.
20 Christiansen, *Hartvig Frisch*, 236–7.
21 Christiansen, *Hartvig Frisch*, 245–7.
22 Christiansen, *Hartvig Frisch*, 244–5.
23 Christiansen, *Hartvig Frisch*, 249–50.
24 Christiansen, *Hartvig Frisch*, 253–5.
25 Christiansen, *Hartvig Frisch*, 258–9.
26 Christiansen, *Hartvig Frisch*, 259–60.
27 Christiansen, *Hartvig Frisch*, 261. The passage translated here is quoted from page 130 of *Tænkt og talt under Krigen* (Copenhagen: Fremad, 1945).
28 *Danmark besat og befriet*, vol. i (Copenhagen: Fremad, 1945), 88–103 and 208.
29 *Danmark besat og befriet*, vol. i, 142–3. For Frisch's attitude to the rupture of Danish–German relations, see also his comment on Alsing Andersen's circular of 2 September 1943 (ibid., 397).
30 *Danmark besat og befriet*, vol. i, 254–7.
31 *Danmark besat og befriet*, vol. iii (Copenhagen: Fremad, 1948), 23–5 and 42.
32 *Danmark besat og befriet*, vol. iii, 251.

33 *Danmark besat og befriet*, vol. iii, 72–4.
34 *Danmark besat og befriet*, vol. iii, 40–1.
35 *Danmark besat og befriet*, vol. iii, 179–80.
36 *Danmark besat og befriet*, vol. iii, 318.
37 *Danmark besat og befriet*, vol. iii, 355–6.
38 For some comparative observations on Hæstrup's and Frisch's consensus interpretations, see H. Dethlefsen, 'Arven fra Hæstrup', in H. Dethlefsen and H. Lundbak (eds), *Fra mellemkrigstid til efterkrigstid* (Copenhagen: Museum Tusculanums Forlag, 1998), 340–1.
39 *Jernbanesabotagen i Danmark under den anden verdenskrig. En krigshistorisk undersøgelse* (Odense University Press, 1971), with a summary in English, 303–16.
40 *Jernbanesabotagen i Danmark*, 12.
41 *Jernbanesabotagen i Danmark*, 293–300.
42 *Jernbanesabotagen i Danmark*, 197.
43 *Jernbanesabotagen i Danmark*, 217–8.
44 For a report, see the daily *Morgenavisen Jyllands-Posten*, October 1971.
45 *Modstandsarbejde i nærbillede. Det illegale arbejde i Syd- og Sønderjylland under den tyske besættelse af Danmark 1940–45* (Odense University Press, 1973). For a summary of Trommer's case against the spontaneity conception of recruitment, see pages 273–83.
46 *Augustoprøret 1943. Samarbejdspolitikkens fald. Forudsætninger og forløb. En studie i collaboration og modstand* (Copenhagen: Gyldendal, 1979), vol. i, 14–15.
47 *Augustoprøret 1943*, vol. ii, 197–200.
48 *Augustoprøret 1943*, vol. ii, 267–70.
49 *Augustoprøret 1943*, vol. ii, 254–5.
50 *Kamp eller tilpasning* (Copenhagen: Gyldendal, 1987). A revised and expanded edition appeared in 2002 under the title *Samarbejde og modstand under besættelsen. En politisk historie* (Odense: Odense Universitetsforlag).
51 *Kamp eller tilpasning*, 9.
52 *Kamp eller tilpasning*, 42–50.
53 *Augustoprøret*, vol i, 18.
54 *1940* (Copenhagen: Gyldendal), 13–14 and 18.
55 *1940*, 11–12 and 454–5.
56 *1940*, 83 and 453.
57 *1940*, 455.
58 *Den 9. april* (Copenhagen: Jurist- og Økonomforbundets Forlag, 1987), 7.
59 *Den 9. april*, 258.
60 *Den 9. april*, 18–19.
61 For a thorough and impartial investigation of the post-war judicial reckoning, see D. Tamm, *Retsopgøret efter besættelsen*, vols i and ii (Copenhagen: Gyldendal, 1984–5; 3rd edn. 1997). For some selected cases of economic collaboration, see C. Jensen, Th. Kristiansen, K.E. Nielsen, *Krigens købmænd* (Copenhagen, 2000).
62 *Under hagekors og dannebrog* (Copenhagen: Aschehoug, 1998), 435.
63 *Under hagekors og dannebrog*, 436–7.
64 V. la Cour (ed.), *Danmark under Besættelsen*, vols i–iii (Copenhagen, 1945–47).
65 *Schalburgkorpset – historien om korpset og dets medlemmer 1943–45* (Odense: Odense Universitetsforlag, 2000), 11–14.
66 *Schalburgkorpset*, 116–21.
67 *Schalburgkorpset*, 192.
68 *Stikkerdrab* (Copenhagen: Aschehoug, 2000), 21 and 176–7. Whatever its scholarly quality, the dramatic subject matter and revisionist moralization of Emkjær's study made it a significant contribution to current public discourse about the occupation period of Danish history. For a scholarly examination of the conduct and punishment of informers, along with other categories of collaborators, see D. Tamm, *Retsopgøret efter besættelsen*.
69 *Stikkerdrab*, 22–4.
70 *Stikkerdrab*, 58–60 and 173.
71 *Stikkerdrab*, 61, 79, 107, 132–3, 160 and 173–4.
72 *Stikkerdrab*, 57 and 160.
73 *Stikkerdrab*, 176–7.
74 *Tyskerpiger* (Copenhagen: Gyldendal, 1994), 66.

75 *Tyskerpiger*, 126–7.
76 *Tyskerpiger*, 193 and 197.
77 *Tyskerpiger*, 198–203.
78 'The Law of the Jungle? Denmark's International Legal Status during the Second World War', in *The International History Review*, 33:2, 2011.
79 J. Gilmour and J. Stephenson (eds), *Hitler's Scandinavian Legacy. The Consequences of the German Invasion for the Scandinavian Countries, Then and Now* (London: Bloomsbury, 2013). The chapter was part of a collection of essays by Scandinavian historians, which had an introduction by Patrick Salmon, who presented a British perspective of the subject, and a conclusion by Allan Little.

The book included also a brief essay with a long title, '"The Five Evil Years": National Self-image, Commemoration and Historiography in Denmark 1945–2010: Trends in Historiography and Commemoration', in which Claus Bundgård Christensen touched upon the political use of occupation history. However, he related the notions and interpretations of that history not so much to the politics of the occupation period itself as to later and recent debates about Danish foreign policy. His examples of such uses of lessons of the past ranged from the debates about membership of NATO in the post-war years and of the EEC in the 1970s to disagreement about participation in military operations in Iraq and Afghanistan and about recent legislation regulating asylum seekers and other immigrants.

Taken as a whole, that book may be seen as an exercise in comparative historiography. As such, it was preceded by H. Stenius, M. Österberg and J. Östling (eds), *Nordic Narratives of the Second World War: National Historiographies Revisited* (Lund: Nordic Academic Press, 2011). The latter work had an essay by Uffe Østergård entitled 'Swords, Shields or Collaborators? Danish Historians and the Debate over the German Occupation', which tackled the central issue of occupation historiography. Like Bundgård Christensen's essay, it touched upon the growing commemoration and self-image literature.
80 New York: Peter Lang, 1998. The pointed title is a quotation from Hitler's order about the way contracts with Danish firms should be drawn up.
81 Odense: Syddansk Universitetsforlag, 2005.
82 S. Andersen, *Danmark i det tyske storrum. Dansk økonomisk tilpasning til Tysklands nyordning af Europa 1940–41* (Copenhagen: Lindhardt & Ringhof, 2003); S. Andersen, *De gjorde Danmark større. Danske entreprenører i krise og krig 1919–1947* (Copenhagen: Lindhardt & Ringhof, 2005).
83 *Hitlers spisekammer: Danmark og den europaeiske nyordning 1940–43* (Copenhagen: Gyldendal, 2005).
84 Copenhagen: Lindhardt & Ringhof, 2005; see also M.R. Nissen, *Landbruget og den danske neutralitet efter udbruddet af den anden verdenskrig*, in *Historie*, 2003.
85 *Med hjælp fra England. Special Operations Executive og den danske modstandskamp 1940–45* (Odense Universitetsforlag, 1998–2000).
86 *Historisk Tidsskrift* (Copenhagen, 2005), vol. 105.
87 *Historisk Tidsskrift* (Copenhagen, 2006), vol. 106.
88 *'Vor kamp vil vokse og styrkes'. Dokumenter til belysning af Danmarks kommunistiske partis og Frit Danmarks virksomhed 1939/44* (Selskabet til Udgivelse af Kilder til Dansk Historie, 2001).
89 *Bjørnen og haren. Sovjetunionen og Danmark 1945–1965* (Odense Universitetsforlag, 1999).
90 '"Folkets vilje – landets lov"? Om DKP's overgangsprogram og demokratiet', in Dethlefsen and Lundbak, 1998 op. cit.
91 For a shortened version in English of the dissertation, see H. Lundbak, *Danish Unity. A Political Party between Fascism and Resistance 1936–1947* (Copenhagen: Museum Tusculanum Press, University of Copenhagen, 2003). For a biography of Kaj Munk, see Per Stig Møller, *Munk* (Copenhagen: Gyldendal, 2000).
92 *Historie*, 2000 (Aarhus: Jysk Selskab for Historie, 2000).
93 *Danskerne og besættelsen. Holdninger og meninger 1939–45* (Copenhagen: Høst & Søn, 2005.
94 Op. cit.
95 Copenhagen: Høst & Søn, 2005.
96 Aarhus Universitetsforlag, 2002.
97 *Historisk Tidsskrift*, vol. 95.
98 *Historisk Tidsskrift*, vol. 101.
99 *Historisk Tidsskrift*, vol. 106.

100 *Besættelsestiden som kollektiv erindring. Historie- og traditionsforvaltning af krig og besættelse 1945–1997* (Roskilde Universitetsforlag, 1998).
101 *Information*, 16 October 2003.
102 *Jyllands-Posten*, 4 May 2005.
103 *Politiken* 8 March, *Berlingske Tidende* 31 March, *Politiken* 4 April and *Jyllands-Posten* 10 April 2005.
104 *Kampen om Danmark 1933–1945* (Copenhagen: Gyldendal, 2005), 559.
105 *Kampen om Danmark*, 563–4 and 575–6.
106 *Kampen om Danmark*, 588–9. A later work, in a contribution to which Lidegaard contrasted Nils Svenningsen and Henrik Kauffmann, focused on the difficult moral and political choices facing influential Danes during the occupation. In *Sådan valgte de* (Thus they chose), seven scholars presented double portraits of different people in different situations making different choices relating to the issue between cooperation and resistance (H. Kirchhoff (ed.); Copenhagen: Gyldendal, 2008).

Conclusion

1 F. Jakobsen, *I Danmarks frihedsråd* (Copenhagen: Gyldendal, 1975), vol. ii, 74.
2 M. Fog, *Efterskrift 1940–45* (Copenhagen: Gyldendal, 1976), 195.
3 Fog, *Efterskrift 1940–45*, 254.
4 Lidegaard, *Kampen om Danmark*, 558.
5 For relations between SOE and the Danish resistance, and British policy towards occupied and liberated Denmark, see translation of K.J.V. Jespersen, *Med hjælp fra England*. Op. cit.: *No Small Achievement. Special Operations Executive and the Danish Resistance 1940–1945*, trans. C. Wade (Odense: University Press of Southern Denmark, 2002).

Works cited

Andersen, S. *Danmark i det tyske storrum. Dansk økonomisk tilpasning til Tysklands nyordning af Europa 1940–41* (Copenhagen: Lindhardt & Ringhof, 2003)

Andersen, S. *De gjorde Danmark større. Danske entreprenører i krise og krig 1919–1947* (Copenhagen: Lindhardt & Ringhof, 2005)

Bjøl, E. *Set i bakspejlet* (Copenhagen: Politikens Forlag, 1993)

Brandenborg Jensen, Ole. *Besættelsestidens Økonomiske og Erhvervmæssige Forhold: Studier i de Økonomiske Relationer mellem Danmark og Tyskland 1940–1945* (Odense: Syddansk Universitetsforlag, 2005)

Branner, Hans. *Den 9. april* (Copenhagen: Jurist- og Økonomforbundets Forlag, 1987)

Bryld, Claus and Anette Warring. *Besættelsestiden som kollektiv erindring. Historie- og traditionsforvaltning af krig og besættelse 1945–1997* (Roskilde Universitetsforlag, 1998)

Bundgaard Christensen, Claus, Niels Bo Poulsen and Peter Scharff Smith. *Under hagekors og dannebrog* (Copenhagen: Aschehoug, 1998)

Bundgaard Christensen, Claus, Joachim Lund, Niels Wium Olesen and Jacob Sørensen, *Danmark besat: Krig og hverdag 1940–45* (Copenhagen: Høst & Søn, 2005)

Christiansen, N.F. *Hartvig Frisch. Mennesket og politikeren. En biografi* (Copenhagen: Christian Ejlers Forlag, 1993)

Dethlefsen, H. 'Arven fra Hæstrup', in H. Dethlefsen and H. Lundbak (eds), *Fra mellemkrigstid til efterkrigstid* (Copenhagen: Museum Tusculanums Forlag, 1998)

Edelberg, Peter. 'Arven fra Hæstrup', *Historisk Tidsskrift* (Copenhagen, 2005), vol. 105

Emkjær, Stefan. *Stikkerdrab* (Copenhagen: Aschehoug, 2000)

Feldbæk, O. *Danmarks historie*, iv: *Tiden 1730–1814* (Copenhagen: Gyldendal, 1982)

Fog, M. *Efterskrift 1940–45* (Copenhagen: Gyldendal, 1976)

Frisch, Hartvig. *Tænkt og talt under Krigen* (Copenhagen: Fremad, 1945)

Frisch, Hartvig. *Danmark besat og befriet*, vols. i–iii (Copenhagen: Fremad, 1945–1948)

Frisch, Hartvig. *Pest over Europa: Bolshevisme – Fascisme – Nazisme* (Copenhagen: Fremad, 1950)

Gilmour, J. and J. Stephenson (eds), *Hitler's Scandinavian Legacy* (London: Bloomsbury, 2013)

Giltner, Philip. *In the Friendliest Manner: German-Danish Economic Cooperation During the Nazi Occupation of 1940–1945* (New York: Peter Lang, 1998)

Gram-Skjoldager, Karen. 'The Law of the Jungle? Denmark's International Legal Status during the Second World War', in *The International History Review*, 33:2, 2011.

Halicz, E. *Danish Neutrality during the Crimean War (1853–1856): Denmark between the Hammer and the Anvil*, trans. J. Cave (Odense: Odense University Press, 1977)

Holbraad, C. *Danish Neutrality: A Study in the Foreign Policy of a Small State* (Oxford: Clarendon Press, 1991)

Hæstrup, J. *Hemmelig alliance. Hovedtræk af den danske modstandsorganisations udvikling 1943–1945*, vols. i, ii (Copenhagen: Thanning og Appels Forlag, 1959)

Hæstrup, J. *...til landets bedste –. Hovedtræk af departementschefsstyrets virke 1943–45*, vols i, ii (Copenhagen: Gyldendal, 1966/1971).

Hæstrup, J. *Dørene åbnes. En forsknings historie* (Odense: Odense Universitetsforlag, 1973)

Hæstrup, J. *Secret Alliance. A Study of the Danish Resistance Movement, 1940–45*, vols i–iii (Odense: Odense Universitetsforlag, 1976–77)

Hæstrup, J. *Europe Ablaze. An Analysis of the History of the European Resistance Movements 1939–45* (Odense: Odense Universitetsforlag, 1978).

Hæstrup, J. et al. (eds), *Kilder til modstandsbevægelsens historie* (Copenhagen: Gyldendal, 1972)

Jakobsen, F. *I Danmarks frihedsråd* (Copenhagen: Gyldendal, 1975), vols i–ii.

Jensen, Bent. *Bjørnen og haren. Sovjetunionen og Danmark 1945–1965* (Odense Universitetsforlag, 1999)

Jensen, C. Th. Kristiansen, K.E. Nielsen, *Krigens købmænd* (Copenhagen, 2000)

Jespersen, Knud J.V. *Med hjælp fra England. 1940–1945*, vols i–ii (Odense Universitetsforlag, 1998–2000)

Jespersen, Knud J. V. *No Small Achievement. Special Operations Executive and the Danish Resistance 1940–1945*, trans. C. Wade (Odense: University Press of Southern Denmark, 2002)

Kirchhoff, Hans. *Augustoprøret 1943. Samarbejdspolitikkens fald. Forudsætninger og forløb. En studie i collaboration og modstand* (Copenhagen: Gyldendal, 1979), vols i–iii.

Kirchhoff, Hans. *Kamp eller tilpasning* (Copenhagen: Gyldendal, 1987)

Kirchhoff, Hans. *Samarbejde og modstand under besættelsen. En politisk historie* (Odense: Odense Universitetsforlag, 2002)

Kirchhoff, Hans. (ed.), *Sådan valgte de* (Copenhagen: Gyldendal, 2008)

Kirchhoff, Hans and Hans Trommer (eds) *'Vor kamp vil vokse og styrkes'. Dokumenter til belysning af Danmarks kommunistiske partis og Frit Danmarks virksomhed 1939/44* (Selskabet til Udgivelse af Kilder til Dansk Historie, 2001)

Kjeldsen, Michael. '"Folkets vilje – landets lov"? Om DKP's overgangsprogram og demokratiet', in H. Dethlefsen and H. Lundbak (eds), *Fra mellemkrigstid til efterkrigstid* (Copenhagen: Museum Tusculanums Forlag, 1998)

la Cour, V. (ed.), *Danmark under Besættelsen*, vols i–iii (Copenhagen, 1945–47)

Lidegaard, Bo *Kampen om Danmark 1933–1945* (Copenhagen: Gyldendal, 2005)

Lund, Joachim. *Hitlers spisekammer: Danmark og den europaeiske nyordning 1940–43* (Copenhagen: Gyldendal, 2005)

Lundbak, H. *Danish Unity. A Political Party between Fascism and Resistance 1936–1947* (Copenhagen: Museum Tusculanum Press, University of Copenhagen, 2003)

Møller, E. *Helstatens Fald*, part 2, 1864 (Copenhagen: G.E.C. Gad, 1958)

Møller, Per Stig. *Munk* (Copenhagen: Gyldendal, 2000)

Nielsen, H. *Dansk udenrigspolitik 1875–1894 med særligt henblik paa beslutningsprocessen* (Odense: Odense Universitetsforlag, 1977)

Nissen, Henrik S. *1940. Studier i forhandlingspolitikken og samarbejdspolitikken* (Doctoral dissertation, 1973) (Copenhagen: Gyldendal)

Nissen, Mogens R. *Landbruget og den danske neutralitet efter udbruddet af den anden verdenskrig*, in *Historie*, 2003.

Nissen, Mogens R. *Til fælles bedste – det danske landbrug under besættelsen* (Copenhagen: Lindhardt & Ringhof, 2005)

Nørregaard, G. *Danmark mellem øst og vest 1824–39* (Copenhagen: Gyldendal, 1969)

Pedersen, Andreas Monrad. *Schalburgkorpset – historien om korpset og dets medlemmer 1943–45* (Odense: Odense Universitetsforlag, 2000)

Poulsen, Henning. 'Hvad mente danskerne?' *Historie* (Aarhus: Jysk Selskab for Historie, 2000)

Poulsen, Henning. *Besættelsesårene 1940–1945* (Aarhus Universitetsforlag, 2002)

Roslyng-Jensen, Palle. *Danskerne og besættelsen. Holdninger og meninger 1939–45* (Copenhagen: Høst & Søn, 2005)

Roslyng-Jensen, Palle. 'Befrielsesjubilæet og den nyeste besættelseslitteratur'. *Historisk Tidsskrift*, vol. 95, 1995.

Roslyng-Jensen, Palle. 'Besættelsesforskningen 1995–2001' *Historisk Tidsskrift*, vol. 101., 2001.

Roslyng-Jensen, Palle. 'Besættelseslitteraturen 2001–2006' *Historisk Tidsskrift*, vol. 106., 2006.

Scavenius, E. *Forhandlingspolitiken under Besættelsen* (Copenhagen: Steen Hasselbalchs Forlag, 1948)

Scavenius, E. *Dansk udenrigspolitik under den første verdenskrig* (Copenhagen: Fremad, 1959)

Sjøqvist, V. *Danmarks udenrigspolitik 1933–1940* (Copenhagen: Gyldendal, 1966)

Sjøqvist, V. *Erik Scavenius: Danmarks udenrigsminister under to verdenskrige. Statsminister 1942–1945* (Copenhagen: Gyldendal, 1973), vol. ii.

Tamm, D. *Retsopgøret efter besættelsen*, vols i and ii (Copenhagen: Gyldendal, 1984–5; 3rd edn. 1997)

Trommer, Aage. *Jernbanesabotagen i Danmark under den anden verdenskrig. En krigshistorisk undersøgelse* (Odense University Press, 1971)

Trommer, Aage. *Modstandsarbejde i nærbillede. Det illegale arbejde i Syd- og Sønderjylland under den tyske besættelse af Danmark 1940–45* (Odense University Press, 1973)

Warring, Anette. *Tyskerpiger – under besættelse og retsopgør* (Copenhagen: Gyldendal, 1994)

Index

www.ingramcontent.com/pod-product-compliance
Lightning Source LLC
LaVergne TN
LVHW022052300826
846742LV00013B/35
* 9 7 8 1 9 1 1 3 0 7 5 0 1 *